The Road Is My Mistress

Tales of a Roustabout Songster

Rik Palieri

National Library of Canada Cataloguing in Publication
ML420.P162A3 2003   781.64.'092   C2003-902943-3

Palieri, Rik
        TheRoad is my Mistress: Tales of a roustabout songster.

First Printing ISBN 1-4120-0403-9
Trafford Publishing, a division of Trafford Holdings, Inc.
Printed in Victoria, Canada

Second Printing ISBN 0-9749874-0-9
Koza Productions
Printed in LaVergne, TN USA
Travelogue

KOZA PRODUCTIONS
66 Koza's Run
Hinesburg, VT 05461 USA
802-482-3185
www.banjo.net

This book is dedicated to the memory of dear departed friends and family. Buzz Potter, Jimmy Driftood, Al Grierson and Veronica Wojdyla & Claudia..

And to my dear wife, Marianna Holtzer, who makes all things possible.

Dear Reader,

This book would not have been possible without the constant nagging and grumbling from an "Old Fellow" from New Hampshire who likes to call himself "The Hobo Minstrel", (a.k.a Fran DeLorenzo). If it were not for Fran's help, guidance, computer skills, perseverance and in general just putting up with me, this book would have not come to life.

It was Fran who first wanted me to write a book and then stepped in and made the big mistake of saying "I'll even help you get it going". After Fran put this silly notion into my head, there was no stopping me. I started going through my journals to see if I had the right starter to get the book going.

If you ever made sourdough bread you will know that you only need a tiny bit of starter to make the bread. By just adding a few simple ingredients to the starter you can make up new loafs for years and even generations to come.

Well the starter for this book can be traced to my early journals. Even though I never liked to write as a child, I started keeping a journal when I lived in Poland in 1984. Like so many of the good things that has happened in my life, it was only after my friend and mentor, singer Pete Seeger, wrote me a letter urging me to keep a journal that I started writing again. Little did I realize how important that one act would be. Following Pete's sound advice, I kept a daily log of my activities in my journal, including vivid descriptions of my travels and detailed information of musical ideas and instructions on how to make and play various musical instruments.

Later, when I was out on the road for three and half years roaming the back roads of America my journal went with me. I sent home news of the people and places and even the loneliness I was feeling. It was often late at night that I would sit in a truck stop or all night diner and just pour out my heart and soul on paper. Besides telling of my daily activities, I also started jotting down some of the stories that I could remember from my early childhood, old family folk lore and my early years of trying to learn my craft as a musician. Anything to keep me writing and forget just how lonely I was. At that time I was not writing for any one but me and never expected that any one else would ever want to read my stories.

For many years I did not pay any mind to those letters from the road and just threw them in a file. As the years went by and my music was getting known, I started getting inquires to write for different magazines.

When writing those first small articles, I discovered that I had a wealth of information and fun stories in my old letters

After a few articles, I soon found out that many people enjoyed my homespun organic writing style. Soon I found myself writing for *Sing Out!*, The Folk Magazine, *Good Citizen*, a local Music magazine, *The Guardian*, a newsletter for The American Sheepdog Club, Motorcycle magazines and one of my favorites a neat little magazine for arm chair travelers called *The Hobo Times*.

As time went by, folks kept asking me, "So when are you going to write a book?" After hearing the same question, like a broken record, over and over, I thought, "Well, maybe I should at least give it a try." Here is where Fran entered the picture. At one of the hobo gatherings Fran convinced me that my stories were worth reading and that he would like to publish my book. For the next two and half years Fran nurtured the project along despite my hemming and hawing and countless spelling and computer mistakes.

After the book started taking shape it was almost like an old fashioned barn raising as friends from all over the country and the world pitched in to help. First from the USA; Sara Shepherd, Ruth O'Neill, Connecticut Shorty, New York Maggie, John & Judy Kane, Walter Lee, Carol Wood, Rick Robins, Lon Austin, Gary Oliver, Lisa Perna, Tina Palieri, Lindy Sax, Mark Moss, Dugan, Jeff Miller, Rick Nestler, Mary Frances D. Collins, The Hobo Nickel Guy, Buzz Potter, Melanie Mardin, Bob Hahn, Amy Collins, Chris Kleeman, Brian Yarwood, Wendi Stein, Dick Boak and the C.F. Martin Guitar Co., Bob of Bob's Auto, the Palieri Family and Marianna Holzer.

Then from the rest of the world! From the UK; Lesley Lewis, Tony Nightingale, Julia and Lev Atlas, Gerald Barry, and Kieth from the Zemaitis Club. From Poland; Zbigniew Zdziennicki and Katarzyna Poloczanska. From Germany; Wilfried Mengs, Bend Harber, Michael Kleff. From Canada; Haywire Brack. And from my friends in Australia; Roger Holdsworth, Dani Voller, Raymond Mow, and Colin Nightingale.

Everyone was willing to pitch in and help make my dream come true. Some special thanks are in order for the following people:

Pete Seeger who took time out of his busy life to help proof read my book and write a quote, and my friend and mentor

U. Utah Phillips who, while locked in a jail cell for his opposition to the war the Iraq, labored over the book's beautiful forward.

My brother Dave "Fish" Palieri and Ken Cantino for the layout and design of the covers.

Photographers; Bob Yahn, Craig Harris, Mark Lamhut, Connecticut Shorty, Ginger (Firecracker) Osborne (Cover Photo), David (Sundance) Querido, Pete Urbaitis, and Marianna Holzer.

Special thanks also to Sing Out Magazine for giving permission to use stories that had previously published by them. Also, thanks and apologies to anyone I may have forgotten to mention.

All of these wonderful people shared advice, proofread and made many other valuable contributions to help me out. I can't thank them enough for without all their support this book would have never been more than a bunch of old letters in my filing cabinet.

* * * * * * * * * *

Even though I never thought of myself as a writer, I have always been a good story teller, for the art of telling a good story seems to just run in my family. I came to appreciate the power of stories at a young age while listening to my mother spin tales around our kitchen table and still, to this day, whenever our clan gathers together stories fill the air.

PS... As with any good story telling, times, events and some of the names may not be precisely accurate or, maybe, even stretched a bit to make a good story.

Introduction by U. Utah Phillips

RIK

We call him Totem Pole. Well, it suits him. Here he comes now, strong, upright, his whole body festooned with instruments : banjo, guitar and a quadriplegic goat he claims to be Polish bagpipes. And they are! Once played, they'll clean the wax out of your ears or make you wish you had more. Tote 'em Pole, that's him. Well, just part of him, the Hobo part. The rest has to do with music, our music. And the road, long stretches of midnight highway, booming on to the next last lost town at the end of the world. You take all the best of who we've become, we Americans ; our plain, honest voice, our wandering soul, the deep, true poetry of all our places, trust, honor, hard-working hands and hearts at peace. Take all of these, stitch them together with our people's common music, the ring of the banjo and happy feet stomping away the darkness -- and somewhere in the middle of all this you'll find Rik.

He has more time and miles on him than a prospector's mule. But he has turned up the gold. It shines from a thousand stages where, night after night he gives back to some of us what he's learned from the rest of us. Always giving, only taking what balances out. Now, this book is part of that balance. The pay-back.

This is an American life only because of all the American lives, past and present, that have flowed into and filled it up. All the hardship, all the open-handed love, the great adventure we're all in whether we know it or not., you'll find it all here in this one, same as you'd find it in all of us. But Rik tells it and lives it and sings it and it all comes out, like the old fiddler said, "finer than snuff and it ain't half as dusty".

Utah Phillips
April, 2003

Utah & Rik on stage at the Philadelphia Folk Festival
(Photo by Pete Urbaitis)

Feral Child

It was back in the mid-fifties, or so I'm told, that my story began. My parents met over a comic book in a grocery store in Hillside, New Jersey. My father, Bill, was in the Navy serving on the aircraft carrier the U.S.S. Randolph. He was home on leave, dressed in his navy whites, when he went down to buy a comic book and spied a pretty Polish girl standing in the store. The beautiful brunette's name was Stephanie, a young eighteen-year old immigrant, newly arrived from Poland. Stephanie was dazzled by Bill's Navy uniform and my dad was equally intrigued by my mother's attractiveness and charm, though she could hardly speak English.

Following a short courtship, this young couple married and, after the wedding, my dad went back to his base in Virginia, while his young wife set up housekeeping. She shared a walk-up apartment in the city of Newark with her new in-laws, Bill's mother Katherine and her sister-in-law Irene. Stephanie and Irene had a lot in common. They were both wed to sailors and soon found out that they were both pregnant.

It was in the darkness of a mid-summer's August night that Stephanie felt the first pains of labor. She was all alone in her tiny flat when her water broke. When she cried out for help, her mother in law heard her screams from down the hall and, with the help of Irene, they made a quick dash to the hospital. Her contractions continued until the next afternoon, when on Tuesday, August 16th at 3:38 PM she brought a little seven pound, two-ounce baby boy into the world.

After three days in the hospital, without my father's presence, the other young mothers in the maternity ward began taunting her, "So where's the father?" My mother tried to explain in her broken English, that she was married to a sailor but the other women didn't believe her and thought that she was another young, unwed mother. One woman said bitingly, "So now babies are having babies." After three days alone in the hospital she too began to wonder, "Where is the father?"

The father in question was hitchhiking his way home from his base in Virginia. Bill hitched a good ride all the way to Newark but, to his surprise, when he arrived at their apartment there was only a letter telling him that his wife was in the delivery room at the hospital. Being a frugal man, Bill knew he had only enough money to buy flowers or a bus ticket. He spent his last bit of cash on a beautiful bouquet of flowers for his wife and decided to walk over to the hospital. He underestimated the distance and the time it would take to walk from Newark to the hospital in Irvington and, by the time he reached her hospital bed, the flowers had all wilted.

The Road Is My Mistress

Together they left the hospital with their new baby. They had decided to name him Richard, after a long debate over using the name Montgomery. Before long, Bill was discharged from the Navy and found a job with Hatfield's Wire and Cable Company.

With a new baby in the house, it was time to think about making a change. Stephanie grew up on the farmlands of her native Poland and she had many happy memories of walking in the woods, picking mushrooms and playing out in the forest. Bill too, had experienced many happy visits at his mother's family farm in Rochester, Massachusetts. Bill liked the idea of having his own little garden and getting a house where they could put down roots. They decided that the city streets were no place to bring up a child so they started looking for a home in the suburbs. After weeks of riding around looking at houses, they found just the right house - a small, three-bedroom ranch, painted barn red with white shutters, in the town of East Brunswick, New Jersey.

Historically, back in the sixteenth century, the first settlers to this area were of English, Scottish, German and Dutch descent. They left the old world for religious freedom and for the adventure of the newly found land. At the time, the woodlands were inhabited by tribes of Indians. The early settlers bought land directly from the Indians and then built a little town near the banks of the South River. The river made it easy for these early pioneers to ship their fresh fruits, vegetables, wood, clay, pottery and bricks to markets in New York and Philadelphia.

Along with the boats and ships sailing the river, a stagecoach route developed and brought more inhabitants to the area. Following the stage, train tracks were laid with big steam engines bringing new people and industry. During the 19th century East Brunswick and the little town of Old Bridge were a hotbed of commercial activity with wood mills, snuff mills, a distillery, shipbuilders and warehouses. To fill the needs of the many blue collar families working in the mills and factories, new houses sprouted like weeds and the town became a sea of small, affordable, ranch style houses often filled by first or second generation emigrants from Europe. After the Second World War, many veterans like my father were able to leave the cities behind and start building a new life out in the suburbs.

My parents settled in a characteristically suburban styled ranch. We lived on one of the president streets, named Roosevelt Avenue. Just down the street from our house was a large lake with railroad tracks running alongside it. Down the tracks from the lake, was an old factory. In the front of its entrance sat two old, rusty rails from the original Camden-Amboy Railroad. There was a historical marker next to the rails indicating that they once were a part of the line where the historic engine, the John Bull, ran. I would often play around these two hunks of steel and imagine the big steam engine puffing and blowing smoke as it ran down the tracks. Even as a young child, I was already fantasizing images of adventure and exotic places. I would spend hours walking up and down the wooden railroad ties and wondering, "Where do these tracks lead?"

I was a bit of a dreamer as a child, a loner, and some could even say a bit melancholy. I lived inside my head most of the time, never liked school and would do anything possible to avoid getting there. Often I would walk backwards to school just so I would not have to look at the building. As I got older I found a more exciting way to reach the schoolyard. Walking alongside the train tracks, I would wait for the early morning train to come. At about 7:30, like clockwork, the big black engine would come rushing by. After the engine had passed I would run alongside the tracks and hop aboard by grabbing onto the side boxcar ladder. When my school came into view, I would leap off the train. I found out that it was a lot easier to hop onto a moving train than to get off of one. When I would let go, the force would throw me to the ground and I would tumble along the hard rocky ballast near the tracks, often scraping up my knees. Of course, my parents had no idea that I was 'hoboing" my way to school. In fact they were both working so hard (my father nights and my mother working days) that they really had no idea of what I was up to at all.

With my father asleep in the house, I would always try to hang out with the older kids. These young adolescents did not like the idea of having a young kid spoiling their good time and were often downright mean. We used to hang out in the woods near the lake right behind the train tracks. One cold November day my older friends were busy building a raft. Being curious I asked them if I could help. They said, "Oh, why sure you can help! You can be our test pilot." Then, after the raft was lashed together, they told me to climb aboard as they pushed the raft into the lake. Of course there was one big problem, I didn't have a paddle. The boys laughed as the raft drifted farther out onto the lake. I got scared and started crying, "How do I get back?" They were all laughing and said, "Jump and swim." I really had no choice, for I was now almost in the middle of the lake, so I jumped into the water and it was cold as ice. I swam back to shore and climbed out of the freezing water soaked to the bone.

By this time the boys had started a little camp fire and told me to stand next to the fire to dry off. Then one boy suggested that, to really get dry, I should take my clothes off and hold them over the fire. Little did I know that these kids were scheming up a plan. Once I had removed all of my clothes, they grabbed them and threw them into the burning hot flames. Even though my clothes were waterlogged they flew into the hot fire and started burning. The boys were howling with laughter as they ran away into the woods. I was standing naked by the fire, watching my clothes burn. I didn't know what to do as I now had no clothes, and it was a long way home. I hid in the woods and waited for the sun to go down then slowly made my way home, hiding behind trees and bushes along the way.

I was not the only one who was at the mercy of these cruel kids. My next door neighbor Dave, who was a year older than me, was also a victim of their nasty pranks. One time, Dave and I wanted to play soldiers with the same big kids. When they caught us, they said they were Japanese warriors and we were their prisoners, so they held us down, tied our hands and feet, and then tied us to a telephone pole. The rope around the pole was also tied around both of our necks so, if either one of us tried to move, we would end up choking each other. The boys then ran away and the clouds opened up and the rain poured down on the two little tykes that were tied steadfast to the pole. Luckily, a man in the neighborhood saw us and kindly cut us loose. As bad as the neighborhood kids were, it was a lot better to be with them than to go home. Their pranks were nothing compared to the horrendous treatment that I had to live with at hands of my father. My dad had his own demons to fight. He was abused as a child. His father would beat him with no mercy.

As a defense against his father, young Bill became interested in boxing. He learned fast and with his quick fists soon had the reputation of being a scrapper. By the time he reached his teens he was known as "Headhunter Bill," one of the best fighters in the school. When my dad became a father, he had no role model for parenting and began to treat me in the same fashion he was raised in. When my father got angry it was like a volcano erupting, the whole house shook and fire seemed to shoot out of his eyes.

Dad worked nights and slept during the day. He was a miserable soul back then and, just like old Rip Van Winkle, was trying to sleep his life away. My mother was not happy either as she was tired of being alone. She needed more in her life than to just sit at home by herself and watch TV. With little hope of her situation changing, she started to go out late at night. After my dad would leave for work she headed straight for the bars. There were many times I would wake to hear the sound of her white Edsel's engine cranking after midnight. By the time I would reach the driveway, I was left behind, holding my blanket in a cloud of smoke. My father knew that she was going out on him and he was infuriated; he would often take his anger out on me by using my body as a punching bag to get over his frustrations. He often got back at her by hurting me, telling me over and over that I was stupid, clumsy and never would amount to anything. After years of this kind of mental and physical abuse I started believing him and my self-esteem shrank down to practically nothing.

My lack of self-confidence, combined with the usual regimen of cruel discipline, began to take its toll until I felt like I was living in the center of a dark cloud. I was developing a bad attitude. I did not care about anyone or anything and my bad reputation grew. When I was in the third grade my father bought me a black leather motorcycle jacket and from the time I put that jacket on, I was pegged as a trouble-making rebel. I did not like to follow directions or listen to authority and I truly didn't care about anything. I soon found out that when you're only a young kid, that kind of thinking can cause you a lot of problems.

As my mother and father were always sleeping or working, I was basically a latchkey kid and would spend most of my time at other people's homes. One of my young friends was a pretty young girl named Gail Prinky. Gail had bright blue eyes, little red cheeks and a pixie haircut. She and I would often walk along the train tracks to school and, sometimes on the way home; we would make a stop at the lake. One early winter afternoon, when the lake was covered over with a sheet of ice, Gail and I ran across the lake. As we ran we heard a crack. Suddenly the ice gave way and Gail went down through a hole in the ice. I quickly ran and grabbed her arm, before she went completely under, and pulled her to safety. Later, when I told my friends and parents what had happened, and how I had rescued Gail, no one believed me. It wasn't surprising, because I wasn't known for this or any kind of good behavior so I rarely got credit for my good deeds. It really didn't matter because I knew I had done the right thing. Besides, Gail knew and she rewarded me with her friendship and an occasional kiss. One day, Gail told me that she was moving. I was so sad to lose my little friend that I went into my mother's jewelry box and picked out a little bracelet of purple rhinestones and gave it to her. I wonder sometimes if she still has it.

MUSIC IN THE AIR

Our neighborhood was always filled with music. Each summer a new bunch of kids seemed to be playing in a band and all the neighbors would turn out for their rehearsals. The first live band I can remember was the Delrays. I can still see those shiny, white Fender Stratocasters playing the songs of the Ventures and the Beach Boys. One member of the Delrays, named Mike Robba, played the saxophone, and lived a couple of houses up the street from me, while the drummer Ralph lived right next door.
Our street really was quite a musical place. Henry Mancini's cousin, Mike, lived on our block and you could hear his children and his students playing their scales every evening. Listening to the sound of music wafting down the street could have made just about anyone want to learn how to play an instrument.

There was music in our house too. My father had a great collection of records that spanned from movie and show tunes to Italian opera. While my dad listened to the old Italians, my mother was listening to pop tunes on the radio. Some of her favorites were the hip-gyrating Elvis, black rhythm and blues man Ray Charles, and the king of calypso, Harry Belafonte. As a small boy, I would entertain my parents and their friends by singing Harry Belafonte's "Banana Boat Song." Everyone laughed to see such a little boy trying to yell out, "Day-O, Day-Ya-Ya-Ya--." Whenever I would hear music playing in the house, it meant that everyone was happy.

As my own love for music grew, I pretended that I was in a band called the Moon Men. My father had a large cardboard drum, stored in the basement, that I would make believe was my drum kit. For my guitar, I used an old bathroom plunger. I would spend hours singing my head off down in the cellar beating on my drum or strumming the old plunger to all of my favorite songs.

Then I got the idea that I wanted to play the saxophone. It must have been the song "Woolly Bully" that was playing constantly on the radio that got to me because now I was hooked on the sax. Indulging in my new hobby, I would seek out the sound of the sax in every song I heard on the radio. When my mother brought me to Polish dances I would stay right next to the stage and stand transfixed as the sax player honked away.

One day there was a musical test given in school. I scored high in the test and was encouraged by teachers to take up an instrument. I immediately said that I wanted to play the saxophone. The music teacher thought I was too young for a big saxophone so she gave me a clarinet instead. Right from the start, I hated that clarinet as it did not look like nor sound like the sax, besides, you can't play "Wooly Bully" on a clarinet! The music teacher taught from a Mel Bay book and, right from the start, we didn't get along. I was pretty nervous around her and often bit the reed of my instrument. When she noticed that I was biting the cane reed she would slap me. Now, not only did I hate the instrument, but I hated her too, and refused to practice. It wasn't long before the clarinet went back into its case and back to Mr. Mancini. My first musical experience had ended in failure.

THE BLACK HAWKS

A few years later, my next door neighbor Dave, told me about a marching band he was in called the Black Hawks. Dave was learning the drums and thought they could use a few more players, so that week my mother drove me to band practice to see if I could get in the band. The band director was happy to have me as they needed more people to march and fill in the ranks during parades. He gave me a long baritone horn that was old and ugly, and smelled like spit, and instructed me to join the other players.

The Black Hawks were a drum and bugle corps that played at parades all over New Jersey and sometimes even traveled out of state. The uniform we wore was a gold satin shirt, black pants with a golden stripe sewn down the side, white socks and shoes and a sharp looking black Australian-styled hat. We played tunes like "Everything's Coming Up Roses," " Night Train," "America," and "Anchors Aweigh." Every week we practiced marching around the parking lot of our high school.

While the Black Hawks were very much into teaching marching, they neglected to give any instruction on playing the bugle. That meant that a few talented children got all the leads while everyone else just blew random notes. Needless to say, we did not win many awards for excellence. Without any idea of how in the world, to play my horn, I decided that it was better not to play at all. Decades before Millie Vanillie, I found that you could be in a band and never play a note of your own. In parades, I would carry my horn but never make a sound. Despite the lack of my musical ability, I still had fun riding in the back of our big yellow school bus while singing with the band as we traveled from town to town.

Most of our shows were at small parades but, to our surprise, we landed a booking at what would become our biggest performance ever - a gig at the New York World's Fair in the New Jersey Pavilion. I couldn't believe it when I learned that my favorite group, Sam the Sham and the Pharaohs were also billed to play that day on the very same stage - the same group that made "Woolly Bully" a hit on the charts. I was thrilled to hear the saxophone player but it made me wonder if I would ever be able to really make any music of my own.

After our performance, we marched the circumference around the big globe sculpture symbol of the Worlds Fair, and were filmed for the evening news on TV. I was experiencing my first taste of a real road tour and I loved it. Unfortunately the magical feeling did not last all that long because shortly afterwards, the band broke up. My marching days were over, at least for a while.

A.M. RADIO AND UNCLE REX'S HILLBILLY GUITAR

In the 60's I grew up with the radio almost glued to my ear. I listened to WABC on the AM dial, with DJ Harry Harrison in The Morning and groovy Cousin Brucey. When the Beatles first came to America, I heard the news broadcast over the school's intercom system. That weekend, when the four Mop Tops played the "Ed Sullivan Show," I, like most of the youth of America, sat in front of the TV set and was completely captivated. It was George Harrison that I immediately took a liking to. George was pegged as the quiet Beatle, a feeling that I could relate to. When I saw him on Ed Sullivan strumming that shiny black Chet Atkins Gretsch guitar, with his long bangs hanging over his forehead, I found another musical hero. I soon became a huge Beatles fan, collecting their records and memorabilia. With the so-called "British Invasion" I was introduced to a whole new world of music. I started listening to groups like The Animals, the Rolling Stones, Freddie and the Dreamers, the Dave Clark Five, Herman's Hermits and so many more. My musical taste was changing with each new group I would hear.

But the rock and roll world was not the only music that I was listening to. When I would visit my father's mother I would be exposed to something totally different than my usual A.M. radio fare, something called Country and Western music. My grandmother, Katherine, (or as every one called her "Kay") was a big country/western fan. Whenever we would come to visit, she would always turn on her Hi Fi and play her favorite songs from singers like Eddy Arnold, Hank Williams and Tennessee Ernie Ford. I loved Hank

Williams and some of the other singers too. I also loved the story songs like "Wolvertin Mountain" and Jimmy Driftwood's "The Battle of New Orleans." It might have been the narratives in those old ballads that caught my ear, as I always loved a good story.

One year Grandma Kay decided to give my cousin Glenn a guitar for Christmas. Glenn was already showing promise that he was the musical one in the family as he had already learned a few guitar chords from his father and was also singing in church. Glen's father, Uncle Rex Ward, originally hailed from Alabama. Rex played a mean Hillbilly guitar style that he learned from a family relative who had played with Hank Williams and the Drifting Cowboys. Uncle Rex knew all of Hank's songs, and many country/western favorites like "Pistol Packing Mama." "Many Sundays we would go over to my Aunt Irene's house and listen to Uncle Rex sing and play while Glen accompanied him. It's not surprising that watching Uncle Rex and Glenn playing made me want to try the guitar too. I begged my mother to buy me a guitar that I had seen at a certain department store. My mother gave in and bought me a shiny red electric guitar. A few weeks later Grandma Wojdyla won a guitar amplifier on the Seaside Beach boardwalk. Now with my guitar and amp I was ready to play, or so I thought, until I realized I hadn't the foggiest notion how to play the bloody thing. Even though I had watched Uncle Rex and Glen happily strumming away, I never could figure out just what they were doing. After a few frustrating attempts of playing a few notes on one string, my guitar just sat in the corner. It felt like another musical failure had struck and perhaps I was just not meant to play an instrument.

COOL LEATHER AND SWITCH BLADES

As I was approaching my teen years I fell in with the wrong crowd. These new friends were all tough guys dressed in high collar shirts, pointy black shoes, slicked back hair and black leather jackets. We were called "greasers" and were proud of it. Many of us carried dog chains and switchblade knifes in our pockets. Back in grade school I had made friends with a young punk named George Vanderveer. George's father was the president of a local motorcycle group called "The Jersey Eagles" and he had two motorcycles parked in their yard: a Harley-Davidson Electra-Glide and an Old Indian. George was a bit out of his mind and was also a tough guy, so we got along just fine. George and I started a little gang we called The Cobras. There were about ten of us, most just barely twelve years old; we thought and acted way beyond our years.

We each had a back patch on our denim jackets; one of us scrawled our club's name on the huge white wall of the supermarket with black spray paint. The Cobras would all hang out together until after dark, often fighting each other for fun, and sometimes going after other kids with our dog chains to scare the hell out of them. George and I both had girlfriends and we would make out with them in the back of the tractor trailer trucks that were parked in back of the shopping center. We were living life big for young kids and I would soon find out what life in the fast lane was all about.

At this time, I had a little switchblade that was the shape of a pistol. When you pulled on the trigger the blade shot out as fast as lighting; I carried it around constantly, showing it off to my friends at every chance. One day a young "jock" kid tried to take my knife away just as I was opening the blade. Click - the blade flew open and went right into the boy's hand. The blood pulsed out of his skin and ran down his arm as he yelled in pain. I quickly withdrew the knife blade and even though I was scared out of my wits, I threatened him with his life if he told anyone. I knew I was in deep trouble and waited for the police to come. The threat must have worked as I never heard anything about it. The kid who I stabbed never said a word to his friends or anyone else. I saw him walking around school for a week with a bandaged hand and every time I walked by he just looked the other way. I never meant to hurt him. It just all happened so quickly.

The switch blade accident made me realize just how quickly your life could change. Not long after that incident my friend and fellow Cobra, Bob, was trying to steal a fishing reel from a store at the shopping center. He asked me to be his lookout. I thought everything was cool and I watched as Bob reached his hand in the glass case and quickly snatched up the reel. He shoved it into the deep pocket of his leather jacket then made for the door. Within seconds a store employee came to the very spot and looked for the reel. When the clerk noticed the reel was gone, he was after Bob in a flash. There was nothing I could do, so I quickly got out of the store. The police were already in the parking lot when the store clerk nabbed Bob. The cops threw Bob into the squad car, whisked him away and I never saw him again. I heard that he was taken away to reform school. With my friend Bob gone, the whole gang started breaking up. It wasn't long before my friend George moved away. I learned that many of my friends were ending up in jail and I soon started re-thinking an old phrase that my father would repeat, "You are the friends you keep." These hard lessons were teaching me that I did not want to follow in my friends' footsteps so I started looking around for some new people to hang with.

With my personal life in a shambles, at least life at home was improving. My mother and father were now working on their marriage, and enlarging the family circle. Soon the babies started rolling in. My sister Lisa was born on my birthday eleven years after me, followed closely behind by my sister Tina and a few years later brother David came along. With all these new crying babies in the house, I knew that I would never be alone again.

ENTER "EXIT"

When I was a little ways into my teen years, music came back into my life. My next door neighbor, Dave, started playing with a few friends who called their band Exit. Exit was your typical teenaged, garage band that played at dances, parties and summer coffee-houses. They had both rhythm and lead guitarists, Kim, (then later Bruce) and Wayne, a bass player - Jimmy, Dave on the drums and two lead singers, Sandy and Billy. They were a good band that could cover anything from the Beatles or Eric Clapton to The Who and the Stones. I was soon asked to be an equipment man or "roadie." I carried and moved the heavy amps, drums, guitars and P.A.. system from gig to gig for the band, and got paid with friendship and hamburgers. The band's manager was an older (college aged) fellow named Mike Robba. Now Mike's musical roots went back to the days when he played sax for the Delrays and even though he no longer played the sax, he did play acoustic guitar. He would often play some songs on his big Fender Villager 12-string when the band would be taking a break.

MARCH ON WASHINGTON

It was 1969 and the drug culture was on the rise. Our junior high school was lost in a cloud of smoke as more and more young kids were turning on (with marijuana), getting involved in political issues and growing their hair long. In those early days, growing your hair was a symbol of your political connections. It meant that you were opposed to the Vietnam War and were part of the so-called counter culture. My father was not thrilled with his son's hair slowly starting to creep over his ears and we got into many fistfights over the length of my hair. Long hair became the issue of the day. Parents and teachers hated it. It divided classmates and encouraged police harassment yet, in spite of all the hassles, it seemed to be worth it as it symbolized freedom.

Even though I was a younger member of the hippie culture I was filled with optimism and determination. When the news spread through our school that there was going to be a march on Washington, against the Vietnam War, I knew I just had to go. My parents caught wind of my plan and I was told I could not leave the house. Early in the morning, I opened my bedroom window, jumped out, and ran down the road. When I reached the New Jersey Turnpike I stuck out my thumb and was picked up by a carload of long-hairs heading to the march.

When we reached Washington D.C., I grabbed my sleeping bag, made my way through a sea of faces and camped out in the large field near the Washington Monument. The next morning people poured in from all over America and soon we were all packed in tighter than a can of sardines. As the day went on, more and more people tried to squeeze in closer to the stage. People started stripping off their clothes in the hot sun as they danced to the music of the Beach Boys. It was quite a scene with naked women dancing, police helicopters buzzing overhead and a huge flag of the Vietcong army flying in the breeze. As the stage filled with famous speakers, thousands of clenched fists were held in the air chanting, "Stop the war! Stop the war now!" As I sat and listened to the speeches I realized that the air was so thick with marijuana that you only had to take a deep breath to get stoned.

The heat of the day became so extreme, that I needed to get up and walk around. As I made my way to the line at the port-a-johns, I saw something that stopped me in my tracks. There, lying on the ground, was a young man who had passed out and much to my disbelief, he had a muddy sneaker print embedded on the front of his face! I just could not believe that someone would care so little about another human that they could just step on their face. I began to get sick and just kept walking until I made my way back out of the rally to the highway where I stuck out my thumb and went home.

On my way home, I was picked up by a soldier who had just come back from Vietnam. I told him about the rally, why I came and how I was I opposed to the war. He agreed and said, "It's an unjust war, and we should get out now." We talked about his experiences in Vietnam. Then he wished me luck and said that maybe our dream will come true and this war will end soon. As he drove away, I realized that I had learned more from talking to this solider than I had from hours of speeches at the rally. I was almost fourteen but I was already experiencing another side of life, and my real lesson was yet to come.

THE LSD TRIP

One day some friends and I were walking to school when one pulled out a pipe. "Have you ever smoked grass?" he asked with a quirky grin. Then he pulled out a bag of the green herb and stuffed some into his pipe. He lit it and then passed it around. I really didn't feel anything that first time but many more experiments were to follow. Grass was everywhere. Even in our junior high school clouds of marijuana drifted around the school while all the potheads chanted Dylan's mantra "Everybody must get stoned!" All of my friends were turning on with pot and we soon started experimenting with LSD.

A friend had told me that he scored some LSD. He had a neighbor who went to California and got some Owlsely Sunshine. "One hit," he said, "and you'll be in outer space." It was decided that we would drop acid the next weekend. We gathered together seven guys and two girls and went, by canoe, to an island in the middle of a nearby lake. The tiny tabs of blotter acid were handed out and three of us swallowed it down. At first it didn't seem like anything out of the ordinary. Everyone was smoking pot, laughing and giggling while waving their hands through the air - then it hit us all at once.

I looked around at my friends and watched as their faces became distorted, almost monster like, creatures with long teeth, big eyes and long arms. One of the girls, who in real life was very petite, started shrinking until she so became so small that I thought she would fit in my pocket! Even the island itself took on a new form, extending its shoreline and growing new trees. The night sky was now transformed into a huge split movie screen with fluorescent-colored bolts of lighting that would crash across the blackness of the sky. The interesting thing was that even though there wasn't a radio with us, I was hearing wild music as the colors swirled around my head!

New patterns appeared and walls of multi-colored dots danced across the air while a huge skull flashed onto the screen of the night. A knife had been plunged deeply into the skull's bone and a stream of dayglow blood dripped down into the lake. Some of the images were too horrible, so I tried to close my eyes to make them disappear but it was no use; the images were burning inside me and would not leave. As I looked behind me I noticed that another screen was filled with horses and chariots circling the stars then racing around the moon. Now the whole island came alive with sound. Trees, plants and bushes took deep breaths and exhaled into a wall of brightly colored haze.

As the hours went by, I began to lose more and more control of myself. One of the older guys, named Rob, came over and tried to help me. "Don't be afraid, you must learn to control the acid or it will rule you," he said. He took me for a walk and showed me how we could gather up the dots of color in the air and roll them into a ball and play catch. As we played with the colors, he used his canoe paddle to beat back the long "plant arms" that reached out in pursuit of us. Soon everyone went to sleep, while I sat holding my finger in the air painting portraits in the sky.

After some time, I was tired of playing and said to myself, "I wish that tree would fall on me." As I looked up, the huge tree started to crack and stagger and then not one, but a hundred "trails" of trees started to crash down on top of me. I yelled out a scream and put up my hands to push back the imaginary trees, then watched the trails return to the trunk of the tree.

It had been hours since I had dropped the acid and I was totally wiped out. I just wanted it all to end and be done with, when something new began to happen. The island started spinning round and round, faster and faster until everything was a blur of whizzing color. I felt like I was falling a thousand miles through the sky, like Dorothy in the Wizard of Oz. Then a loud voice called to me; it was as if the acid was talking to me. "I'm stronger than you are. This is not your path. Don't you ever come back to my door." As the voice trailed off into the great unknown I felt like I had hit the ground and finally returned to earth.

My "trip" was suddenly over. I felt a sharp pain in my head and collapsed from exhaustion. In the morning I opened my eyes to a new world rich in color. The trees were so green, and the sky was such a beautiful shade of blue that I felt as if I was viewing the world like I had never seen it before. I was so happy to be normal again but I knew that, after this trip, I would never be the same.

THE RINGING OF THE BANJO

Back at school, I had started hanging out with all of the school musicians and I was interested in learning how to play my own music. I didn't want to play rock music like my friends. I was hearing something different. I wasn't sure what kind of music I was searching for, but I began to hear the ring of the banjo echoing in my head. I don't really know where it came from, but something inside me was drawing me to this exotic Afro American instrument. I had heard stories from my father that great grandpa Palieri played a banjo and we had even had his old banjo at our house until my dad gave it away. Perhaps it was the spirit of my ancestor calling me to his favorite instrument. To hear the sound of a banjo was pretty rare back in the early 70's. Except for the rippling bluegrass banjo of Earl Scruggs on The Beverly Hillbilies or an occasional radio air play of "Foggy Mountain Breakdown" from the soundtrack of Bonnie & Clyde, the banjo was rarely heard any-where.

Then I heard from my friend Mike about a tall, skinny, bearded banjo player who often played the banjo on Sesame Street on TV. Soon I found myself getting up early just to catch a glimpse of this fellow, Pete Seeger. In a short time I was hooked, and the banjo became my life. I bought one of Pete's records, Young vs. Old, and practically wore it out. I also started reading up on Pete and he became almost like a father figure to me.

Pete was born in 1919, in New York City, into a family of musicians. His father was a musicologist and his mother taught classical violin. Pete caught the banjo bug by learning the tenor banjo at a private school; then he switched to the 5-string at the age of 17, after going to The Appalachian Folk and Dance Festival and getting a lesson from ace banjo player Bascom Lamar Lunsferd. Pete, at the same time, had a scholarship to Harvard, but got so interested in politics that he lost it and had to drop out at age 19. He then decided to travel the country by thumb and freight train, searching for the America he had heard of in these old ballads and fiddle tunes that he was learning. He traveled throughout the country picking up new songs and banjo picking styles everywhere he went.

In 1940 he hooked up with one of America's greatest balladeers, Woody Guthrie. Woody and Pete hit it off right away, and started doing some traveling together. One year later they joined a group of radicals and formed a band called The Almanac Singers, named after the "Farmer's Almanac." The group was comprised of Lee Hays, Mill Lampel, Peter Hawes, Bess Lomax and later, accordionist Sis Cunningham. These young singers were heavily involved in the labor movement, not only in collecting old songs but making up their own.. The Almanacs played at union rallies, strikes and picket lines, taking their music right to where it was needed most, straight to the people.

The group lived communally in a loft in Greenwich Village they dubbed The Almanac House, which soon became the meeting place for anyone who sang folk songs. In 1941 they recorded two albums, called Sod Buster Ballads and Deep Sea Shanties, and used the funds to finance their first cross country tour. The tour took them to union halls from Pittsburgh, PA to striking longshoremen in San Francisco. After the official tour ended, Woody and Pete traveled on. They went up to Seattle, where they played at a little benefit the workers called a "hootenanny." Intrigued by the strange word, they asked what it meant and the organizer told them, "We were looking for a new word to call our monthly parties and the word "Hootenanny" won out over "Wing Ding" by a nose. Hootenanny means a big country style music party. So after their trip, Pete and Woody brought to New York this new term to use for their own rent parties. Every month the Almanacs held a party to pay the rent and these hootenannies soon became well known in Greenwich Village. The Almanacs were gaining in popularity, especially among the more progressive crowd. They recorded a controversial album called Songs For John Doe. This album was filled with anti war songs recorded before the United States got into World War II. They changed their tune after Germany attacked Russia and started writing songs in support of the war. It was a bit of a flip flop, but politics often makes strange bedfellows. They later recorded an album called Talking Unions, their tribute to the labor movement. Soon their voices were heard on the radio, but before too long most of the members were called off to war and the group disbanded.

After the war Pete and fellow Almanac, Lee Hays, along with a bunch of friends, helped create a new folk magazine called People's Songs to continue their idea of spreading the folk music gospel. People's Songs was started in 1946 and went broke in 1950. After that went under the same group started the magazine Sing Out, which is still going today. Lee also asked Pete to form a new group with young singers Ronnie Gilbert and Fred Hellerman. The group started out as the No Name Quartet but soon changed to The Weavers. In a short time they went from a gig at a small nightclub in the village to recording some major hits that would be played on the radio. They recorded old folk songs like "On Top of Old Smoky" and "When the Saints Go Marching In" and had a number one hit with "Good Night Irene," a song from their good friend, black blues singer, Leadbelly.

Huddie Ledbetter was already a legendary figure in folk music circles. He played a big old Stella 12-string guitar, recorded songs for the Library of Congress, and even sang his way out of prison at one point. He was a big hit with the college crowd. He had his own radio program too. Leadbelly was a favorite at the Almanac's hootenannies and often played together with Woody and Pete. Even though Leadbelly was a great performer and song stylist he, like so many of his contemporaries, was just eking out a living. He always knew that one day he would become famous but he never lived to see his dream come true. Just six months after Leadbelly died, the Weavers recorded his song "Good Night Irene" with an accompanying band arrangement by the famous band leader Gordon Jenkins. No one could have predicted that this recording on the Decca label, would not only revolutionize the pop music world by jumping to the number one song on The Hit Parade, but also would create a new interest in old folk songs.

With their big hit, Pete and the Weavers, were the talk of the town. As Pete would later say, "You couldn't turn on the radio in 1950 without hearing that song. I was in a diner one time when I heard a customer say, 'Will someone turn that damn song off? I heard it ten times today!'"

But soon the happy times for the Weavers would come to an abrupt stop. America was in a state of fear. The Rosenbergs and the German scientist Klaus Fuchs had been arrested and accused of passing the secret of the atomic bomb to the Russian Government. The country went into a patriotic hysteria, questioning everyone about their affiliations with progressive movements, especially affiliations with the Communist Party. As the Weavers were considered to be progressive, they too were questioned. A book called The Red Channels was published, and inside was a list of entertainers, including actors and writers, who had questionable backgrounds. Pete's name was in the book and his troubles were just beginning. In Washington D.C., the U.S. House of Representatives' Un-American Activities Committee (HUAC) was created to look into these matters. Both Pete and Lee Hays were eventually questioned before the committee.

The Weavers had a vision of a world living in peace, but their thinking was before its time. To most Americans, the idea that you could trust the Russians, or befriend an African-American, was unthinkable. The Weavers' concerts were a gathering place for the left and at the height of their success they ran smack into the HUAC's hands. Concerts and TV appearances were canceled and radio stations stopped playing their records. At one concert, a stink bomb was set off and even threats of violence were aimed at the band members.

In 1955 Pete was ordered to come before the HUAC Committee to testify. Most of the liberal minded were pleading the Fifth Amendment saying that they would not testify against themselves and walked away with just a dent or two in their armor. Pete believed that he had to take a stronger stand and confounded the committee by declaring that no one has the right to ask any American questions about their personal religious or political beliefs. The judge charged Pete with ten counts of contempt of court and sentenced him to jail. Pete's wife, Toshi, and his friends raised bail and freed him from his cell.

While blacklisted, Pete kept on singing despite HUAC's attempt to silence him. He had always sung for kids in schools, colleges and summer camps. In 1953, when the

Weavers had to quit, many of the younger school kids he'd sung to were now in college and asked him to come to their schools. Oberlin, Antioch and, soon other colleges would follow. Pete would later say that, despite HUAC's attempt to hurt him they unwittingly gave him free publicity. For a long time to come Pete would be tied up with court battles. Meanwhile, folk music was exploding in the music industry. A group called the Kingston Trio, who were inspired by the Weavers, recorded a song by an old mountain banjo player named Frank Profit. The song was an old murder ballad called "Tom Dooley" and the melody was so infectious that it shot up quickly in the music charts. A folk music boom was underway. Colleges all over the country were forming little coffeehouses and having hootenannies where young folk singers would sing ballads and hillbilly songs. Everyone seemed to be riding the folk music bandwagon. Young singers following the Kingston Trio's lead were almost commonplace. Record companies embraced the trend and record-ed dozens of new folk singers; a show called Hootenanny aired on network television. Young girls danced around in hootenanny boots and every college had scores of young-sters strumming away on guitars and long necked banjos.

The new interest in folk music was also bringing a lot of the old timers out of the closet. People like the Father of Bluegrass - Bill Monroe, blues musicians Sonny Terry and Brownie McGee, Elizabeth Cotton, flat picker Doc Watson, Ozark balladeer Jimmy Driftwood and the Irish group, the Clancy Brothers and Tommy Makem, were packing houses and now appearing on TV shows. A long new line-up of new folk stars were becoming known with names like Joan Baez, Judy Collins, Bob Dylan, Peter Paul and Mary and the ever-popular bluegrass of Flat and Scruggs, and all that music was filling the air waves.

While all of the folk music hoopla was going on, Pete was still fighting his court case. He was blacklisted from TV and some of the concert presenters wouldn't touch him with a ten foot pole. In 1962 his long court battle was finally over. He won his case on a technicality. With his case now over, he was able to travel anywhere and re-establish his place in the music community.

His original songs were being recorded by younger singers like Peter Paul and Mary and the rock group, the Byrds. His songs, "Where Have All the Flowers Gone?" "Turn, Turn, Turn" and a song he penned with Lee Hays, "If I Had a Hammer," became popular hits on the radio and were now sweeping the nation.
He joined together with some friends and help organize the Newport Folk Festival, then later created an educational TV program called Rainbow Quest introducing new and old faces of the folk music crowd.

After his battle with HUAC, Pete became a symbol of the radical movement. Whenever and wherever an event took place that cried out against injustice, Pete was there with his banjo in hand. As a young man Pete fought for the unions, struggled for civil rights and now in his forties was heavily involved campaigning against the Vietnam War.

PETE SEEGER COMES TO TOWN

One day I heard that Pete Seeger was doing a concert at Douglas College, not far from where I lived, so I played hooky from school and hitchhiked to the show. It was the early 70s, and Vietnam was on everybody's minds. The college campus was filled with long hairs. My own hair was now past my shoulders, so I fit right in, and slipped into the church where it was to be. What happened next transformed me. When I saw Pete singing in that church something clicked inside and I said to myself, "This is what I want to do with my life." After the show Pete mentioned that he would be backstage and that there was a petition to sign. I went backstage and saw Pete and his wife Toshi surrounded by reporters, students, even some young toddlers. I stepped up to him and asked a dumb question, "Pete, why do you play the banjo?" He replied with a smile, "Because I like the tone." As I walked away from the concert I felt as if my life was about to change. For the first time in my life, the darkness in me was lifting and a bright light was now shining in my eyes.

After Pete's concert I knew I just had to get a banjo. When I told my mother about my new interest she said, "So now it's the banjo you want to play." She shook her head, laughed and told me that I should at least take lessons. In the beginning I didn't know that there were different kinds of banjos, so when I called the local music store they answered, "Sure, we can teach you the banjo. What kind do you want? We have 4- string, 5-string, even 12-string banjos." Being a 15-year old, I told him I would take the 12-string. He said, "Well, we're all out of 12-strings, but I do have a 4-string here." I told him I'd take it.

My new banjo teacher did not know how to play banjo at all. He was teaching me on a Les Paul electric guitar with the aid of a Mel Bay instruction book. One day I discovered Pete's TV show called Rainbow Quest, and saw that he played a 5-string banjo. The next week, when I went into my lesson, I told my teacher about how I wanted to play a 5-string banjo. He said, "Listen kid, you learn how to play this four string and then we will tack another string on."

I realized that he knew nothing about the banjo and quit my lessons. I soon sold my 4-string and my mother thought that I had given up the idea altogether, but I hadn't. Instead I got a Pete Seeger: How To Play the 5-String Banjo Book and read it every single night. I pretended that I had a banjo and practiced the right hand movements on my pillow or on the tabletops at school. Often I would go into a music store, take a banjo off the rack and practice until the salesman would throw me out.

THE GIBSON RB 180 LONG NECK

After Pete's concert, I became even more obsessed with getting a banjo. I saved every penny that I could get from birthdays and chores and even stopped eating lunch at school just to save a few more pennies toward getting my own 5-string banjo. After months of saving, I had a little over $200. Then my mother realized how much I had saved and how I really did want a banjo. She offered to help me out. My dream was a long neck banjo, like Pete's but they were hard to find and expensive too but to my good fortune, I stumbled on an ad in a phone book about a musical warehouse that carried all kinds of instruments.

When I called, much to my delight, I found they had one old, long neck Gibson banjo that had never been bought. They would be happy to sell it to me for $250 with a case and the man even offered to drive it over to my house. I quickly convinced my mother that I had to have this banjo and the next day the man pulled up to our house with a long, black banjo case. As he opened the case, you could smell the aroma of the wood and that wonderful scent of a new instrument. The banjo was a Gibson RB 180 Long neck, made in the 1960s, with a pearl Gibson crest on the peg head. After my purchase, I ran with my banjo over to Dave's, where his band was rehearsing. They all marveled over my new banjo, then one member laughed and said, "But he'll never play it. It's hard to play banjo, besides his fingers are too short." Mike came over and was really excited. "Hey maybe we can really play a few songs together now.." Mike and I had tried to play songs with my tenor banjo and now, with this new banjo, the possibilities were within reach.

I brought my banjo to school the next day in hopes of finding someone to tune it. I remembered a short, stocky fellow whom I had seen at school and at the Pete Seeger concert, who I thought might have been playing hooky too. I walked up to this bearded long-hair and asked him if he played the banjo. Then I showed him my new instrument. He smiled an elfish grin and tuned my banjo right away and started singing some of Pete's songs. At once, I knew I had found a new friend. His name was Neil Jacob. Neil taught me how to tune the banjo and then showed me Pete's basic strum. I was bowled over as Neil's fingers swept over the strings creating that bubbly banjo sound that I so loved and admired. With my new friend's help, I was on my way. I went home and got right to work practicing until my fingers bled. My banjo became like an outgrowth of my own limbs. When I found that I needed a strap to play my banjo while standing, I found a young kid who made me a leather one in exchange for my old switchblade. I knew now that the banjo was my life. There was no need to hold onto the past.

I played for hours and hours until my parents couldn't stand it any longer and would yell out, "He's crazy! Our son is crazy with that banjo!" When I was not practicing, I was listening to records or reading books about folk music. Soon my room turned into a mini folk music shrine, with pictures of Leadbelly, Woody Guthrie and Pete plastered all over the walls. I took my banjo everywhere and I even brought it to school each day, carrying the big case to every class I had. During lunch I would sit outside and play banjo tunes to my astonished friends who'd never heard such music before. Even in classes, I started practicing banjo rolls on my desktop until some of my teachers would give in and let me play a song or two for the class.

By the summer's end I was able to play together with Mike and we even decided to form our own folk duo called the Twinkle Town Detective Agency, inspired by a wacky sign we had seen along the roadside. We would spend evenings at my mother's kitchen learning chords and songs, and on weekends we would host hootenannies in my basement, gathering together a rat's nest of beginning guitar pickers and singers.

OUR FIRST GIG

Mike worked at the Home News newspaper in the advertising department. When he heard that another newspaper, the Newark News, was on strike, he thought that this was just the right opportunity to try out some of those old union songs that we had been learning. We jumped in Mike's old station wagon, with our guitar and banjo, and headed out. When we got there, rain was in the air and the picket line looked a little bleak. Now Newark, New Jersey is not necessarily the best place to be - even on a nice day - so with daylight almost gone and puddles of rain dotting the sidewalk, it was very uninspiring. Mike talked to the head fellow on the picket line and explained that we had come to sing for the workers. The old fellow looked at us with a queer stare and asked "You want to do what?" Mike repeated our desire to sing on the picket line. The old fellow looked at the rain falling on the soaked picket signs and said, "Go ahead." We then pulled out our instruments and started walking through the pickets singing Woody Guthrie's "Union Maid." When the pickets heard that infectious chorus "Oh you can't scare me, I'm sticking to the Union," their spirits lifted a bit and they began to sing along.

One fellow started doing a dance as he waved his picket sign up and down the block and even a few passersby stopped to join in with the singing. Another, a big black man, carrying a huge delivery of meat, danced along the sidewalk, almost juggling the half a cow he was holding. One song led to another until we had sung every song we knew. The Union official stepped forward and said, "You guys are great! Can we get you a sandwich and something to drink?" We walked over to a small trailer and, with smiling faces all around, enjoyed our first professional job earnings of two ham sandwiches and two Cokes.

BALLAD HUNTING IN THE PINES

As a young banjo picker, I sometimes had to go to great lengths to learn new tunes. Back in the early 70s there were too few banjo books so you had to learn the old fashioned way and go out and find someone to teach you. I had often heard of a place called "Albert's Cabin," in the Pine Barrens. Not known by your average tourist, the Pine Barrens is a kind of remote exotic wonderland down in south Jersey. In southern New Jersey the land changes from the rich soil that earns the state its nickname of "The Garden State" to a sandy land of pine trees, creeks and swamps. A lot of the land is still untamed and left in a wild state. The people who inhabit the region, known as "Pineys," are just as unique as the land itself, for it is from this very region that the stories of the Jersey Devil sprang up and some still say that you can hear the lost child of Mrs. Leeds screeching through the midnight air.

Albert's Cabin was said to be owned by two brothers who used it as a hunting lodge. It soon turned into a Mecca for all who loved the sound of the fiddle and banjo and where the Pineys would gather every Saturday night to play some of the best hillbilly music this side of heaven. I was still in high school at the time and didn't have a car or any money. I somehow convinced my pal, Dwayne Gross, that we could hitch-hike down to south Jersey and find this unusual place. I grabbed my banjo and Dwayne, his mandolin; we strapped our sleeping bags to our backs and started off down the highway.

We got as far as Mount Holly where we found a tiny music store. They had some really nice banjos and guitars there and I asked the owner of the store if he had ever heard of Albert's Cabin. The tall middle-aged owner replied that he went there often and, in fact, he was heading over there that night and if we would like to come, he would be happy to take us along.

We piled into his station wagon and rode down to a town called Waretown where, at a junction, we took off down a series of darkly lit back roads. I looked at Dwayne and we both started getting the creeps. Then the driver drove the wrong way down the Parkway and turned onto a dirt road between a row of bushes. Now our worst fears were racing around our young minds. After all, who was this man? We had just met him and didn't know a thing about him. He kept swerving around and through the pine trees, past abandoned TV sets, washing machines and stacks of old tires. As we passed a tall tree we saw an old bullet-riddled stop sign poking through it's branches. Now we both gasped as we were convinced this man was some kind of an axe murderer and was taking us faraway to kill us!

Just as we were about to scream, we heard something. It was the friendly sound of people playing music. At once, our fears ended as our car pulled into the grassy parking lot. Our driver smiled and said, "Well boys... we're here." Soon our new friend was introducing us all around and we pulled out our instruments and joined right in with the crowd of pickers standing around the porch. As I looked around, I saw two other banjo players. One was a youngster like me and the other a real old timer who played what looked like some kind of homemade instrument. I picked out the tune of "Cripple Creek" and noticed the old man was smiling as he watched my fingers beat over the head of my banjo. The old fellow introduced himself, "My name is Sam Hunt... and I have been playing this banjo for over 40 years. Yep, I even make 'em myself. Cut the wood on my own wood saw. This one here I made awhile back... You know I get letters from all over the world saying they want one of my banjos... Yep... I even make boats too. Yep... I'm one of the last of the Barnagat sneak-box boat builders... You ever heard of it? Well, we used to use 'em around here for duck hunting. Not many people do anymore... but I still make 'em. Even cut the wood from my own trees..."

Well, old Sam went on like that without hardly taking a breath of air in between sentences. I'd never heard anyone talk so fast and furious in my whole life! I liked Sam. There was something almost primeval about this old fellow. He was off the true vine. Soon Sam and I started playing a bit of music together. Even though I was still a rank beginner, I could frail the banjo, a style that was not too common. When I started frailing, a crowd soon gathered and before long both Dwayne and I were the hit of the evening. As we shifted from one song to the next a tune caught my ear. It was like nothing I'd ever heard before. I asked, "Hey, what's that tune called?" Sam shouted back, "Why that's the 'Old Joe Clark'... ain't you never heard of that one?" "No," was my reply. "Well," Sam said, "Well then, why don't we just learn it?" Soon Sam and the young banjo player, named Max, were showing me how to find the notes. "It's easy," said Sam, "most of the song just plays itself... why you just tune to open G-tuning, and then just slide right on into the notes." That whole night I kept working on that one song. The party was just about over and I was still sliding my finger about down the 1st string and singing softly, "Fare Thee Well, Old Joe Clark, fare thee well I say, I traveled around a thousand miles to hear your banjo play."

Later we all nestled down into our sleeping bags and fell asleep on a blanket of pine needles. I learned many songs that night - old ballads, country tunes and fiddle tunes, but of all the songs, the simple banjo song "Old Joe Clark" has stayed with me through the years, and has mellowed like fine vintage wine.

THE COMMUNE

Mike had been living at my parents' house, but eventually he found a new home at a musicians' commune just outside of Princeton, NJ. The commune was an old run-down Victorian farmhouse, decorated with tie-dyed curtains, yard sale furniture, a motorcycle parked in the living room and a goat that we milked, and painted red so the hunters wouldn't shoot it. The commune was rented by a rock and roll band, called Yesih, and was everything a young hippie could dream of or hope for. Mike rented a room and naturally, I spent weekends (almost the whole summer) hanging out there. We filled Mike's room with guitars, books and records and continued to live out our folk music fantasy.

The members of the band would often take in strays, and I had fit right in with the rest of the drifters who filled the big rooms of the old house. One day I was at a concert with one of the band members and we brought home this young girl who made herself at home and soon started doing all the cooking so they aptly named her Mom. Mom became the anchor of the house; she nurtured the band and gave the house a kind and friendly feeling. There were other folks who came to live at the commune and each had their own distinct personality. Omad was a large black man, with a shaved head, who would practice kung fu every morning, and had a black belt in karate. Then there was Ron, a tall long-haired fellow who would always be in the kitchen baking bread. Just a stone's throw from the farmhouse was a wooden A-frame where a nice couple lived with their baby son. They used the stream that ran by their house to bathe in and drink from. They were really into getting back to the land, living off the land and being one with nature. I spent many evenings in their tiny house eating natural food and chanting "oohhhmmm". The band was always rehearsing, so there were guitars and drums always set up and ready to go in the living room next to Nick's motorcycle. It was a fun place to live until the band got into drugs. That summer Mike and I played almost nonstop. We were encouraged by the band to go and experience the Philadelphia Folk Festival and, as we had never heard about this festival before, we thought we should give it a try.

THE PHILLY FOLK FESTIVAL

Near the end of the summer we went to our first folk festival. The Philadelphia Folk Festival in Swanksville, Pennsylvania is one of the oldest and biggest folk festivals in the United States. For years, it has been bringing some of the giants of folk music to the open fields of Mr. Pool's farm. The year was 1971, with Woodstock still fresh in every-ones' mind, we drove Mike's station wagon down through the grassy hills and joined thousands of folkies as we set up camp. I had never experienced anything like this before, and it was as if all my dreams were coming to life. I walked around with my banjo from tent to tent, amazed at all the people singing and strumming away at all those songs that I loved. It was at Philly that I first saw some of the people I had only read about: Doc Watson, Bill Monroe, The Lilly Brothers, Mike Seeger, Oscar Brand, and some brand new faces like Utah Phillips. I was in folk heaven and was even able to pick up a few playing tips from the other banjo players.

That night a storm broke loose. It wasn't just any storm, it was a hurricane. Soon the grassy fields were pelted with rain and they quickly turned into an ocean of mud. The rain continued all night and by morning the mud was so thick and deep that it covered everything in sight. Tents, cars, instrument cases and people were caked with thick mud. Many of the evening concerts were canceled and the morning workshops were late. As I walked around in the rain that morning, I watched in disbelief as some campers actually fell into pits of knee-deep mud and some even seemed to completely disappear as they went down into the muck. Mike had picked up a festival girlfriend who was so covered with mud that you could not really tell what she looked like. Later when he drove her back to the commune, she took a shower and revealed such a homely face that Mike's only comment was, "Well, she looked good in the mud." It was still the feeling of the 60's so everyone just got into the moment and enjoyed the mud. They played mudsliding games and on the last day, when the rain had let up, half the festival walked down the road and had a big skinny dipping party a la Woodstock. At the festival's end, we climbed into Mike's station wagon that had to be pulled out of the mud by an old tractor.

THE BUST

The commune was getting crazier and crazier. One of The Breed motorcycle gang had moved in and brought with him a plethora of drugs and guns, not to mention a line of motorcycles parked in the living room. Marijuana was always pretty common on the farm, but now there was cocaine, and even heroin, floating around and the once calm feelings turned into a constant state of paranoia. One evening, Nick, the leader of the band, was sitting in the kitchen with other band members, getting high, when a big rat ran by. Nick jumped up, grabbed a rifle, and pulled the trigger. Boom! The gun went off and missed the rat but landed smack into the leg of the lead guitar player. Blood spattered the floor as Lennie, the drummer, reached up and called an ambulance for help. The ambulance, complete with screaming siren came quickly down the quiet backroads, with a police car trailing behind. They loaded Chris into the ambulance and rushed him off to the hospital while the police stayed behind and questioned everyone. The police had been keeping their eyes on this place and knew that it was getting out of hand. They walked around and took down notes about everyone who lived there. It was not long after the shooting that they returned, this time to bust the place. Mike had gone for the weekend, but later heard what happened. The police planned a major raid and they had requested backup units from a few neighboring counties to get the job done.

Early that morning, they hid in the woods and fields, then fired tear gas into the windows of the farmhouse and stampeded through, smashing down doors and clubbing everyone in sight. When they got to Omad, who was a black belt in karate, they found him sleeping in a sleeping bag, and began beating him while he was stuck in the bag, while taunting him, "What are you going to do now with your black belt?" The whole farm was smashed to bits as they looked for drugs and then hauled everyone down to jail. Mike said it was horrible. They beat everyone including the girls. He said he never heard from or saw any of them again.

GLEN GARDENER

When I returned to high school that fall, I noticed a cute young girl named Janie. Janie had long blond hair, wire rim glasses and just like me, walked around in a buckskin coat. Janie and I soon became friends and she invited me to meet up with her foster parents who also played folk music. Mike and I drove over together and we brought our instruments. That night became another turning point in our lives. Janie's foster parents, Robin and Bill, both played guitar and in their younger days, were involved in the folk singing scene in Greenwich Village. Bill had a great flat-picking style and could finger-pick too. Robin was a fine singer and captivated me with her voice and stories about her days in the Village.

A surprise guest was Robin's cousin, Chuck Iroje, who was a fantastic all-around musician. Chuck was a recognized sideman, who played bass for Judy Collins and many other we-known acts. The night was filled with intensity, and I learned many of the songs that would soon be a part of my early repertoire, like "The Cuckoo Bird," "The MTA," "Rolling In My Sweet Baby's Arms," "Salty Dog," "Worried Man Blues," and the ever-popular, "I Won't Go Hunting With You Jake, But I'll Go Chase Some Women." Robin and Bill soon moved into the country and invited me to visit them in their new country home in northern New Jersey. The town of Glen Gardener was like a brand new world with open country roads nestled in between softly rolling hills. Just down the road from their new home lived another family that were soon to be very important in my life: the Kanes, John and Judy Kane lived there with their three children and a huge sheepdog named Tattoo.

John knew a lot of songs from his own Irish ethnic background and songs from the days of the 60s folk revival. Judy did not play an instrument but was a true folk fan and hosted many of the parties that soon sprang up in the tiny town. Judy also loved horses and, together with Robin, taught me the basics of horseback riding. We would spend hours out riding Robin's two horses, Rusty and Jughead. I liked to ride bareback, using my legs to hold on and often I would ride Jughead, who must have known that I, without a saddle, was an easy mark as he ran under a low branch and knocked me to the ground. I spent almost a whole summer hanging out at John and Judy's practicing my banjo and trying to learn how to play the guitar. Every morning, John would go over the finger-picking style inspired by Elizabeth Cotton and tell me that my job was to practice as he went off to work at his job as a pipe coverer (Asbestos Worker, Local # 32), only to find me crouched over the same table with a cup of coffee, still picking away when he returned at night. Taking a trip up to Glen Gardener became almost a weekly event; I would just throw my banjo over my back, stick out my thumb and hitch a ride.

One time I was hitchhiking, not far from my home, when a car made a U- turn to pick me up. At first I was a bit startled by the wide-eyed driver, until I saw his banjo lying in the back seat. "Where're you going?" he asked. "Oh up near Route 287 to Clinton," I replied. "Do you have any time to play a bit of music first?" Then the fellow, who's name turned out to be Frank, told me that he had a friend named John Burger who also played the banjo and was a great guitar picker too. Frank drove me over to meet his friend and we pulled out our instruments and played for a couple of hours before we all climbed back in Frank's car and drove up to see John and Judy. John and Frank were incredible musicians. They could play all the songs that we knew, and some we had never heard of. John's mastery of the finger style guitar was awe-inspiring as were Frank's riffs on the mandolin and metal body dobro guitar. That night, the music flowed as freely as the Jack Daniel's, so we played until the sun came up and all the whisky in the house was gone.

The arrival of Frank and John brought a whole new level of musicianship to our little group and before long; everyone was reaching out to expand their musical horizons. As I was still in high school, the idea of showcasing my new friends came into focus. I got together with my old junior high art teacher, Bob Hust, and told him of the plan. After meeting everyone Bob agreed that it was worth trying, so he helped organize a concert at my high school in East Brunswick. The idea of a concert was enough to pull everyone into shape. Soon we were all working out set lists and talking about performance techniques. I was to perform both with my friend Mike Robba, who was also to be the MC, and to do a set with Bill Boyd. Now Bill had a lot of experience, as he had been with a bluegrass band back in his college years. He knew that I had no real stage experience so he advised me on how to use a microphone. Bill suggested that at home I practice, by standing next to my doorknob and moving the banjo next to it for more volume, then away when I was singing. It made a lot of sense to me, but certainly looked strange to my parents as I became almost glued to the doorknob. Finally, the big day approached. My mother went out and bought a spangled, cream colored cowboy shirt for my first performance. The show was really wonderful with everyone doing a terrific job. I was scared to death as I stood in the big auditorium but as I was only a back up banjo player, I didn't have to be in the limelight. I was thrilled just to be a part of things and from that concert on, my name started getting around as one of the school musicians. That night I also met a young girl named Claudia, who would become a big part of my life.

The Road Is My Mistress

CLAUDIA

Claudia, at that time, was a light-haired, green-eyed girl with a cherub-like face. She was only fifteen years old, but seemed to know a lot for her young age. She had a girlfriend who was in one of my classes at school, so it was easy to set up a date. As the date was coming closer, another friend named Jim told me that he had once met Claudia at a party where he pulled her name out of a hat. This story delighted me and made me even more interested to meet her. At that time I was already having musical parties in my basement so it was easy to invite her to come. That night turned into one of the best hootenannies that we had ever had. Many of the young rock and rollers turned up, plus my banjo pal Neil and of course, Mike. Claudia sat there the whole time soaking in all the music and getting a taste of a new lifestyle. After the night was over, I gave her a kiss and we made plans to see each other again.

Soon Claudia was becoming a part of the regular gang and she started traveling around with Mike and me in his big station wagon. One time we spent the day playing music at a park, up in northern New Jersey, where they had a fantastic little waterfall way back in the woods. Claudia decided that it would be fun to take a little swim and jumped into the water. She then removed her shirt as she played under the falling water and laughed urging me to follow her. I joined her in the water and realized that this young girl had some ideas and plans of her own and they were not only about music.

MIKE'S PLAN

Mike and I had this plan of us hitchhiking across America, singing songs for nickels and dimes, and becoming real folk singers. I saved up all the money from my high school graduation and then, a few weeks later, planned to take off down the highway. Claudia was just getting into learning leather work and she made me a leather shoulder strap for my banjo case for easier traveling. My mother helped me pack and loaded up my knapsack with canned goods and clothes. When I picked up my sack, it seemed to weigh a ton but I thought I could get used to it. We climbed into Mike's station wagon for a short ride to Glen Gardener, where he would be parking his car. Our planned route was to hitchhike on Interstate 80 all the way to San Francisco.

That night we had a little party with our friends, and then made an early start the next morning. I soon realized that I had overpacked, and that the idea of carrying this knapsack loaded with canned foods, plus my heavy banjo, was going to be impossible. We had not walked but a few miles when I went to take a step and simply fell backwards from the sheer weight of the pack on my back. Mike laughed and helped me off the ground and said, "We have a long way to go; this is just the beginning." We trotted onward and made it to the entrance of the interstate. We were so thrilled. "Now we're really on our way," we shouted. We walked out to the highway and stuck our thumbs out, waiting for a ride but there was not a car in sight. We walked down the road for an hour or more, but still not one car came in either direction. I said to Mike, "I guess not too many people use this road." Mike just smiled and urged me to continue. A few hours had passed and still not one car had driven by, and now the hot summer sun was heavy upon us and our clothes were soaked with sweat as we carried our heavy loads down this endless road.

Suddenly, a car came screaming down the wrong side of the highway with a wild driver shouting, "Hey, you ***holes! This highway isn't open yet!" As we stood dumbfounded he turned the car around, drove back toward us and said, "Okay, get in." He drove us a few miles to where the interstate really started, shook his head and wished us luck as we got out of his car. Now that we were on a real highway the cars were flying by and it didn't take long to catch our first ride. It was a young couple heading out to Wisconsin. For some reason, Mike didn't want to go to Wisconsin (as it was not part of the plan), so after pretty much an all night drive, we got out the next morning near downtown Chicago. What a mistake this turned out to be! We stayed at that exit for hours without getting anyone to stop for us. Soon other hitchhikers joined us, so now there was a whole army of us hoping to catch a ride. The was sun beating down, our shirts stained with sweat, and just when you thought things could not possibly get any worse, two cop cars pulled over to talk to us. Chicago cops were not known for their kindness back in the early 70s, especially towards two long-haired hippies carrying instruments.

"Okay, boys, let's see some identification. Do you know it's illegal to hitchhike on an Interstate highway in the state of Illinois? Where are you going? Do you have any money?" The cops kept firing out questions while looking us over. I tried to be polite and said, "We're sorry, but where can we hitchhike?" The cops looked at my young face and said "It's illegal to hitchhike on an Interstate." I replied, "Can we hitchhike on that road?" and pointed to the next road over. The Cop said, "No, that's an Interstate." "How about that one?" I asked. "No, that's an Interstate too." Frustrated I moaned, "Well, where can we hitchhike?" The two cops looked at each other and laughed. "See that road over there?" he said, pointing to what almost looked like someone's driveway. "You can hitchhike there. "Now get going, because if we catch you out here again, and we will, it will be 30 days and 60 dollars. Now git!"

This road that we were now on could hardly be called a road at all; it was more like a side road for farm tractors. We walked and walked, having absolutely no idea of where we were going, until a big pickup started heading in our direction. Without thinking, I jumped in front of the truck and yelled, "Please help us!" The farmer took pity on us, stopped, and told us to hop in the back. "Where you boys going?" he asked, looking at our instrument cases and packs. "Just out of here," we replied. "Well I'm going into

Joliet, so I can take you there." We nodded and off we went.

In Joliet, Mike came up with a new idea. He said, "Rik, lets look into taking a bus," so we made our way to the bus station and found out that we could get an "Ameri-pass" and travel the whole country for not too much money. As I still had the money from my high school graduation, I thought this was a good deal and went and bought the tickets. Traveling by bus seemed to suit our style and we soon made ourselves right at home, at the back of the bus, playing songs for all the passengers. We'd get off every once in a while to check out a city here or there, only to be climbing aboard yet another bus by nightfall. We'd often open our instrument cases to earn a few dollars for our breakfast. We were on a tight budget, eating pancakes and chili most of the time. Music became our passport and we used it at every opportunity. One time, in the middle of Kansas, two burly men came on board. They were covered with tattoos and had short butch-type haircuts. Every time they looked our way they sneered. Mike and I thought we were in trouble and braced ourselves. At one point, we pulled out our instruments and started playing quietly in the back of the bus. One of the big men moved out of his seat, heading in our direction and we thought, "Well, this is it." When he reached our seats, we noticed that he was smiling and he said, "You boys sure play some good music. My friend was wondering if you knew any Hank Williams songs." With that, Mike broke into a rousing version of "Jambalaya" followed by "Your Cheating Heart" and a foot-stomping, "I Saw the Light." The two fellows and the rest of the bus, burst out into applause. The bus driver soon called us to the front of the bus to use his microphone and lead everyone in song. Our little songfest lasted all the way through Kansas until the bus made a stop and we had to make a change at the station.

As this was my first trip west, I marveled at the scenery. Riding through western Kansas we saw herds of buffalo and passed through the old western town of Dodge City. We passed fields of golden wheat with huge grain elevators, and were awestruck by the majestic Rocky Mountains. I was seeing things that I had only read about, and experiencing firsthand the true beauty of America. We spent a night walking through the gambling casinos of Reno, Nevada where even the gas stations were lined with one-armed bandits. The lounge acts in these dives had sleazy women dressed in sparkly sequins, with only pasties covering their breasts.

Eventually, we reached California and around mid afternoon our bus pulled into San Francisco. I was so excited; I didn't know what to do first. Plans raced through my head for seeing Alcatraz Island, eating a fish dinner on Fisherman's Wharf, or going over to Haight-Ashbury to see all the trendy "head shops." While my mind was swimming in thoughts of our next adventure, Mike said, "I need to go and get a post card. I'll be right back." A few minutes later, Mike popped his postcard into a mailbox and said, "Well, we made it and now it's time to go home." "Home!?" I screamed. "Home? We just traveled all the way across America, riding on smelly busses for a week, eating only pancakes and chili beans and you are already wanting to go back home?" I was filled with anger. Mike said, "Well Rik, staying here is not in the plan and I have to be back at work in two weeks so we have to go back." I was so confused. "You said that we were going to stay here and that you had quit your job." Mike said sheepishly, "Well, I never actually thought that you believed me. I didn't really quit, this is just my vacation and I do have to get back." I was crushed. I knew that I was not ready to stay on in California by myself, so I had to give in and go along with Mike's plan once again. Then Mike said, "Don't feel bad. We can spend the day enjoying Fisherman's Wharf and then get back on the bus and take the slow way back home." I looked at Mike and said, "Let's make the most of it then." With that, we headed down to the wharf to enjoy a meal of Chinese LoMein, and climb around the tall ships in dock. By nighttime, we were back aboard another Greyhound, riding through tall redwood trees all the way along the rocky coast to Oregon.

Near Portland, two young musicians got on our bus. One was toting a bluegrass banjo and the other, a box filled with harmonicas. Soon we had a hot and heavy jam going at the back of bus. With two banjos, Mike's booming guitar, and the wail of a harmonica, we made that bus rock. We played 'til evening when the bus driver said, "Ok fellows, lights out!"

When we hit Seattle, we spent the day basking near the Space Needle. The sun was shining brightly which, we learned, is a rare occasion, so everyone was out enjoying the warm rays. We were earning a few pennies as street musicians, when a young woman came by and said she loved our music and would like to show us her town. We packed up our instruments and spent the rest of the day walking the streets with our new friend. By nightfall, our lady friend suggested that we could stay at her house. She said, "My husband is out of town and it would be fun to have you as my house guests." Mike looked at me and winked. From past experience I knew what trouble an offer like this could lead to, so even though it was extinguishing Mike's fantasies, I told our fan that we'd better be hitting the road. Now it was Mike who was not the happy camper, but he agreed to go with my plan this time.

From Seattle, we rode to the mining town of Butte, Montana. In Butte we walked into a dark tavern. As we entered we saw a bunch of unfriendly faces at the bar and decided that our music was not going to do the trick this time and ran out the door. We got back on the bus just missing getting our faces rearranged.

The bus drove over the misty mountains of Montana, past the endless flatlands of North Dakota and all the way to the windy city of Chicago. In Chicago we found a little festival going on and met a few guitar pickers to jam with but we couldn't get too excited as both Mike and I knew that we were nearing the end of our trip and we would soon be back in New Jersey. We boarded the bus again to our last stop in Easton, Pennsylvania. We reached Easton in the middle of the night and slept in the train station on a hard wooden bench. We woke up to the gruff sound of a policeman's voice telling us to, "Get up, boys, you'd better get moving before you get in trouble." We picked up our gear, stuck out our thumbs and headed for home.

HATFIELD'S

By the time I got back home from my musical odyssey, my parents informed me that it was time for me to get a real job. My father was always a hard-working man sometimes working two or even three jobs just to keep up with the bills. One of his part-time jobs was at a department store and, through his contacts, he was able to get me a job unloading trucks. My first day on the job was unloading a truckload of heavy air conditioners. My arms ached at the end of the day, but I really didn't mind the job. All of the truck unloaders had long hair (hence - why we were unloading trucks), so it was always a bit of a party time in the back of the truck. After about a month I got bored and thought I should try something else. I had this idea of learning to make musical instruments by taking a job at the Oscar Smith Auto Harp Company. I went to their offices for an interview, brimming with enthusiasm. The interviewer must have thought I was a bit crazy as he knew that this was nothing more than a sweatshop job. I got the job of cutting out sound holes. At first I was still a romantic about the job but soon I couldn't tell if I was cutting out sound holes or holes for doorknobs, as it all seemed the same. I got bored and quit and my mother suggested that perhaps I could get a job with my father at Hatfield's making wire and cable. She ended her plea with "You can make good money at Hatfield's."

All of my life I had watched my father get up at nine o'clock at night, eat dinner (actually, his breakfast), and go to work at Hatfield's. My father was almost nonexistent in my life as he was always working. I would soon find out why my father was always so tired and miserable. My dad signed me up and now, just like him, I too was working at Hatfield's. I had never been in a factory before and certainly never worked the midnight or what they call the "graveyard shift." The building was colossal, with machines reaching all the way to the ceilings and the noise was almost deafening. You could hardly talk to anyone unless you shouted. There was also a menacing, unhealthy, almost dangerous, atmosphere to the place. On my first day at work, my father introduced me to all of the guys that he had worked with since he left the Navy. I found out that he had a nickname. Here at work they called him "Willy." All of the other guys had monikers too. There was Big Daddy - the boss, Mulligan Stew - who liked his Irish whisky, the Hawk - who had a huge nose, Cadillac Bob - who was a smart dresser, Bubba - a really big fellow and plenty more. These guys all looked mean. Just the sight of them made you understand why they worked the midnight shift as you didn't want to be seeing them in the daylight. At first, they weren't friendly, as they did not like long hairs, but after a while they started warming up and calling me "Willie's son."

To say that I did not like Hatfield's would be putting it way too mildly as I really hated this place - it was awful. The work was hard, the hours were bad and it was just a damned dangerous place to be. No one worried about any environmental hazards (in those days). The air was filled with lead-dust and many of the employees would never reach the age of retirement. The worst thing, for me, was that you could never get away from the place. You worked all night and by the time you got home, you were too wide awake to sleep. When you finally fell asleep, you dreamt about Hatfield's and then you'd wake up to get ready to go back. No, you never could leave Hatfield's.

One morning my father and I rushed into work only to find a machine on fire. The guy who was watching the machine said, "My shift is over, now this is your problem." My dad jumped into action and, with his big arms, started pulling the cable off the reel and out of the fire. While he and I were holding the line, another worker grabbed a fire extinguisher and put out the blaze. Not wanting to lose a minute of work, someone pushed the start button. All at once, the coil of cable started snapping off the ground and one loop grabbed my leg. I shot up into the air while my father looked on in horror. "Cut the line! Cut the power," my father shouted in panic. By now, I was hanging upside down suspended from the cable and was heading straight into the mouth of the machine. They killed the power just in time and had to cut me loose. My father said "You are lucky, we almost lost you."   A few weeks later, I was walking on a high catwalk and was so tired that I almost lost my balance. I caught myself just in time, before going over the railing. Once again, I saw my father look at me and shake his head. Then just for a moment, it was as if I saw my own face in his. Almost like a peek into my future and what I saw scared me to death. I knew I had to get out of this hellhole, but it seemed like a lost cause as most of the people who worked here stayed on forever.

Then one night, at around three in the morning, my prayers were answered. It was a slow night, the cable was running smoothly and there was not much to do. I had brought along my tape recorder and was trying to work on a new piece of banjo music by an old timer named Wade Ward. The name of the tune was "June Apple" and as the reels of cable went round, the guys on the floor started to tease me about the square dance music that I was listening to. Then two of the guys playfully joined arms and started to dance. Before long the rest of these big burly fellows were all in a big circle dancing around the machinery. A few minutes later Big Daddy, the boss, came in and took one look at me, my tape recorder and his men dancing and called everything to a stop. The men jumped back to work and I had to go into the office for a little talk. It turns out that they didn't think that I was right for Hatfield's, which was fine with me. They offered to lay me off, and the next day I was a free man. The layoff entitled me to collect unemployment. Back in the mid-seventies, work was hard to find so I also got extended benefits and after that, extended-extended benefits. With years of employment checks heading my way I had enough time to really figure out how I could make a living with my music.

LESSONS WITH ERIC DARLING

While I was working at Hatfield's I was able to do a few good things to help my music along. The first was to buy my first Martin guitar and the second was to take a few lessons from one of the all-time great banjo players Eric Darling. Eric was a leading figure in the 60's folk revival and worked as a replacement for Pete Seeger when Pete left the Weavers. He later started a group of his own called the Roof Top Singers who had a top ten hit with an old blues song called "Walk Right In" by Old Gus Cannon.
Eric lived at the edge of Central Park, in New York City and once a week I would take a bus from Jersey and then ride the subway to get my lesson. Inside Eric's apartment I saw a wall of gold records from his many achievements and, also some of the instruments that I recognized from his albums. Eric was friendly and a good teacher. At the time, we were working on learning bluegrass rolls, when one day he surprised me. He said, "Rik, we are going to do something a little different today. I have to do a few errands and I was wondering if you'd like to come. We can talk on the way."   I didn't realize it, but I was about to get one of the most important music lessons in my life.

We left his apartment and rode the subway. While riding along underground, Eric spoke of his days touring with the Weavers and making hit records. Then, sounding a bit somber, he said, "Rik, you are young, just starting out, and I want to tell you a little bit about my life so that you won't stumble into any pitfalls." Then he went on to say, "There will come a time, if you stick with it, that your music will hit a plateau, a wall that might stop you in your tracks. You will have to understand that to get over it you will either have to work even harder or sometimes just get away from it." He then talked about how hard it is to get a big hit, and then later, try as you will, you may not be able to create that magic again. When we came back to his apartment I stared at the gold records on his wall and his smiling face. At the time, it was almost too much information for a youngster, but as I grew in my music and reached a few musical blocks of my own, his words of wisdom and advice rang clear and true to me.

ZEMAITIS, GUITARS & GARETH - The Gypsy Minstrel

It all happened back in 1973. I was still in high school, playing my long-necked Pete Seeger style banjo, when an English fellow came to visit our school. Gareth Hedges was visiting America and was invited to perform during an arts festival. I can still remember Gareth cradling that Zemaitis rosewood 6-string guitar, while playing the Reverend Gary Davis's version of "Candy Man." My eyes popped out as I gazed at the colorful wooden inlay around the strange D shaped sound hole. It was like no other guitar I had ever seen, with an ebony neck, embedded with flecks of iridescent pearl, ending in a carved fleur-de-lis. At the very top of the wispy, curved headstock sat a long metal engraved shield with the word Zemaitis inscribed into a border of flowers and scrolls. Gareth's fine finger style captured and mesmerized me and the mellow balanced tone of his rosewood Z guitar, rang straight to my heart. It was not long before Gareth and I became best of friends and spent many hours together playing music. Gareth was very involved with the British folk scene, learning his music firsthand from guitar masters like Davy Gram, Ralph McTell, and John Renbourn. He also spent time with many American folk icons, like Gary Davis, Mississippi Fred McDowell, Doc Watson, Son House, Big Boy Crudup, Bill Monroe, Clarence Ashley and Tex Isley. At the time, Gareth was my link to the masters. He became my mentor and after I left Hatfield's, we spent years together hoboing around the country roads of America.

While I was still living at home, Gareth persuaded me to borrow the family Volkswagen and make a trip to Washington, D.C. to see some old friends. It sounded like a great idea, so we headed down the highway and drove until dark. Then Gareth pulled off the highway and parked the VW bug in this small town right in the center of a middle class housing development. I asked, "Gareth, what are going to do here?" Gareth said, "Get some sleep." So Gareth and I, together with all of our instruments, bedded down for a few crowded hours of sleep. When the sun came up, we rushed off again and headed to downtown D.C. to meet Gareth's friends. We came to this big apartment building and knocked on the door of the dazed occupants. Gareth did the talking so at first, I was unaware that they really didn't have the vaguest idea of who we were. Gareth told me that he needed to borrow my car for an hour and that I should go in and get some sleep. I gave him the keys and he roared off. When I went inside, I was getting the strangest looks. I assumed that Gareth had explained everything, so I just made my way in and said, "Oh we had a long drive. I'll just take a little nap." When I woke up, I found out that no one who lived in that house had ever heard of Gareth. After a few very uncomfortable hours Gareth returned and said, "Oh well, I guess my old friends have moved on. We will have to be moving along." Then we left.

During another of our rambles, Gareth and I drove to a tiny shore bungalow on the seaside in Point Pleasant, New Jersey. Before we reached our destination, Gareth was going on and on about his good friend John who we were about to visit. When we pulled up in front of John's house we noticed that there weren't any lights on and that the door was locked tight too. Gareth paid no mind to the lock and simply looked for a window to crawl in. I was getting a little nervous, but Gareth reassured me that he and John were good friends and there was no need to worry.

Once inside we made ourselves at home and played a bit of music. Gareth asked if I was getting hungry and then proceeded to look around the kitchen. He found a few eggs and potatoes and started to cook up dinner. While the food was cooking, we picked up our instruments and played a few more tunes. In the middle of a rousing banjo break, the door swung open and a tall bearded man screamed out, "Who are you and what are you doing in my house?" Gareth said in his sweet English accent, "Oh John, it's me Gareth. Don't you remember, we met at a party and you said to pop in if I'm ever in the area?" All of a sudden my stomach was twisting into a knot as I realized that Gareth only vaguely knew this man and that, we not only had broken into his house but were eating his food too. As we all stood in silence Gareth picked up his Zemaitis guitar and asked John if he would like us to play for him. I reluctantly grabbed my banjo and struck up a fast fiddle tune. Within seconds, John's frown turned into a smile as he sat down to listen. After a few songs our dinner was ready, and by now, John was an old friend and was delighted to have us join him for a meal. In fact, he did not want us to leave, so we ended up spending the summer.

Soon, John's cottage, as we called it, became the hangout for our group, The Union Valley String Band with bandmate John Berger. John was a giant of a man who could play the most delicate finger style ragtime guitar and at the time was just learning the fiddle. We played all kinds of low-life dives like Nolan's, in Perth Amboy, NJ. Nolan's was a rough bar with just a postage stamp sized stage. Often my long necked banjo would almost clip Gareth as I moved about the stage. Despite the primitive conditions at Nolan's, it was the place to be. Often times, the bar was taken over by our fans with the young ladies doing belly dances to our mountain music, or a fight would break out and we would have to keep on playing to try and settle the crowd until the fighters would spill out into the dark alleyway.

There was always some kind of activity going on at the cottage, from voice lessons to learning new songs from old LP's. As John's cottage was right on the seashore it also meant that there were female fans, visitors and tourists in the area. Right next to John's cottage was a hotel filled with young college girls for the summer. One day Gareth decided to erect a sun-bathing room in the backyard, so he nailed a few large walls of plywood together, placed a few chairs and a little table for fruit and wine in it, disrobed, put on his sun glasses, and enjoyed the sun. Of course it didn't take the young girls long to spot Gareth from the high hotel windows and he developed quite a fan club. Soon these young women were hanging out the windows and calling to Gareth and later, many decided to join him. Many a time, I found myself being called to deliver another bottle of wine or some fresh cheese to Gareth and his naked harem.

We stayed at the cottage until fall and then, as the chilly autumn winds blew across the lonely boardwalk, we all migrated to The Farm, another hangout for all kinds of destitute musicians.

THE CARTERET SERENADERS

When I was not hanging out with the band, I was doing volunteer work with a group called The Carteret Serenaders. The group was made up mostly of middle aged women who liked to sing at hospitals, nursing homes and for other charities. I realized that being with this group was a good way to introduce myself to different audiences and give me more stage experience. The shows were sort of a rag tag event, with the ladies covering old pop standards and me playing the banjo. These were not easy gigs as often the audience was barely in control and would scream sometimes, or throw up during the performance. As I got more comfortable with the group, I challenged them to book a show at the notorious Rahway Penitentiary. The show finally came to pass and we were escorted inside the main gates where we were asked to take off our coats and empty our pockets. Our instruments and sound gear were rolled away to be thoroughly checked out before they brought everything up to the performance area. Once we were cleared, we walked into another room with a big steel door locking behind us. Then another big door was opened and we all walked into the main building.

The prisoners were, to our amazement, not only polite but downright friendly as they welcomed us into the huge auditorium with coffee and cake. Above our heads, painted over the stage, was a huge green monstrous head with an even more ghoulish creature rising from it's skull. That painting reminded us that we were not playing for a Saturday afternoon bridge club. The show was very well received but I think it was just the idea of having mostly women in the building that brought the most applause. When we were leaving some of the people from the program committee walked us back to the big steel door and you could see in their eyes the longing to walk out with us through the door to freedom. We said good-bye to our friends as the big door slammed behind us and was then locked up tight.

THE DYSFUNCTIONAL THANKSGIVING

It was back in about 1976, when I was trying to make a living by giving private music lessons that I had the weirdest Thanksgiving that can remember. It was just a few days before Thanksgiving that my car broke down and I had to borrow the family auto to make a trip out to Clinton, New Jersey to give a few guitar lessons. That fall I was experiencing many automotive problems, with blown engines, car accidents and even vandalism. It was with great trepidation that I asked my mother for the keys to her powder blue

Eldorado Cadillac. That car was like a boat on wheels and ate enough gas to drain an oil tanker, but it was my last hope to make a few bucks so I decided it was worth the risk. On the trip over to Clinton, I noticed that the car was smoking! When I got to my student's house, I found that my engine was on fire. We put out the blaze and later carefully nursed it back home. I was too afraid to tell my parents about my little mishap, so I just kept my mouth shut. My mother did not use her car till Thanksgiving Day. On that day a whole mob of relatives came to our house. My mother was in the kitchen cooking up the big feed, when she realized that she needed a few things at the store. "Oh Bill," she yelled to my dad. "Can you go to the store and pick up a few things." He looked around and saw that his car was blocked in. Then she yelled "Oh just take MY car."

As I heard her words, my stomach sank. I wondered if now was the best time to tell them about my little problem. When I thought about all the yelling that might take place, I said to myself "I made it home with out any problems - maybe it will be ok!" The Cadillac was parked at the near the end of the driveway making it the best choice for the trip. My father jumped in the driver's seat and cranked up the engine, but it stalled. He tried again and this time it would not even turn over. By this time my aunt's boyfriend who owned a garage got into the action. "Hey Bill, having problems? Maybe I can help." Old Jerry opened up the hood and listened to the motor and then said "Maybe we should put a bit of gasoline in the carburetor." Jerry went over and filled a glass jar with a bit of gas and told my dad to crank her up! As my dad cranked the motor a big plume of fire shot out of the engine and caught the jar aflame. Jerry, in a panic, threw the jar over his head, landing into the next door neighbor's yard.

Our neighbor, who was not at home, had a big pile of leaves in the yard which immediately caught fire. Just at that moment my mother was taking the big bird out of the oven. When she looked out the window, she saw that almost the whole back yard was in flames. Seeing everyone scrambling around trying to put out the fire made her arms weak and she dropped the turkey on the floor. We managed to put out the fire before we had to call the fire department and before any real damage was done. My mother washed off the turkey and put it back on the serving platter and we all ate our meal. Hardly a word was said as we ate that big bird. Then My Mother looked at me and said, "Were you the last one to drive my car?"

THE SLOOP CLEARWATER

I first heard about the Sloop Clearwater at one of Pete Seeger's concerts. I wrote to Pete for more information and he wrote back telling me where and when the next meeting would be. It didn't take me very long to get involved. The sloop's story itself is interesting. Back in the mid 1960's Pete was getting interested in sailing. He had this bathtub of a sailboat and would often spend days and nights learning to tack and jibe with the currents of the Hudson River. One day, a friend who was interested in both sailing and music handed Pete an old book about big cargo sloops on the Hudson. The book told stories of the old sloops that once graced the Hudson. There were stories of the sloops being the main traffic on the river hauling cargo from New York City upstate to Albany. The book fired up Pete's imagination, and he began thinking about the idea of building a replica of one of the sloops to help save the Hudson River from pollution. Most people thought he was a bit off his rocker, but he started setting up concerts to raise money for the project. It took awhile but more and more people started getting involved with Pete's dream, and as the money came in, the plans were drawn up. She would be about seventy-six feet on deck, from bow to stern, and would be built along the characteristic lines of the sloops of long ago. By 1969, the ship was built and had her maiden voyage sailing down from the ship yard where she was built, in Maine, all the way down to New York City. Along the way, there were free riverfront concerts featuring the crew of musicians who were aboard her.

Every year, the Sloop would do a special Pumpkin Sail, where they would load the deck of the boat with pumpkins and sell them in riverfront community concerts up and down the Hudson River. It was exciting to go down to South Street where the sloop would make her final stop in New York City. I would head down there early in the morning and stay right to the very end each night. Pete would be there, as well as a host of talented musicians who were known as The Hudson River Sloop Singers. One of the crew was a curly headed fellow named Bob Killian. Bob was a songwriter and a banjo player too, and after we played a few songs together Bob said, "Rik, you should think about sailing with us and maybe you'll get a chance to play a bit of music too." Bob's friendly welcoming manner made me feel like perhaps I should be more involved with this organization. A few months passed, and I decided to join up and become a member of what then was called The Hudson River Sloop Restoration Project, and started receiving the monthly newsletter. As I was still a teenager in high school, I thought that I would need to take some sort of training course on sailing to get on board. I signed up for an after school evening course on Sailboat Safety sponsored by the Coast Guard. Here I was with my shoulder length hair and jean jacket, mixing with a bunch of "Yachties," dressed in captain hats, white belts, monogrammed blue blazers and deck shoes. At first, it was an uncomfortable mix of age and lifestyle but through the course I learned that small differences often disappear when you are reaching for a bigger goal. I later learned that you don't need to have any sailing experience on the Clearwater as they teach you everything you need to know.

MEETING PETE

I had read that Pete was going to do a free evening concert at Central Park, with Arlo Guthrie. I marked that day on my calendar, and was anxious for the big day to arrive. Little did I know that earlier that same day my mother would take my two young sisters to the park to visit a few museums. After they finished looking around the museums, they all went over to Central Park to have a little picnic and play with the other children. While they were at the park, they saw a huge crowd gathering as they were setting down blankets. My mother was curious about what was going on and asked one of the young girls who was already sitting down if she knew. The girl replied that there was a free concert with Pete Seeger and Arlo Guthrie. When my sister Lisa heard that Pete was playing, she remembered that I was also planning to be at this show and for some strange reason thought that I was going to be playing there too. They told my mother that they were going off to look for me and headed for the stage area. They were both only tiny tots at the time, about nine and six years old, so when they met one of the stage hands and told him that they were looking for their brother, who is a friend of Pete Seeger, he brought them to the trailer where Pete and his wife Toshi were getting prepared for the evening's show. Lisa remembers walking into the trailer; "It was so strange as we were only two little girls and did not realize where we were, but as soon as the door opened, I recognized the big tall fellow with a gray bushy beard, holding a banjo. I knew it was none other than Pete Seeger."

After a few moments of stunned silence Lisa blurted out, "I know you. You're Pete Seeger." Pete replied, "Where do you know me from?" Lisa said, "From watching Sesame Street. Do you know if my brother is here?" Pete, a little perplexed, asked, "Your brother?" Lisa continued, "My brother is big fan of yours and he plays the banjo, too. He is really good. I thought he said he was coming to see your show. Is he here?" Lisa went on about her brother until Pete then asked, "Who is he?" Lisa said, "His name is Rik Palieri and, you know, he has some of your records, too." Pete laughed and told her, "No, he isn't here." Then he asked his wife, Toshi, to make the girls some sandwiches, he gave them some water and then sent them back out to play. My sisters left the trailer and told my mother what had just happened. My mother really did not believe them but told them, "That's nice." She told them that it was getting too crowded and that they'd better leave for home. A few hours later, I arrived with Claudia and sat down to enjoy the show. That night at the concert, Pete said, "Tomorrow I will be performing at a riverfront festival in Hoboken, NJ, to benefit the Clearwater. Everyone's invited."

As Hoboken was just a stone's throw away from my parents' new home, Claudia and I planned to go. The next morning, at breakfast, my sister said, "I met Pete Seeger yesterday." I looked at her like she was crazy." "He was filing his nails," she snapped back.

Unaware of my sisters' little promotional campaign, I just shook my head and walked out the door with my banjo slung over my back. When Claudia and I arrived there were already a few musicians playing together in a little circle so I pulled out my banjo and joined right in. We played for while a when someone called out, "Hey, Pete's here!" Pete was dressed in a bright yellow T-shirt and black Greek fisherman's cap. He joined our circle, unzipped his leather guitar case and took out his big 12-string guitar and played along. After a few songs he introduced himself. When he came to me he said, "And who are you?" I stuttered out, "Hi I... I'm... Ri..k Rik Pal... ieri." Pete looked at me, cocked his head and said, "You know Rik, I met your sisters yesterday and they told me you are a good banjo player. Why don't you come up on stage with me and we'll sing a few songs together with the rest of the group?" I stood in shock thinking, "You met my sisters? You want me to join you on stage?" Pete smiled and later welcomed me up onto the tall waterfront stage.

After meeting and performing with Pete in Hoboken, he started calling me and encouraging me to get more involved with the Clearwater Organization. I started going to more meetings and met an Italian woman named Claire Dameo. Claire was a real activist and had plans for starting a New Jersey sloop club. I decided that it would be good to work together so we started seeing each other often. Claire was also involved with a little coffeehouse in Jersey City called Not for Bread Alone. She ran the place with the help of a group of young kids and often with the help of Rev. Kirk, or Brother Kirk, as we called him. Brother Kirk was a giant of a man, with a raspy, strong voice and a heart of gold. Kirk was a friend of Pete Seeger's and sang often with Pete at Clearwater events and once on the TV show Sesame Street. Kirk also ran a similar coffeehouse in New York City called the Hey Brother Coffee House and was now mentoring these young kids along with Claire. The idea came up of doing a benefit to get this fledgling sloop club off the ground. Pete was contacted, along with Brother Kirk, and I recruited a few more of my friends to round out the evening.

The concert was held at Jersey City College and we performed to a small but enthusiastic house. After the show with Pete and Kirk, we had enough funds and people to start our club and, as I went to more and more meetings, I started getting to know a lot of the musicians who hung around the boat. The group was made up of about a dozen or so music makers who would support the sloop at any kind of gathering. As I always had my banjo with me, I would often be asked to join in too. After a while I became a regular member of The Hudson River Sloop Singers and soon found my calendar filled with Sloop Singer shows.

While singing with the Sloop Singers, Pete suggested that I should consider trying to put on a riverfront community festival like his in Beacon, but more in my area like in Perth Amboy. It's tough to say no to Pete, so I went headfirst into the project. I went down to the harbor area as Pete suggested and tried to imagine how a festival could take place there. I contacted my old junior high school art teacher Bob Husth. Bob was a good guitar player and singer and was also interested in the environment. I told him about Pete's suggestion and he was more than willing to roll up his sleeves and join in to help. Bob started calling up Pete for more ideas and soon we all did a few concerts together and talked about doing a festival in the summer. As Pete was already booked, he suggested that Harry Chapin might be available. Bob contacted Harry and not only did he agree to come, but said he would contact Bob McGrath from the kids show Sesame Street to come along. There were weeks of preparation, including a special trip up to Pete's log cabin to borrow a big pot to make stone soup, an old Clearwater tradition. We spent weekends making signs and getting everything ready, including making our own silk-screened T-shirts. The festival arrived with the Sloop Clearwater docking at the harbor and a makeshift stage, a few environmental booths and our T-shirts. I was the emcee, and sang a few songs in between introducing the acts. It was a small festival with perhaps a thousand people showing up. Harry Chapin was in top form and he led us through many of his hits. Then he introduced a new song "Cats in the Cradle," which, he said that he wrote for his son. Then he asked if anyone was having a birthday today? My younger brother David called out and ran up to the stage (it really wasn't his birthday, but he would always use this trick to get a little attention). Harry lifted my brother onto his shoulders as he sang. For his last song, he invited me and a couple others to join him on stage and I stood next to Harry and joined in the fun. Then Bob McGrath asked me to play a little banjo background behind one of his songs. I was having such a great time; it was really hard to get off the stage when the time came.

At the end of the festival I was invited by Bob to play some music with him on a special moonlight wine and cheese sail on the sloop. Even though I had seen this magnificent sailing ship many times in the past, I had never had the chance to go out for a sail. We walked along the gangplank that led to the Sloop's main deck. The lines were cast off, the sloop's auxiliary diesel motor kicked in and we pulled away from the dock. As we headed out of the harbor, Captain Peter Wilcox called for "All hands on deck!" We all prepared to raise the huge mainsail; two lines had formed on each side as we picked up the heavy rope that would eventually raise this huge sail. Then the first mate cried out an old sea song, or as they call 'em, sea chanteys.

"In South Australia I was born .. Heave away.. Haul away..
South Australia, round Cape Horn and we're bound for South Australia!"

As he gave the command we all pulled hard on the line; pulling the heavy rope in rhythm actually made this heavy work fun. As the singer sang out "Heave away... Haul away," we pulled with all our might and the heavy wooden boom lifted higher and higher. With a few last, hearty tugs the huge canvas sail caught the wind and we were riding the surf as we tightened all the lines and made way for the open sea.

We sailed out towards Sandy Hook with wine corks popping and fresh cheese being passed around the deck. Bob McGrath asked me to get my banjo so we could play a few tunes together. In moments, the deck was filled with music and we sang until the wine and cheese had disappeared. As Bob and the last guests were leaving, the crew asked if I could stay on board as there were more festivals to do. They needed a few extra hands to help sail the boat and they also said that being a musician, I could also help sing at the festivals. I liked this taste of life on the "rolling sea." I had no real commitments as Claudia and I had split when she left for college, so I agreed to stay on for another week.

After everyone left the boat and the crew settled in for a good night's rest, I climbed down into the main cabin and placed my sleeping bag in a row of bunks. I soon found out just how tight the bunks were when a young blond girl named Heather bedded down next to me. I recognized her from the festival, as she was one of the singers who joined Harry and me up on stage in Perth Amboy. That first night, the boat was pitching back and forth and I started getting a bit queasy in my stomach. Heather came by and could tell, just by the look on my face, that I was getting seasick. She told me in a reassuring voice that the same thing happened to her when she first got on board. Then she said, "Just think of the motion as if the boat is rocking you to sleep." After her words of advice, I just slept like a baby.

Every morning, rain or shine, we had to get out and do "deck wash." Everything had to be cleared off the deck, then out came the big buckets and brooms. The salt water was stored in big wooden barrels on deck. As the Clearwater's deck was made of a soft wood the deck needed the salt to keep from rotting. Little buckets were filled with the salt water and thrown to the deck, and as the worked progressed water was flying in every direction. Every one who was not getting water grabbed a broom and started scrubbing away at the dirt on the deck while more buckets washed away the grit. As I was busy scrubbing away, I noticed that my bunkmate Heather was throwing more water on me than on the deck. I could tell by her devilish smile that she wanted to get to know me better and I thought that getting to know her too would be well worth it. Heather had been aboard the Clearwater for some time, as she was part of the permanent crew. She had her shoulder length blond hair tied up in a blue bandanna and wore a T-shirt and short shorts with a sailor's knife swinging from a rope around her waist. We started hanging around laughing and singing together. We would eat together in the cozy crew's cabin and late at night did the midnight watch together looking up and down the river for passing tugs and ships. During one sail, we climbed the rigging up to the crow's nest at the top of the mast and sat high above the boat, locked in each other arms as the boat rocked against the waves. Once, while we were in dock, Heather climbed halfway up the mast and then shouted, "Hey Rik, look up." I looked up the mast and saw that Heather wasn't wearing anything under her shorts. She laughed with a sly grin as she came down to the deck. I knew that Heather and I liked each other but I wasn't ready to get involved in that way. We continued to be friendly bunkmates 'til the end of my stay.

After a week, I had to get back to my real life, such as it was, so I packed up my gear and said goodbye to my friends. As I stood on the dock the signal was raised to leave. Heather and the crew untied the long ropes that held the sloop to the dock and as the diesel motor fired up, the sloop slowly started pulling away with everyone shouting goodbye. I looked at Heather's face getting smaller as the boat headed out of the bay. One of the crew was singing one of my favorite songs while the rest of us sang along. From the dock, I too sang:

"Bye, Bye, Bye, Bye. Bye, Bye, Bye,
Bye, Bye my Roseanne.
Bye, Bye, Bye, Bye. Bye, Bye, Bye , Bye, Bye.
And I won't be home tomorrow."

THE LAST OF THE GYPSIES

Claudia missed her life in New Jersey. After a semester, she returned from college in Vermont and we reunited. She enrolled at Rutgers University in New Brunswick. At first, she moved in with my family but there was a lot of chaos, what with parents and kids, so we saved up money and found a place to set up on our own. We roomed with some of Claudia's friends from the craft world. Claudia was now making extra money doing leatherwork, a skill that she had learned when we first met. She specialized in hand carving, a technique that was hard to master and she became very good at it. The house we moved into was owned by some of Claudia's friends that she had met at a craft show. They were a lot older than we, but being crafters, they were young at heart. The woman named Mary, was from the south and had a deep southern accent. She was a doll maker and would dress the part, wearing a long pinafore dress. Her partner was a little younger and he was also a toymaker, but instead of dolls, he made trucks and trains cut from blocks of wood. At craft shows Bob dressed like a cross between Robin Hood and a hobbit and, needless to say, they always attracted attention at these shows.

The house we all lived in was a hangout for any crafter that was in the area and the living room was often filled with strange oddball characters. There was Alan, a silversmith, a fellow called Scott the Shot, who used to work at a mayonnaise factory catching the bottles as they rolled off the assembly line and, two of the strangest people, Tomorrow and

Schmitdy who were both afraid of daylight, and only came out after dark. During the day the house was busy as a beehive with every one working away at their craft, but nights were filled with a long line of guests who seemed to always stay the night.

We were pretty young and innocent about a lot of things, so it came as quite a shock to learn that our landlords were not only crafters but swingers too, there was all kinds of pornography littered around the house and people popping in and out at strange hours. I was away for most of the week, giving banjo lessons and staying with friends, so I really didn't understand what Claudia was going through but she would tell me stories of how Mary would often mop the floor bare-breasted, and walk around the house stark naked. While Bob had his own little harem, all wearing short half unbuttoned skirts. Sometimes, all the guests would end up in the same bed together and watch porno flicks all night long. There were mirrors on the ceiling of both their bedrooms and bathrooms, and even Bob's workshops had erotica pinned over his tools. Later I found out that Mary was even using her sexual favors as barter, swapping a night in the sack for new wheels for their truck. Things were getting pretty strange.

Trying to get away from all the madness, Claudia immersed herself in her school-work. She was also now getting her leatherwork in craft shows all over the northeast. Her parents bought her a beautiful emerald green Ford Econoline van and soon we started living the life of traveling gypsies, driving from show to show. Being around so many craft workers, a song sprang up in my mind and started taking shape. I had written songs before but they were mostly novelty songs with my friend Mike. Nothing had ever happened like this. It was almost as if the song was being channeled to me from deep within myself. Days went by as new words twisted around into sentences in my mind, then linked together to form a new verse. After a week it was done and I called it "Last of the Gypsies" and dedicated it to Claudia and all her crafty friends.

The Last Of The Gypsies

Early morning rising, miles of open road.
Battered station wagon, filled with bracelets, rings and gold
A mustached man, in a blue work shirt, sips his coffee in the cold
Talks of life and yesterday, things he should have sold
Chorus

The last of the gypsies, the last of the clan.
try to make a rainbow, and sell it if you can
Broken down jalopies, in a gamblers caravan
Blowin' down the highway on a endless one-night stand.

Hands made of callous, fingers stained with dye.
A flowing wisp of golden hair, silhouettes the sky
Looking for tomorrow, with a fire in her eye.
carving out a living, from a leather piece of hide.
Chorus

Ivory bones and polished stones, pots made out of clay
Wooden planes and stuffed toy trains, hung out on display.
The tired eyes who made the prize, sit behind the empty trays.
Shoes with holes on worn out soles, who live from day to day.
Chorus

Now the show is over, booths all taken down
Let's brew a cup of coffee, relax and mill around.
Talk to friends and neighbors, find out where they are bound.
Get up in the morning, pull the tent peg's from the ground.
Chorus

Claudia met some new friends, John and Nancy, at another craft show, who had a nice apartment to rent. We both knew it was time to leave Mary and Bob's. The apartment was in the little town of Helmetta, not far from Old Bridge where I grew up. The main feature of town was an old brick snuff factory owned by the Helm family. The town was named after one of their young girls, Etta, and became known as Helmetta. The house we moved into was an older home, set right next to the train tracks and we learned just how close to the tracks we actually were the first night we slept there. When the bright light of the engine lit up the house and a rumbling shook it so badly, the cups vibrated right off the table and broke as they hit the floor. Besides the train, we had an old cook stove that burned soft pine wood and, since John was a woodworker, there were always plenty of scraps to burn but as he used soft pine, the stove would start to smoke like a chimney. Often Claudia and I had to tie bandannas around our faces while we scrambled to open the windows to let the smoke out. Despite the problems, we liked it at John and Nancy's. Our friends liked it too, and our little apartment was becoming a beacon to guitar pickers and singer/songwriters. It also became the meeting place for the new Central Jersey Clearwater Sloop Club.

THE FESTIVAL OF BLUEBERRIES

Ever since the Perth Amboy festival in 1976, Pete was urging me to get a bigger environmental festival going in that town. I took on the challenge and started dreaming up an idea of using the little riverfront park hillside as a kind of natural amphitheater, with a stage in the center of the harbor down below. Claudia wanted to organize a crafters area and other members had ideas for making and selling freshly picked blueberries, or baking them into muffins and cookies, to benefit the Clearwater. Armed with everyone's enthusiasm I went down to the mayor's office to see if we could get this project off the ground. At the time, my hair length was down the middle of my back and I dressed in a faded old denim jacket, certainly not the kind of visitor that Mayor Otlawsky was used to receiving. As I walked into his office, the mayor took one look at me and said with a grumble, "Where's your tie? Everyone who comes to my office wears a tie." I looked at the mayor with a smile and said, "Mayor, if I had a tie I would wear it." He laughed and said, "Okay kid, what do you want from me?" I first reminded him of the little festival we'd had a few years ago with Harry Chapin and Bob McGrath. He nodded his head and said, "That worked out pretty well for Perth Amboy, we had over a thousand people come down to the waterfront." I then told him about my idea of expanding the event to include a bigger stage and a craft show, environmental booths, homemade blueberry pastries, and sails on the Clearwater. The Mayor said, "You can do this?" I replied, "With your help, I think I can. "Well," said the Mayor, "I'm going to give you a chance, but I want you to work with my recreation department head, Mr. Bandola." It was agreed and I went back home to tell everyone the good news.

I started meeting Mr. Bandola weekly. At our meetings we would discuss what we needed and what progress our club was making. Pete volunteered to come and so did Bob McGrath. Soon performers from the Sloop and eventually from all over the state, started sending in letters asking to be a part of the show. At each meeting we handed out new assignments for the many signs, posters and programs that we would need. Mr. Bandola talked to the police and ambulance people and reserved a large stage. Our group made a trip down to southern Jersey where we spent a day picking our own blueberries and then spent days baking them into muffins, pies and cookies to sell. We had T-shirts made and had talked to Pete about bringing along his big iron pot to make the stone soup. We had no budget at all but through early T-shirt sales, we scraped up the money to get everything we needed to make the festival work. The night before the festival the weather report called for rain. Claudia and the rest of the group continued making signs for parking, knowing that if it rained we were at risk of losing all our hard work. The morning of the festival it was still drizzling but I loaded up Claudia's van and headed out to the festival site praying for the rain to stop. As I neared the site, I noticed that the clouds were clearing right over the harbor where the stage was being put into place. It was like a gift. The sun soon pierced the dark clouds and shone down on the stage and I knew my prayers were answered. It turned out to be a beautiful day.

The performers started showing up, as well as the crafts people, and the whole area was alive with the sounds of happy people putting up displays. The Sloop Clearwater came up the river and docked not far from the stage and Mr. Bandola and the mayor were happily walking around smiling at all of our efforts coming to life. Pete arrived, shook the mayor's hand, and then walked around the festival. He too could feel the energy and was pleased. I climbed up on the stage and welcomed everyone to the Festival of Blueberries and everyone was thrilled as the crowd grew to over five thousand. When Pete took the stage he asked me to come up and join him in one of his favorite tunes "John Henry." I asked Pete what key he played it in and after a short run-through we were ready. As I walked out on the stage with Pete I saw my dream had come to life. There, before me, were my friends and family and thousands of other people. Pete shot into the song,

"When John Henry was a little baby, sitting on his mama's knee.
He picked up a hammer, a little piece of steel saying ..
This hammer's gonna be the death of me."
I joined in, "Lord .. Lord, hammer's gonna be the death of me."

Pete sung out the ballad of the black hero who beat down the machine with his determination and will power, getting the audience to join in the chorus. After the song ended the crowd jumped to its feet and Pete called out, "Rik, how bout another one? Do you know this?.".. "I'm gonna lay down my sword and shield, Down by the riverside..." In minutes, the hill rang out in song and before long I left the stage to let Pete do his thing. After Pete's set, Mayor Otlawsky came up on stage and handed Pete the key to the city. The festival continued with all the performers getting their chance on the stage and then enjoying the stone soup from Pete's big kettle. Even though no one made a penny, as every one had volunteered, they were all happy to be a part of the fun. After the festival, Pete, Mr. Bandola and our Sloop Group went out for a dinner. My father decided to join us and sat right next to Pete. As I looked across the table, I saw my father talking and smiling with Pete. I could still remember when I had first played Pete's record at home and my dad yelling, "Get that Commie off our Hi-fi!" Now they were like old friends. We all had come a long way.

International Vagabond

POLISH BAGPIPES

Circa 1978

My introduction to Polish folk culture came when I stumbled across an article called "Springtime Hope For Poland" in a 1972 issue of National Geographic. Flipping through the article, I noticed a photo of a Polish bagpiper. There he was standing in the middle of a green pasture holding a big hairy bag, with a wooden goat head at the top. I stared at this photo for hours. "Polish bagpipes?" I had never heard of Polish bagpipes before, so I was curious to find out more information. The only clue about the pipes, in the article, was that it was called a Kobza. Being of Polish heritage, and in love with folk music, I thought, why couldn't I try to get one of these things and learn how to play it? Little did I realize what I was getting myself into. A few weeks later I went to the Rutgers Library to see if I could find out any thing else about the Polish bagpipe. At the time, all that was available was from Groves Musical Encyclopedia, which said: "There are eight types of Polish Bagpipes. The word for bagpipes in Polish is Dudy or Gajdy, not Kobza, although that is the word most Poles use. Polish pipes are both mouth and bellows blown. They are found in the mountains of southern Poland and in the region of Wielkopolska though they are very rare today." That was all I could find for a while but my curiosity was fired up and I knew that somehow I would find one of these things and learn how to play it.

Years went by, and I slowly gathered more and more bagpipe information; the bagpipe came to Poland by way of India, dating back to 1527. At that time, bagpipes were found at many village inns, peasant weddings and later in royal courts. Because of their wide popularity, bagpipers were taxed as highly as water mills.

Five of the eight types of pipes come from the Poznan region of northern Poland. These included two small, high pitched Wielkopolska bagpipes; the Siesienki, a practice pipe made out of a pigs bladder; the Koziol, a black bagged pipe, used before weddings; and the huge White Koziol, the biggest pipe of all, with a large wooden goat head, amber eyes and long horns made from wild boar. This pipe was played during wedding nuptials. The remaining pipes are from the mountainous regions: The Gajdy or Silesia bagpipe, the Zywiec Dudy (a mouth blown pipe very similar to the gajdy) and another mouth blown pipe from the high Tatra Mountains of Zakopane, called the Dudy Podhalinski, also known as Koza. (a word for goat in Polish.)

Polish bagpipes are made up of four elements: A melody pipe, a longer bass drone pipe, a goat skin bag and either a wooden bellows or a blow pipe - used to inflate the bag. Inside the chanter and the drone pipes sits a wooden cane reed that is tuned with string and bees wax. The wood is usually made from fruitwood: pear, plum, apple, or sometimes it can be of ebony or yew. As with most bagpipes, they were often played by shepherds while tending their sheep. They were also played at village festivities where they were accompanied by a fiddle or, in the case of the Wielkopolska polka pipes, a whole band of pipers accompanied by high pitched fiddles, clarinets and trumpets. It was the Koza pipe from Zakopane that I first saw in that picture, but still I had no idea what on earth they sounded like. I started calling up local Polish organizations. Most thought that I was putting them on, but one mentioned a young fellow named Peter Stroniack, who, he thought had one. I tracked Peter down and invited him over for a meeting and found that Peter also played the Scottish pipes. It was his interest in the Scottish bagpipe, plus his Polish heritage that led him to trying the Polish pipes.

He went to Poland, with his parents and came across a Polish mountaineer who played them. His parents set up lessons for Peter and he was able to buy a set of pipes from his teacher. Peter's pipes looked almost like the ones I had seen in the photo. They had a gray goat bag, with a beautifully carved wooden goat's head. Peter told me they put the goat's head on the top of the chanter, to remember the spirit of the animal. "Do they really have a spirit?" I asked. "The mountaineers say they do," he replied, and then added, "If you learn to play them, you will find out."

The first thing you experience about these pipes is the very strange sound. There are three reeds in the melody pipe and one reed in the drone pipe and altogether it gives off a big cluster of sound. I watched with amazement as Peter blew up this big goat bag, filling the room with my first taste of the exotic notes of the Polish mountains. Peter was kind and let me give it a try and, as I put my mouth on the wooden blowpipe, I could smell and almost taste the goat.

It reminded me of a story my mother had told me about her experience as a child. There was a man in her village of Cmolas, who had a bagpipe (he must have moved there from the mountains) and she remembers the day when he let her try to blow into the bag. She said she took a deep breath then blew into the bag, but then she could smell the odor of the goat and ran away. The man just laughed and laughed.

Me, not having any experience with bagpipes, could hardly blow up the bag, never mind try to play it. Nonetheless, I was hooked drone and chanter on becoming a Polish piper. Peter packed up his pipes and wished me luck when he left. He had no idea how I could get a set of Polish pipes, without going to Poland. A little while later I received a phone call from a Jacek Marek, a leading Polish choreographer. He told me he had heard of my interest in Polish folk music, and wanted me to know, that three Polish pipers would be coming to the Smithsonian Festival of Folk Life. The pipers were organized by Jim

Kimbell. At the time Jim was head over heels in love with the Polish pipes; he was writing his thesis on the pipes, while collecting music from the Poznan region. The pipers were just fantastic. They were all dressed in their Native costumes and they each had a Polish bagpipe under their arm. They had pipes from Poznan, Zakopane and Zywiec and I loved them all, but it was the sound of the Zywiec pipe that captured my heart. That deep ancient drone filled my romantic image of what the Polish mountains must be like. After their performance I tried to talk to the pipers but to my absolute horror, I found they did not speak English. Only then did I realize what I was getting into. Not only was I looking for a rare instrument but, in order to learn how to play it, I would have to learn to speak Polish too!

FIRST TRIP TO POLAND

July 1980

I soon became obsessed with the idea of getting and learning how to play the Polish pipes. I started writing to anyone who had even the most remote connection with Poland and eventually, I found a fellow from a dance band who was heading over to Poland. He arranged to bring me back a set of pipes if he found one. To my good fortune, he did come back with a beautiful set of pipes which were made in the village of Ustron by a pipe maker named Suhi. The workmanship was outstanding, with a beautifully hand carved, wooden bellows, intricate inlays of metal in the drone pipe and even a carved wooden goat's head sitting on top of the hairy white goat bag. I was thrilled! I sold an extra banjo I had and used the money to pay for my pipes. I also found a few recordings that had Polish bagpipe music on them and soon found myself locked in my room trying to learn how to play my pipes. To say it was not easy would be an understatement. The bellows had to be pumped up with your right arm to fill up the bag, then the goat bag had to be squeezed just right with your left arm or the reeds would shriek or cut out. While you were pumping and squeaking, you had to cover all the holes and lift only one finger at a time to play something that sounded like music. It seemed hopeless, but after months of practice I was able to play a short tune. Well, I guess it depends on who you talk to as some might have called it more noise than music. About the same time I was doing a concert tour on the Sloop Clearwater for the Pumpkin Sail. At one of the shows we had to row out from the sloop to do a concert with Pete Seeger in a folk club on shore. At the show I decided to take a risk and try to play my pipes. To everyone's surprise, I pulled out my big white goat, strapped it to my body, pumped it up and did, in fact, play a short tune. Pete was so impressed that on the ride back to the boat, as we were so cramped for space, he said, "Hey Rik, you can sit on my lap." He then asked me all about my pipes. Pete was encouraging me to keep up the good work, but we both knew that I had a long, long way to go.

    I knew that I what I really needed, was to see and hear someone who could really play; so once again I started writing letters, this time to the Polish Embassy. From my letter writing I received an unusual letter from the Polonia Society in Poland, inviting me to a festival of Polish folk music in the city of Rzeszow. I was stunned. It took a while to scrape up all the cash but somehow I managed. Claudia's family background was also Polish so she planned to come along and, together, we packed up our big suitcases and headed for the airport. We arrived in Warsaw at a crammed airport surrounded by military guards. Everyone was busy chattering away in Polish and we didn't understand a thing that was going on. Before panic struck, a tall, friendly man rushed to our aid. "Are you Rik Palieri from America?" he asked in a strong Polish accent. At once, the throngs of people parted to let us through. The man was from the festival and was here to escort us and welcome us to Poland. We cleared customs in minutes, with his help, and soon found ourselves sitting at the bar sampling our first taste of Polish vodka. At the time, I was pretty much a teetotaler so downing this shot in the Polish way (Drink it all in one big gulp!) was quite a task. Soon a few more festival representatives joined us and the vodka was flowing like water. Once we were well lubricated, they put us on a bus with some of the groups that were also taking the long bus ride bound for Rzeszow.

    The trip took almost the whole day and, as the hours passed, I looked out the windows and discovered for myself the land of my ancestors. One of the first things that I noticed was the beautiful flower gardens that stood in the front of almost every house. Around each house stood a big heavy metal fence decorated with colorful patterns in the chain links. Many of the houses were made of wood, similar to our American log cabins, but painted in white or yellow. Some houses were blue; I later found out that a blue house marked the residence of an unmarried woman. Blue paint also helped keep the flies away. Others were made of brick or even cinder blocks. At the time building materials were scarce and treated like gold. Most houses had a big pile of wood, bricks and cement standing proudly out in the front yard. As we passed through the farmlands you could see dome shaped haystacks glittering in the sun and the sounds of the many red cows that were out in the pasture. As the bus rolled through the countryside, it would often make a pit stop for the bathroom. It was always ladies to right, men to left. We were discovering that we were a long way from home.

    When the bus reached the festival, we were marched up to a room in a college dorm for orientation. The festival organizers welcomed us to the "World Festival" and handed out stacks of papers to fill out. To our disbelief, all the speeches and paper work were in Polish. One of the organizers saw our discomfort and asked in broken English, "You mean you don't speak Polish?" I shook my head and he replied, "Don't worry. We will find someone to help you." A few moments later a young bearded man named Jan came walking in with a happy smile said, "How can I help you?" To our relief he not only spoke English, but was very knowledgeable about Polish folklore. When I told Jan about my interest in Polish bagpipes he, and everyone else, picked up their arms and rocked them imitating the motions of a bagpiper, back and forth while laughing their heads off! "But why are you laughing?" I asked. Jan, while in the middle of a laugh blurted out, "No one wants to play bagpipes any more." But, as their laughter faded away, I heard a curious sound coming from the next building. I left the room and headed straight for what sounded to me like a bagpipes drone. I followed the sound into and up through the next building right to the top floor but, just as I reached the hallway, the sound stopped. I waited a while and then started climbing back down the stairway thinking that I must be imaging things after my long flight. Then the sound started again and I rushed back up the stairs and ran to the door of the mysterious notes. I knocked on the door and found, to my surprise and delight, a young American. Around his waist was what looked like a Polish bagpipe. As I looked further into the room, there was an old man with another bagpipe playing into a tape recorder. I realized I had just hit the jackpot so I asked if I could stay and watch. The American said, "Sure, I'm not really into this instrument. My group wants me to learn but it's awfully hard." I stood in amazement as I watched the old man pump up the little bellows that inflated the tiny black bag. I looked closer and saw that the melody pipe was decorated with a small carved goat's head, complete with eyes of Polish amber.

The American explained that this was a bagpipe from the region of Poznan. It had a high pitched melody pipe and a low bass drone made from the horn of a cow. The old man was noticing my interest and asked this young student if I wanted to learn too. I jumped at the chance and even though he could not speak English, we worked out a daily lesson plan. In these lessons he would pump up his bagpipe and play a basic tune then strap the bagpipe on me and place my fingers over the holes. He would then pump up the bellows and show me how to keep the bag full of air. As the young American student had said, "It was not easy." We had to take little breaks in between songs, as my arm would ache from pumping up the bellows. After a few days, I was starting to get the knack of it and was able to squeak out a few notes without losing the air pressure. By this time, we had worked out a simple code. He would smile when I did something right and shake his head when I was wrong. Even though we could not speak to each other I was learning and he was overjoyed that a young person from America was trying so earnestly to learn the instrument that he loved.

A few days later a big parade was planned and all the groups were lined up and marched down the street. Just before the parade began one of the Festival officials asked me if I had a costume for the parade. When I said I didn't, they told me of a booth at the festival where I could get one. As I had brought along a bagpipe from the region of the Silesian Mountains they pointed out the costume from that area and said, "You need a costume from Istebna." I said, "Istebna, what's that?" They laughed and replied, "That is where your bagpipes hail from." I looked at the heavy woolen pants, embroidered shirt and bright red vest and said, "You mean I have to wear that?" I soon put on my new outfit and, while holding my set of pipes, joined in the line. I was a bit nervous as the bagpipes that I had brought along had a problem. Somehow, while on the plane, something happened to the bagpipe reeds and it refused to play. Even my new Polish bagpipe teacher could not fix them, so there I stood, all dressed up, with a polish bagpipe that would not utter a sound.

As I stood there forlorn, a middle-aged man asked me in English if I could play him a tune. Embarrassed, I tried to explain that the pipes would not play. The man continued, "They must play, for they were made by me and my father-in law." I must have been nervous for, as he spoke to me, I started to pump up the bellows and to everyone's surprise, the reeds came back to life. He smiled and said, "But of course they play!" He then lifted his young son to pet the hairy white goat bag. I had heard of old folk tales of bagpipers believing in the spirit of the goat. They even carved a wooden head, to thank the animal for its hide to make the instrument. After this experience, I too was a believer.

The man pulled some photos out from his wallet. "See, here is our shop. My father-in law, Suhi, makes the pipes but I'm learning and soon will take over his business." He wished me well and said he would be back to show me some more of their instruments before the festival was through. The following day they had scheduled a contest for all the instrumentalists of the festival and, once again, I was told "You must perform." While waiting my turn, and enjoying the other contestants, I spied a man dressed in a similar costume to what I was wearing. He had a long beard and wore the hat of a mountaineer. I soon found out that he was one of the judges and his name was Jozef Broda. I sat there watching him and thinking, "Broda, I have heard that name before." Then it hit me that one of my Polish records had a cut on it with a Polish bagpiper named Jozef Broda. In fact, it was his song that I was planning on playing. When my turn came, I played a few songs on the banjo and then tried to play the one song I knew on the bagpipes, "Groniczki, Groniczki." As I struggled with my goat, the bearded man smiled and clapped his approval. I soon found out that I had won the contest and was awarded a folk doll and proclamation saying that I was the festival's "Outstanding Solo Instrumentalist."

With my award, the press came to do a photo shoot, with Mr. Broda and me. Jan (from the festival) was so happy that I had won that he soon became my official interpreter. After the press had gone, Jozef Broda told Jan and I that he was thrilled to see me trying to play such an old and difficult Polish folk instrument and he would be happy to teach me if I was interested. I could not believe my good fortune for, not only had I won the festival award, but now had the opportunity to study with a master piper! A few hours later, we joined Jozef who had just finished another press interview and had his own bagpipe ready for my lesson. The reporters were from one of Poland's most famous magazines, Panorama Poland. They were interested in meeting this young American who was in love with Polish folk culture and asked if they could stay. Broda went to work and brought out his big, brown goat-skinned pipes. His bellows was decorated with a tasteful folk motif and the wood of his pipes seemed to be hundreds of years old; I was in awe. Jozef stood proudly with his chin pointing up to the sky, while pumping up his goat bag, and sang the beautiful song that I had just stumbled through. My ears had never heard such a wondrous sound; he played flawlessly. Broda then came over and started instructing me on the correct stance of the Polish piper. He then had me pump up my bag and keep it inflated until the bass chanter note and the drone note flowed steadily. After a few more simple instructions, he wished me well and told me that he usually will not teach bagpipes to a tourist, as it is too hard to master. He then said something that lit a spark in me, "If you truly want to learn you must come and live here in Poland with me and I will teach you."

FAMILY REUNION

My mother was born in the tiny village of Cmolas, not far from the festival. Ever since I can remember, my mother would tell me stories of her childhood and of her native Poland. She was born in a small, whitewashed log house with a thatched roof, in the open fields of the village of Cmolas, outside of the city of Rzeszow. Her father's family emigrated to America in the late 1800s to work in the coal mines of Donora, Pennsylvania. My Grandfather, John Wojdyla, was born in Donora but the whole family left America soon after his birth. His father had developed black lung from working in the mines and went back to Poland to try and recuperate. Most of my mother's tales were about her childhood in Poland during the Second World War.

She can still remember the day that war broke out: "I was just a child at the time; my grandmother told me that something horrible had just occurred in the neighboring town. She walked with me down the long road towards the village of Kolbuszowa. There I saw the carnage of war. Men and horses lay dead on the ground with the smell of death still lingering in the air. My grandmother said, 'See the tragedy of war. I brought you here so you would never forget what war is.' To this day I can still see the truck loading the bodies. It was so horrible!'"

Because Cmolas was on the main road, it was being occupied by both Germany and Russia and it was always filled with lines of soldiers. The Nazis sent a line of trucks to collect all the men from Cmolas and only the very young or very old were left behind. They took these men to work as slaves for the Third Reich on farms in Germany. My mother and her brother were raised by their grandmother while her mother, Veronica, traveled to markets to sell material to support the family. Sometimes my mother accompanied her mother to market and on one trip, she saw a very young boy singing a song in the center of the square. The boy was singing (alternating words in Polish and German) *"Butter... Butter "Water Water. All you Nazi's can kiss my a**."*

A soldier heard the little boy's song and - boom - fired his rifle and shot him dead. My mother cried as they moved the boy's body from the marketplace. She was learning first hand how cruel war was and that everyone in it had a price to pay.

One sunny afternoon, while she was playing out in the meadows, she saw something like she had never seen before - tiny drops of sparkling rain. She ran over to try and catch the raindrops that were falling so hard they made tiny holes in the ground. Then she looked up and saw two airplanes circling and diving. One burst into flames and crashed into the field.

Soon the roads were filled with soldiers, while the dead bodies of men, horses and livestock littered the streets. The soldiers often raided the homes of the villagers, taking everything in sight, and they would eat and sleep and then move on. Sometimes they stayed for weeks while my mother's family hid in the woods. The food that my family brought with them soon ran out, leaving them with only the fruit from an old pear tree and mushrooms to survive on. Finally, the army moved on, but our family never felt safe again. In fact, to this very day, my grandmother buries canned goods in the garden, just in case.

One of my favorite stories took place at the beginning of the war, before they took Grandpa away. The Nazis were bombing a nearby city and all the men from Cmolas banded together to loot the burning stores. Most of the men took watches, gold rings or whatever money they could find. My grandfather, Big John, took only one thing, a huge bag of noodles. All the men chuckled as Big John carried the big noodle bag, dodging the bombshells all the way back to Cmolas. When he got back home, everybody laughed at John for taking only the noodles when he could have filled his pockets with riches but soon everyone understood, as the roads became filled with Nazis and food became scarce. Not only did our family have food but they shared the big bag of noodles with all their neighbors, and everyone realized food was even more valuable than gold.

My mother would tell me tales of how deep the snows were in Poland and how they used to have to make a tunnel from the house to the barn to take care of their livestock. During the long winter she and her brother Matthew would trap rabbits which, because of the cold nights, would freeze solid. Then she and Matt would pretend they were cowboys and ride the stiff rabbits through the snow. She also told me of her favorite cow, Whistle, and how she would lead her out to pasture. One day poor Whistle got caught in a patch of quicksand and it took most of the village men to get a rope round her and hoist her out of danger.

Thinking back on all her stories, and being so close to her village, I just had to find a way to visit the family and especially, 90 year-old great grandma. We found a woman from one of the dance groups, who could speak Polish, and she was delighted to come along for a family reunion. We took a taxi and located the town, but had a hard time finding the house. Then I remembered that the family made hats. At once, one old man pointed to a long road.

I remembered my mother telling stories about how she had lived on a long road that went east to west. Her words echoed through my mind as I stared down the long road to try to search out their home. I thought I remembered my mother telling me that she was born in an old wooden log home with a thatched roof but I remembered that house was knocked down years ago, and they built a new home with dollars after working in America. Still having difficulty, the taxi driver asked a man standing on the street. He yelled, "Do you know of the Pastula's?" The man looked puzzled and I remembered again that they made hats. The driver yelled again, "They have a hat shop." "Oh, Pastula the hat maker," the man replied and pointed to a cement and brick house just down the road. When we pulled up to number 16, there was my great grandmother busy at work sweeping the dirt out the door with an old broom. Through our interpreter we called out, "Grandma, it is Stephanie's son from America." "Oh, my God! Stephanie's son from Ameri-ca," her voice rang across the fields.

Soon all of my cousins and uncles rushed onto the porch. They asked us to come into the house and poured us some coffee. They apologized that they did not know we were coming and that they had only a little food. Then they complained about the strikes and the food shortages. They said all the food from Cmolas was being sent into Rzeszow for the festival and my heart sank. I realized that the bountiful meals that we had been enjoying at the festival were coming from the neighboring Polish communities. I was basically taking the food from my family's mouth. And strikes? We never heard about any strikes. Then they explained that there was a new union called "Solidarity." The Union was staging strikes all over the country and was trying to gain new freedoms from the Soviets. Everyone looked worried as these were dangerous and forbidden words that they were speaking aloud and in a moment's notice, the conversation shifted.

Great grandma smiled at our lady friend, who was doing the translating, "See this old bed? Your mother was born on this bed and your grandmother was also born on this very bed, and even I, as old as I am, was also born on this bed!" Tears welled up in my eyes as I imagined the ghosts of my ancestors filling the room.

My family opened one of the few cans of meat that they had and, once again, apologized for the lack of food. We sat there and ate ham sandwiches, sipped on tea and cookies and then all had a strong shot of vodka before departing.

After our trip to Poland everything at home seemed dull in comparison. I kept things running with the Sloop Club, the Festival of Blueberries and playing at small coffeehouses for a few years but both Claudia and I knew it was time for a change. John and Nancy were having some marital problems and many of our friends were leaving the area so we decided that we would move up to Vermont where her family lived. We packed up all the books, instruments, and Claudia's leather tools, and rode up to the Green Mountains. We soon found out we had made a huge mistake!

THE BROCCOLI YEARS

1981 to 1984

1981 was for me the beginning of "The Broccoli Years," a time of hardly any money, few friends and nothing but a long hard road ahead. When we first thought of moving to Vermont our choice was based on the fact that it seemed to have a thriving folk and craft scene. By the time we moved there, most of the folk clubs had closed, and we realized that the craft shows were, in fact, few and far between. Even the town of Springfield that we had just moved to was on hard times. This one-time giant hub of the tool industry had lost its glory to Japanese competitors. Now, many of the factories were boarded up and the empty store fronts and rundown houses along Main Street seemed to echo the frustrations of the once prosperous workingman's town. In one word, it was dismal. Springfield was never a music or arts community, but as Claudia's parents needed some caretakers to watch their home while they spent time in Florida, we decided that it was worth trying out so we moved in with them and prayed for things to get better. Despite the gloomy atmosphere, Claudia still had the dream of her leatherwork becoming a full time leather craft business. When we lived in Jersey, we had spent most weekends going to craft shows. Now that this was her full time occupation, almost every minute of the day was devoted to her leatherwork.

Claudia set up her workshop in the basement of her parent's home. In her tiny workroom she would cut, die, carve and sew her leather work, all by hand. I would sometimes help her punch holes and even help skive the leather hides. The room was so small, that we would bump our heads together as we dragged the large leather skins across the sharp skiving blade. By the end of her workday, Claudia would be covered in chocolate brown dye, but her shelves would be filled with a wide array of new belts, wallets and pocketbooks.

When we lived in New Jersey, I had enough gigs and students to keep us going. After moving to Vermont I had to start back at zero. There was only one bar left that would feature acoustic music and though I played there often, my gigs just barely put bread on the table.

In spite of our seemingly romantic life style, having two artists trying to survive on only their art income was sometimes just impractical. Even though Claudia was getting into many of the most prestigious craft shows, we would often come home with just enough money to get back down the highway. It was obvious that winter that we were having a difficult time living in Vermont, so we packed up the van and moved on in search of the sun.

LIFE'S A BEACH!

We left for sunny Florida, with the idea of doing craft shows throughout the winter and then heading back to Vermont for the summer craft show season. As both sets of our parents now lived in Florida, we thought it would be easy to just go and live with them for a few months. In a way, the arrangement wasn't all that bad; I was able to get a job teaching banjo at the Banjo Man's Picking Parlor and Claudia was able to do many crafts and art shows along the Florida coast. We were not married, so there was no way that we could live together under our parent's rules. Claudia's folks lived more than an hour away from my parent's house, so we each did our own thing and we'd only meet up when we could.

With our separation, it also gave me more time to reconnect with my family. It was during this time that my father and I were finally starting to interact like a father and son but the seeds of our new found friendship had only come about recently.

It was on the Father's Day before we went to Florida that I began thinking about the difficulties in my relationship with my dad. I had a rough childhood with my dad always working or sleeping. We never had much of a life together and in fact, when we were in the same room we hardly spoke to one another. The longer I pondered our situation, the more I realized that it went far beyond just my father and me. This kind of estrangement went all the way back to my grandfather and his father. As I thought back to all the fights and arguments that we had while I was growing up, I realized I was carrying around too much baggage from my childhood, and it was time to unload. Now was time to break the chain. I went down into the basement grabbed a pencil and set my thoughts to paper.

"Fathers and Sons"

Fathers and Sons, since time begun,
iron clad hearts weighing a ton.
A shake of the hand - a slap on the back,
old memories from a worn leather strap

Chorus;
The hardest thing for a father to do,
isn't swinging an ax or tying little shoes,
so open your heart, you've got nothing to lose
and show your son your love,

My father and me would never agree,
fussing & fighting since the day I was three.
A giant of steel, who just couldn't feel
how to show his son his love,
Chorus

The autumn winds blew as the young child grew
as he cursed at a man, that he never knew.
While doing the chores, he cursed him much more
and never gave his father his love.
Chorus

Too many days have come and have passed
and the days of my childhood are out of my grasp.
Now my father and I both want to cry,
thinking back on the time that we were denied
Chorus

After I finished that song, I knew that I had to sing it for my father. It was only a short time after the song was written that I got that chance. In November my family came up from Florida. They came north to bring in the holidays at a gathering at my grandma's house. As the kitchen filled with the sweet aroma of Polish sausage and cabbage, everyone was busy setting the table and preparing for the big meal. Before we sat down to eat, I told my parents that I had planned something special. When I nervously picked up my guitar the room was still filled with noisy dinner chatter. But as I sang, the room quieted down with my family listening to every word. When I finished, they were all sobbing around grandma's kitchen table. As the last notes of my guitar still rang in the kitchen walls, my dad came over and gave me a hug and said "Son, I'm sorry. Though we can't change the past, we can try to make the future better." With everyone still in tears, I sang a few more songs before we ate. Singing this song became a major turning point in our relationship.

A FISH STORY

My folks live in a little bungalow town in central Florida. Living near the ocean I found plenty of time to relax on the beach, look for manatees and even go fishing. Thinking back on those fishing trips, there is one fish story I'll never forget.

One day my younger brother David and I decided to go fishing. When we went looking for David's pole we could not find it so my brother decided to just take Dad's favorite pole and off we went. We pulled our car near a little dock next to the big bay and then we brought out a bucket of shrimp for bait and spent the next few hours trying our luck. Later in the day, somehow, David dropped my father's pole and it rolled off the dock into the ocean. My brother jumped in the water trying to retrieve the pole but it was no use as the bay was too deep. After a few more attempts we realized that my father's pole must have sunk to the bottom and it was gone forever. We were planning to replace my dad's pole but before we had the chance, he had the urge to go fishing. My dad searched the house for his pole and kept asking, "Did you see my pole?" Nervously we replied, "No, I haven't seen it in days." After a while he gave up the search and grabbed another pole. We went back to the very same spot we had been to on our previous fishing trip, threw in our lines and waited for the fish to start biting. We were not there very long when my father thought he had a bite. "Look," he said as his pole bent over, "I think I have a big one." He reeled and reeled till his fishing pole was so bent over that it nearly touched the dock.

By this time a little crowd had gathered as it looked like my dad had caught himself a real prize. Well, in a way he did. When his hook came out of the water it was attached to two large horseshoe crabs clutching on to, you guessed it, his old fishing pole! My father was astounded at the similarities of this pole, that he just dragged out of the bay, and the pole he thought he had in his closet. By the time we got home he was so excited about comparing these two poles that we just had to break down and tell him the truth. After hearing the whole story he said, "How could I be so lucky as to catch my own pole?"

BACK HOME AGAIN

Despite having fun in the sun, Claudia and I found Florida to be unproductive. We felt that we were living in everyone else's world and not our own so, after a few years of playing cat and mouse and running back and forth, we decided to just stay in Vermont. The next winter was a real test. Vermont winters can be harsh with snow sometimes falling for days and even weeks at a time. The first winter we stayed in Vermont was one of those tough years. We were snowed in most of the time and often so broke that we were turning the furniture upside down hoping to find a bit of change just to buy groceries.   About the only thing we could afford was broccoli and eating it day after day was getting tiresome. We were getting to the end of our rope when I decided to do something I had never done before, play rock guitar in a bar band. I found a few local musicians who played weddings, dances and bars and joined up with their band. I put an ad in the paper looking for an old Gretsch hollow body electric and much to my surprise was able to find a 1950's Tennessean for only fifty bucks. A friend gave me an old amp and I was ready to rock and roll!

Ok, I was never a great guitar player and, to be honest, with this electric guitar I was worse than ever, but the amazing thing was the crowd liked it. At every show we played the people would hoot and holler yelling, "Turn up the guitar," and then, after the gigs, would treat us like we were rock stars. The whole thing was ridiculous - the music that we played was awful, covers of the Eagles, Beatles, Elvis, Country- Rock, wedding songs and a lot more too hokey to mention. Now it is not to say that these songs themselves were bad, it was just that the way that I played them sounded heartless. I felt like a prostitute, for I knew I was only doing it for the money.

Back at home, I was still teaching both banjo and folk guitar. As I used folk music to teach my students, I was finding out that I was looking forward to giving my lessons much more than doing band gigs. It was around that time that I also got a job teaching guitar, at Vermont Community College. The course gave me a whole batch of new students and after the course was through many of the students started taking private lessons, so I had enough money to help pay bills, and leave the band.

WEDDING ON THE RIVER

By this time Claudia was tired of living just hand to mouth and started thinking about enrolling in a school in southern California to learn how to make horse saddles. We were having all kinds of personal and money problems and were just ready to go off on our separate ways, when I did the strangest thing - I asked her to marry me. Yes, for some reason I thought, well maybe if we get married, our life would start coming back together, so one day while we were pulling up weeds in the garden I popped the question.
It took Claudia a few days to say yes and then tell her parents. Needless to say, hearing that your daughter is about to marry a musician is not exactly the best news, but after a while everyone became busy with wedding plans. As most of our friends lived in New Jersey it was logical that we hold the wedding there.

An old friend, Mac Babcock, had a beautiful house along the Raritan River and offered his back yard to hold the event. After multiple trips down the Garden State Parkway the big day had arrived. The night before the wedding we all went down to Jersey. Claudia went off for a night with her relatives and I went over to Mac's house and set up the chairs and tables. Mac's wife Rennie had decorated a little metal archway with flowers and made the back yard look absolutely gorgeous. Later that night I went out to eat hamburgers with my friends and then slept in the back of a pickup truck.

The next morning Mac, Rennie and I went over the plans and waited to receive the guests. When my father arrived he found he was so nervous that he forgotten to take his white shirt but his mother showed up to save the day, bringing his shirt and tie just in time for the wedding to begin. By the time the Unitarian minister showed up, most of the guests had arrived. It was a sunny June afternoon when Claudia walked out into the garden and made her way to the flower draped archway.

Claudia had wanted to be married in a leather wedding dress but the pattern did not work out, so she chose a simple antique white gown with lavender trim. I was wearing a white suite with a lavender shirt and tie and had given in to Claudia's father's wishes and even cut my hair. For the ceremony, we wrote our own vows. We used Walt Whitman's poetry and had the preacher stress how important our individuality was. Our vows were so convoluted and unreligious that after the wedding my mother quizzed the preacher to see proof that he was a real minister. After the quick service it was time to party and with so many guitars and banjos floating around, I spent the rest of the evening singing and playing music with our friends.

After we had packed up the chairs and tables, while singing old work songs, Claudia and I headed over to a nearby hotel. While Claudia was busy looking over all the wedding gifts and cards, like most men I had only one thing on my mind. Even though we had had problems with sex in the past, I felt that now that we were married everything would change for the better. Claudia kept putting me off, till she finally gave in and said, "Ok, let's get it over with!" At that moment I realized that maybe I had just made another big mistake.

HONEYMOONING IN ITALY

A few days later we were back in Vermont care-taking her parents' home. By the time her folks came back they were on the warpath about getting a job and living like normal people. Needless to say we counted the days 'til we went off and spent all of our wedding money on a trip to Italy.

As an art historian, Claudia had planned a honeymoon that any art lover would love. She found a cheap tour package that would take us to Milan, Venice, Naples, and Rome.

When we were getting ready to leave, I started packing up my banjo, only to hear Claudia say, "No banjo or other instruments. We are going to see art. You won't have time to play and we already have too much baggage." She was right about the luggage as she had packed almost everything she owned into to two large suitcases that I had to carry all over Italy. I have to laugh now, as I realize that one of the suitcases was never even opened.

MILAN

When we landed in Milan we had just enough time to get into the church that housed the famous painting The Last Supper. We were still jet-lagged, and it was at the end of the day so we were still in a bit of a haze, but once we saw that painting we could feel the absolute beauty in this work. The church itself was almost destroyed during the Second World War but, miraculously, this one wall survived intact. As I was looking at this huge fresco I felt a feeling of inner peace. It was the first of many wonderful moments on this trip

GENOA

The next day instead of joining the group we went out on our own path and visited a banjo player named Silvio who wrote for the banjo newsletter and lived in Genoa. We took a long train ride and met Silvio at the train station. Silvio was delighted to show us around his town and brought us to the birthplace of Columbus then down through the narrow streets to a seafood restaurant. The area is noted for its seafood, so we were excited to sample the local cuisine. When we looked over the menu we noticed that almost every entry included some type of octopus. I was a little squeamish about eating anything with eight legs, so I finally spotted one meal that just said fried fish. When Silvio placed the order he ignored my request and told them that we were his guests and for them to give them the best dish on the house. The house specialty was of course filled with octopus. We had octopus in the salad, octopus and pasta, fried octopus, by the end of the meal we had eaten over eight varieties of these strange looking creatures and, you know, it didn't taste bad. After our meal we headed over to Silvio's house for a bit of music. As I knew that this would be perhaps the only time on this trip that I would be able to hold a banjo, we made the most of it and played until it was time to catch the train.

VENICE

The next few days were filled with typical tourist trips: walking into a thousand churches, sight seeing, and spending hours waiting on the bus for the tour director to find missing tourists. Then we went to such an enchanted place that it made me forget about all my frustrations!

When I first laid my eyes on Venice I almost cried from the sheer beauty that surrounded me. On the tour we were told that centuries ago the people of this area brought immense trees to the waters edge and drove them into the mud. On top of these wood pilings they built a magnificent city, right in the canal. Over the years the water level rose up to the buildings and soon spilled over into the lower doorways and windows. Today most of the houses of Venice are slowly sinking into the canal and, even though the city is sinking, it is still one of the most beautiful places in the world.

I knew from reading about Venice that I would like this town, but seeing it in real life I fell head over heels in love with it. I loved the canals, the red terra-cotta roofs and the unusual lifestyle that is all a part of the Venice way of life.

One of the special attractions of this city is the sleek black boats they called gondolas. They use these boats to navigate the tight twists and turns of the narrow canals and at night each end of the gondola is lit with a tiny candle. This tiny light helps the gondolier as he paddles and sings his way through the dark passages of the narrow waterways.

As evening fell upon us, the noisy crowds went home and, one by one, the lights in the houses along the canal lit up like a scene in a Walt Disney movie. Soon all you could hear was the sound of the gondolier's paddle lapping into the dark blue water. I have never experienced such beauty or felt as romantic about life as I did when I was in Venice. As we glided under one of the bridges, our gondolier broke out in song. He sang the famous song from Naples, "O Solo Mio," in a high tenor. His strong voice boomed through the narrow canal and echoed against the buildings with its glorious sound

Hearing his voice made me realize that there was something in the night air that unlocked the negativity that was burrowing in my soul. The music had unchained me and made me happy just to be able to savor this moment. I could have stayed in Venice for the rest of my life, but as the tour moved on I had to follow.

As our trip went south, we made our way down to the land of my father's ancestors in Naples. I never knew much about my Italian roots, other than that my great-grandfather had come from this area. I was told that he grew up in a convent, because his parents were actors. In those days it was unheard of to have children traveling with entertainers so it was very common to leave them to be raised at a convent. Great grandpa was skilled in both music and the arts and later in life played mandolin and banjo. As I looked into the bustling streets of Naples, I could almost feel Great grandpa welcoming me back to the city of his birth.

NAPLES

It is said that in Naples the streets are so crowded that it is the only place in Italy where you will see three people riding a Vespa motor scooter. Much to my surprise, that, in fact, was one of the first sights I saw while circling the big bay. The hotel that we stayed at was the most picturesque hotel of our whole trip. The immense marble building sat right along the bay and had a terrace where you could look out to the Isle of Capri. Everything in Naples was exhilarating; the people were animated and passionate, the traffic was mind boggling and the food was mouth-watering.

The restaurants not only had excellent food but also had a whole range of street musicians to entertain you while you ate. These musicians seem to have a bit of a pecking order. Some could only play near the curb, while others would be able to play on the sidewalk. Only the best musicians would be allowed to enter the restaurant and sing at the tables. The one thing that they all seem to share was that they all carried an extra large tambourine. These are not only used for percussion accompaniment but they also used them to collect tips.

Speaking of music, I must mention that this area is also home to the Italian bagpipe. The instrument looks like a large sheepskin sack with four legs and a blow pipe. It has two long chanters and two drones and it has a carnival like sound. It is called the Zampogna and is one of the oldest bagpipes. It was said that Nero once played the pipes and also had them inscribed on a roman coin. The Zampogna is usually played around Christmas. This goes back to an old legend that when the Virgin Mary was in labor she called for the shepherds to play her the bagpipe to soothe her pains. Whether the old story is true or not it has inspired a wealth of Christmas songs played on the pipes. Each year starting on November 12th, the shepherds come down from the hills to play their Zampogna. They often play on the streets but also will come to play at churches and parties. Years ago the pipers would leave carved wooden spoons in the doorways of the houses that they were to play at. Unfortunately, as we had come in October, there were no bagpipes to be found. When I asked about them, one old fellow shook his head and said, "They play from November to January, and believe me that is enough! So, if you want hear them come back at Christmas."

From Naples we took a bus over to see the ruins of Pompeii. It is amazing to think of how advanced this old culture was before it was destroyed by Mount Vesuvius. As we looked around we saw not only ruins but some of the actual people, trapped at the moment of their death, entombed in a thick crust of lava ash. As I gawked into their ghoulish faces, I wondered if these poor souls knew that when the volcano erupted that they would be here forever. As we walked back to catch the bus, I, too, realized that our time in Italy was running out. In just a few days this storybook trip would be over and we would be returning to a very uncertain future. But, why worry about that now while we can still enjoy, as the Italians say, "La Dolce Vita."

The last night we sipped wine on the marble terrace while bats swooped wildly over our heads. These furry creatures were almost like Naples itself, dark, wild and mysterious. As we went inside for the evening, our little furry friends also left and waved farewell with their leathery wings as they flew off over the moonlit bay.

The next morning I was sad to leave Naples, but we had to move on, as we were headed to our last stop the eternal city of Rome

ROME

It has been said that "All roads lead to Rome" and, after you see the enormous buildings, you can understand why. I had heard of the gigantic Roman Coliseum and the Spanish Steps but, surprisingly, I never heard anything about the gargantuan Monument to Victor Emanuel. This building dwarfs everything in sight. While not the most attractive building it sure is big. Besides walking the streets and gazing at buildings we also made a trip the Vatican to see the Sistine Chapel, sampled some Italian ice cream and right before we left threw our coins into the famous Trevi Fountain hoping for a return trip.

SPRINGFIELD, VERMONT

It did not take long for the fun memories of the Italy trip to fade and for us to return to our separate lives. We were still having the same problems that we had before the wedding and instead of life getting better it was just getting worse. Claudia and I never worked on our personal problems and even though we were great friends, our views of sex were miles apart. She was deeply involved with her work and art and basically just wanted to be celibate. Every thing would have been great if I shared her view but I didn't and I found it very difficult to be in a relationship with someone who did not want to sleep with me. To top things off my life was going down the drain. I lost most of my students by going off to Italy, so now I had no work, no money and no sex. I was losing my self-confidence and falling back under that dark cloud of my childhood. I knew I had to find a way out but I did not have a clue how to do it. In the middle of my darkness, I was still holding on to the hope that someday I would become the musician of my youthful dreams but how? Then a crazy idea struck, why not get a grant to study the Polish bag-pipes! It sounded silly at first but the more I thought about it the more I realized that it was possible.

While I was struggling with my own demons, Claudia was rethinking her idea of being a leather worker. Seeing all of her favorite paintings in Italy inspired her to want to become an art teacher. To achieve her new goal, she began to substitute teach and work at getting her teaching degree. It was only a few months from returning from our trip, while we were having our Thanksgiving turkey that I had the strange feeling that we would not be together next year. Little did I know what life had in store!

THE GRANT TO POLAND

1984

The idea of studying in Poland was planted during my last trip back in 1980. Jozef Broda, the famous Polish folksinger and bagpiper told me, "The only way to truly learn this instrument is by living in Poland. We don't teach bagpipes to tourists but if you come back I will teach you." He did give me a few lessons but after a couple of months of practice, back at home, I could see I was getting nowhere. The worst part was that I was involved in the New Jersey folk scene and I was asked to play the pipes at folk festivals. Though I tried my best I was not making very good music. It was during this time that Pete Seeger wrote to me. Pete had been watching my development with the pipes and even though he was excited he knew I needed help. In the letter he wrote, "You are getting to be a much better banjo picker than you were when I first sang with you. Which reminds me, Rik, I really urge you practice more on the Polish bagpipes before you play too much in public on them. Eventually, you'll be damn good on them, but Poles who know what a high art good piping can be, won't be charitable to us."

Pete's letter started me thinking. I knew he was right, but how was I going to learn? I did not know of anyone who could teach me here in America so there was only one thing to do. I would have to go and study in Poland!

I jumped into this new project and went to work. I went into the library, found a book on foundations and looked for anything connected with Poland. I found one that looked promising, The Kosciuszko Foundation's American Center for Polish Culture. This foundation is one of the oldest Polish American organizations and they sponsor art, music and cultural events as well as provide fellowships to students and run summer studies' programs in Poland.

I sent a letter telling them of my desire to study the Polish bagpipe and a few months later I was told, "We are sorry, but we have no interest in this type of study program at this time." I did not give up but continued to send letters to other possible sponsors. One letter went to Hillshire Farm Kielbasa Co. They wished me luck and sent along a huge book of coupons for free kielbasa. I guess they did not know how to help but did not want me to starve. A year went by and I tried the Kosciuszko Foundation again. No luck, rejected again.

I kept practicing day after day, but I did not see much hope ahead. Once more I tried the Kosciuszko people and this time I got back a big fat envelope filled with papers to fill out. They were interested.

Now the real work began. I had to get together health certificates, a formal proposal of my plan of study and three recommendations from educators or experts in my field. Oh, there was another small detail; I had to start learning to speak Polish. For the recommendations I sent out a letter to one of my old high school music teachers, Chris Christensen, The Vermont Community College where I was teaching at the time, and one to Pete Seeger. Everyone was delighted to help. Then I found out about a Polish language course being offered by a Polish priest named Father Felix Reczek. Father Felix was from the Franciscan order. He grew up near Pittsburgh, PA and went to a Polish high school. Later, his family moved out to West Rutland, a small community of Poles who came to Vermont to work in the marble quarries. We started out as a whole class of determined Polish-Americans, who wanted to get back to their roots. Father Reczek was a stickler for pronunciation and the alphabet. The course ended, but I kept coming for my weekly lesson - ("tak" means "yes," "nie" means "no," "dziekuje" means "thank you," "dobry" means "good!") I took lessons right up to the time of my departure. A letter arrived from Poland informing me that I was going to be Poland's first fellowship student of the Polish Bagpipe.

SINGING ON THE TRAIN

I left America in October 24, 1984, loaded down with my suitcase, bagpipes and long necked banjo flying from Boston to JFK to Brussels.

I had to wait about five or six hours for my train to Warsaw and when I boarded the train I sat in a compartment with two English speaking students. One was a fellow from England, the other an American woman, named Pauline, who was studying in Poland.

Soon the train started its long journey through Germany. At every stop more and more people crowded into our car and, by now, the train was a flutter with Germanic and Slavic tongues. The suitcases piled higher and higher till the train was as tight as a sardine can. It was at this moment that I pulled out my banjo and started playing. Immediately, the talking stopped, and all eyes stared at this long-haired banjoist. At first, I played some fast hoedowns, but I could see by their faces that they could not make sense of it. I then switched gears and tried the softer classical sound of Beethoven. This worked much better, and before long everyone was humming along. After a while I went back to some American tunes. This time, now that I tried to meet them halfway, they all joined in. Soon the train car was filled with "Red River Valley," "Oh Susanna," "My Bonnie Lies Over the Ocean," and even "You Are My Sunshine." Just when I was teaching them the old African-American song "Kum-by-ya," the door bolted open and an East German Soldier entered to check our passports and papers. We had reached Berlin.

At once the train car was silent, as the border guard looked over everyone's documents. One soldier was carrying a machine gun strapped around his shoulder and another guard stood by with a huge German shepherd, chained beside him. You could tell by everyone's eyes in the car that this was a serious moment. When they came to Pauline, the guard's face turned nasty and, as he started yelling at her, everyone in the train car looked worried. Pauline began to cry as they started to move her out of the car. I asked her, "What is the problem? What is going on?" She said, "I do not have the right papers with me. I left them back with a friend in Brussels. They want me to pay a fine, but I do not have any hard currency with me, so they are going to take me with them." I asked, "How much do you need?" She replied, "About 20 dollars." I reached into my shirt for the little leather pouch tied around my neck. I withdrew the money and handed over the cash. The guard smiled, and then left as Pauline walked back inside the car.

Again inside, this once unfriendly mob of strangers were now reaching into their wooden baskets, handing out bread, cheese, apples, pears, wine and vodka. They looked at Pauline and me with eyes that told of another victory in defeating the giant. "Now, it's time to celebrate." Soon our voices rang out in joy as our train sped into eastern Poland.

Reaching Poland, our train car was unhitched and we had to wait for a new engine to take us to Warsaw. It was a few hours before the engine came to pick us up and then we headed towards the city of Poznan. I began to feel a little travel weary and started worrying about my getting to Warsaw at nighttime. Pauline was worried too as she now knew that I hardly knew any Polish and with all my baggage it would be hard for me to get around. She suggested that I get off with her in Poznan, spend a night in a student's hotel, then she would help me find a train in the morning. I was so tired, that I would agree to just about anything so I said, "Why not?" After a nice warm bath, as I started dozing off to sleep, the radio was on and I heard a bagpipe and what sounded like Broda's voice. I fell asleep wondering if I was only dreaming or was this the voice of the man who I was to study with?

The next morning, Pauline walked me over to the train station. She told me, "Remember, your train is called Pociag, your ticket is billet, and your ticket is to Wisla. Then you have to find your way from there to Istebna. The name for track is "peron." You need track four." She said goodbye, and watched me as I walked down to find the train platform. I was still in a haze and I had placed my heavy suitcase down to look for Peron Four, when, out of nowhere, a man ran off with my bag. I yelled out, "STOP!" and then "Help!" A group of elderly women saw the man run off and they began yelling something in Polish. The man dropped my bag and kept on running. I picked up my bag and tried to thank the ladies. They smiled and laughed when they heard me try to say "Dziekuje" and at this moment I realized just how vulnerable I really was. My command of the Polish language was terrible and I had a very long trip to get to this place called Istebna. I must have looked confused because one woman came over and glanced at my ticket, and then pointed to a waiting train. I jumped aboard, and walked down the car corridor looking for an empty seat. I found one and it was not long before a young man with black hair sat down next to me. The train started rolling, and I looked out the window as Poznan rolled out of view. After a while I tried to talk with my new neighbor. He understood me enough to tell me his name was Tom and after a while longer he told me he was going to Bielsko Biala. I told him about going to Istebna to study with Jozef Broda. He told me that he had seen Broda on TV and once in a school concert, and then told me that he would help get me to Istebna. After a while, I took out my banjo and started playing. Tom and the rest of the passengers were all fascinated with this strange instrument. I had already learned my lesson about playing fast and unfamiliar tunes so I started out with some slow tunes and then I even tried to play along to tunes that Tom would sing. The music kept up for a while, then the train came to a stop and Tom signaled that we had to get off. We got on another train, then rode on two buses and then back on another train. I was so confused I felt like a pull toy, with Tom leading from place to place. At last we reached Wisla. It was already dark. Tom asked around and we boarded another bus.

The bus stopped at a crossroads near a lumberyard and a round faced woman, who was listening to my story through Tom, motioned for us to get off here. She told Tom to follow her as she wandered through the narrow wooded road. We were walking for quite a while when my hands, holding my heavy suitcase, gave out. The woman, who we learned was named Theresa, picked up my suitcase and kept walking. Soon a home-made tractor roared down the road, and stopped to pick us up. We climbed aboard and made our way to the top of a small mountain. The tractor rolled right up into a schoolyard and the driver shut off his motor. Teresa brought us to a big, blocky cement building where we walked up the stairs, to the first apartment, and knocked on the door. The door opened and Jozef Broda's children, Kasia and Joszko, greeted us with warm smiles. I handed a bouquet of flowers to Jozef's wife Marisa, and walked in to what would become my new home.

ISTEBNA

The village of Istebna goes back hundreds of years and, like most mountain towns, was first just a sheep pasture where shepherds would tend their flock. Then, because of its location, sitting right on the boarder between Slovak and Poland, it became a trading post for lumber and wool. Istebna sat right at the top of a small mountain range separating Poland from Slovakia. The architecture was almost as old as the town it self. Huge wooded log houses, with wooden terraces, sharp peaked roofs, and long overhangs dotted the old streets and mountain fields. This was a town right out of an old folk tale. Even the air seemed magical with a natural echo adding to the atmosphere.

JOZEF

When I walked into the Broda's small apartment I was told that Jozef was still in Warsaw waiting for me. He was also on the radio last night and I told them that I thought I had heard his voice while I was in Poznan. Marisa sent her son, Joszko, to the school to call Warsaw (the school had one of two phones in Istebna, the other was at the Post Office.) and let Jozef know that I was already here.

Jozef arrived the next morning, glad that I made the trip safely, and said, "We were worried when we did not see you come off the train." He then called the children into the living room. Jozko and Kasia brought in Jozef's gajdy, a violin and some wooden flutes. Jozef called out a few words and the children began to sing and play "U Kowala Kuznia Murowno" The ancient melody came to life, with Jozef pumping away on his bagpipe, young Joszko playing the fiddle and Kasia playing the wooden flute called fujarka. This is what I traveled all these miles for. I was so happy and excited that I had hardly any words to express myself. I reached over, pulled out my banjo, and joined right in. Smiles filled the room, as my fingers dashed across the five strings of my Gibson, and we drifted from one old song to the next. Then I played a few songs from the mountains of my home. Jozef put down his pipes and reached for his fiddle. In a few moments his bow sawed out "Cripple Creek" and the room was filled with laughter as Jozef struggled to get out the tune.

Our little session went on for a few hours with more and more people filling the tiny apartment. If I was worried about how I was going to get along without a good command of Polish, I was learning that I could speak volumes without saying a word just by playing my banjo. Soon the music stopped and everyone was talking a mile a minute. I listened for any familiar word, but the words flew by before I could even guess what they were. Then Jozef looked right at me. I could tell he wanted me to do something, but I wasn't sure what it was. I thought that maybe he wanted me to close the door, so I did. Everyone laughed, then I tried to close the window and once again I failed. Jozef walked over to the wall, lifted his finger and turned off the light.

All at once my fears returned. I slowly put away my banjo and walked into the small spare room where they told me I would be staying. I looked around and closed the door. I soon learned that as long as I was in this room I was safe and I felt in control. This room would become my refuge.

The next day I went off with Jozef, back to Warsaw. We boarded the train at night and made it to Warsaw by morning. On the train Jozef talked slowly and I began to understand a few words, linked them all together and came out with some idea of what he was talking about. I could tell he was also excited about my coming to study with him, and he also wanted to learn a bit of English.

By the time we reached the old town streets of Warsaw we were like old pals. We soon came to a big white building with the word "Polonia" over the door. I remembered that Polonia sponsored my 1980 trip to the world festival and that they were in charge of all the cultural events in the country. We were met by an English-speaking woman and a few men. We drank endless cups of tea as we talked about my study program. "We don't know what to expect from your program. It is the first of its type. More of what you call an experiment," the attractive woman said as she smiled and looked at Broda and me. "We will be giving you a monthly stipend, plus a ration card, to get sugar, butter, meat, coal etc. You will be covered by our country's health plan and you will be housed with Mr. Broda's family in Istebna. As far as your study program," she went on to say, "You and Jozef will have to work that out yourselves. We understand that you are also a performer and we hope that you will share your talents in concerts with Mr. Broda. There is one more condition, you must register with the police every month and let them know what you are doing and the places you have been." Soon a bottle of vodka appeared and we all drank a toast to the success of their "experiment."

FIRST LESSONS

When we came back to Istebna our program began. Jozef brought me over to the school, where he taught gym and music. The room was completely stuffed with instruments, tools, costumes and awards hanging on the wall. Jozef asked to see my bagpipe and as he looked it over he said, "It will take a lot of work to make this into a real gajdy, but we have time for that. We may also make a visit to Mr. Pan Suhi, the luthier who made your pipes, but for now I will let you practice on my gajdy." Jozef handed me his prized possession, a big brown goat bag, with wooden parts that went back hundreds of years. I asked him, "Why don't you have the carved wooden goat on your pipe?" He said, "It is not traditionally found in this village and, if you want to play music from Istebna, we will have to remove the goat head from your instrument."

We stayed in his workshop for hours, until it was dark, had a dinner, that was basically the same little meat roll that we had for breakfast, and then went for a walk. Jozef loved the outdoors. He was an avid sports enthusiast and he liked to run, hike and ski. I was a basic American, lazy and out of shape, but I was in for a rude awaking. That first night we walked for hours, up and down, through the hills, fields and forests. I was exhausted and fell fast asleep. The next day it was the same routine, study with the bagpipes doing basic exercises, then a long walk at night. On this walk I began to notice that we had passed the same house three or four times that evening. On the next evenings walk, I said to Jozef, "Didn't we pass that house just a few minutes ago?" He laughed and told me, "You're learning. We won't have to walk this walk again."

The next day, we left school early and Jozef said that he wanted me to come with him to the center of Istebna to get a few things from the store. We walked just a short distance on the main road and then headed into the woods. As Jozef was telling me about all the native trees and mushrooms he kept asking me, "Are you paying attention?" I told him, "Yes," and he kept walking, twisting and turning our way through the thick forest. We finally came out of the woods and walked down the center of the town. I was amazed at all the beautiful old log houses that we passed on the way to the store. We walked into the store, where the shelves were almost bare, but there were a few items left and two long sausages hanging from a meat hook. Jozef remembered about a letter we had to mail, so we went next door to the post office. When we returned Jozef's face dropped. We looked up and saw that the sausages were gone, with only two tiny ends of meat left suspended from the hook. Jozef filled the knapsack we were carrying with a few loafs of bread and some vegetables. As we walked out the door he said, "I have some business to take care of, so I want you to walk back home with this knapsack, by yourself. You were paying attention, weren't you?"

He then jumped onto a bus and disappeared into the hills. I didn't know my way back on the main road so I had only one choice and that was to go back the way I came, through the fields. At first I was angry. I had only been here a few days, a stranger in a strange land, and now I had to find my way home on my own. Then I stood on a high hill, and I could see the school in the distance. It looked far but if I could navigate my way down the hill, then through the woods, I thought I could make it. It took me about a half an hour or so to get down the hill. By then it was getting dark and I still had to get through the woods. As I slowly retraced our trail my mind flashed back to our journey in. Was it at this tree we turned, or was it that one? I concentrated slowly working my way through the tall spruce trees. At last I saw the opening to the main road, with the school just ahead. I had made it.

Jozef's wife scolded him for leaving me behind. Jozef said, "Life is hard. It was good for him to learn that, even in an unfamiliar place, you can find your way, if you pay attention to your surroundings." It was in his plans to let me struggle to learn.

The next month was filled with new discoveries and even a simple walk in the woods turned into a new and important lesson. There were new words to learn, samples of organic herbs to taste and music everywhere. Once, while we were walking along a frozen river stream, Jozef called me over to look at the ice. "Ryki, its early Cubism." We laughed, and then he pointed to an opening in the forest with a crystal clear panoramic view of the snow topped mountains. He smiled and said, "Many artists have tried to capture the beauty that exists in nature, but none can put down on canvas what you see before your eyes."

From these little walks, I began to see nature in a whole new perspective. Even though I had been living in Vermont for years I had never appreciated the life style or the natural gifts of Vermont living. Now I relished the moments of walking through the woods, hiking the hills and singing by the river. Slowly, I found myself transforming into a new person or perhaps just letting out the spirit that was trapped inside.

JANKO'S HOUSE

After one evening hike, we walked down into a small valley to a small farmhouse. There was a light burning inside and the sound of music flowing from within. When Jozef opened the old wooden door I looked into the tiny, sparsely furnished room. Inside stood a tall friendly man playing the fiddle and a much younger fellow pumping away on a gajdy. The music stopped as greetings were exchanged. The tall man's name was Janko, one of the best known of the regional musicians. He was teaching some new songs to Zbigniew Walach, who was just starting to gain his place in this regional hierarchy. Janko was delighted to hear that I was from America. He pointed to a faded photograph taped to the wooden bellows of his old set of pipes and said, "My father played the gajdy too and he could sing like a bird. He left for America years ago to go to Chicago. Maybe you have seen him?" Then he took out a very old Czech accordion and began singing "Red River Valley." I had my banjo on my back and in no time was playing along with Jozef as Zbigniew joined in on fiddle. Hours passed, lost in shots of strong vodka and freshly picked mushrooms. At one point Janko went into his closet and pulled out his old worn red woolen vest and his white big brimmed hat. He motioned for me to put these on, then handed me his old set of pipes. He told me, "These are the oldest pipes in town. My father taught me how to play them, I then taught Jozef and others, and now we will teach you. Then you can go back to America and play our music just like my father did years ago." As I looked around at Janko's rubbery comic book face and his warm smile I knew that I was becoming part of an old community and that in the future, I would always try to honor that commitment but, for now, I was totally filled with love and joy for this land and these people. I really felt like I had come home.

THE COMMUNITY

Istebna was filled with all kinds of characters, from the cleaning woman, Mrs. Wypinski and her husband, who took care of the school and answered the telephone, to the Broda's friends Edek and Stasha Zajac. There was also the group of teenagers in Jozef's dance and song ensemble. They ranged in age from thirteen into their early twenties. The group performed at festivals, concerts, radio and on TV programs throughout Europe. They had many appearances on Polish National TV. At the core of the group were Broda's two children, Joszko and Kasia, Edek's daughter Marzina, his niece Wiesia, a beautiful blond fiddler named Monika and her sisters, and a few big strong boys named Stash, Adam and Walter. Most of the group, which in all numbered around twenty-five, came right from Jozef's school and had been with him for years.

At first it was hard to be taken in by the group. After all, I was almost thirty years old, I could hardly speak Polish and I was an awful dancer but they did enjoy my banjo playing and with the help of Jozsko and Kasia, it was not to long before we were one big happy family. They even gave me a new nickname, "Ryki," which jokingly refers to my loud voice and means "Song of the Elk." Broda's closest friends were Edek and Stasha Zajac (Rabbit). Stasha was a true Gorali Mountain woman and her mother and sister lived right behind her house in an old log home. Edek was a big, rotund jolly soul, who always had some hot tea and kielbasa on the table. Edek and Stasha also loved to have parties, with singing and dancing all night long.

Jozef and I would often stop by their house, after a walk through the hills, and instead of knocking on the door, we'd play a tune on our instruments until the heavy wooden door opened wide to let us in.

WIESIA

Wiesia! Her eyes were bright blue, and her long hair was braided down to her waist. She had a voice like a dove and she drove all the young boys crazy.

To me, she represented everything that I loved about Istebna. Because Wiesia lived just behind Edek's house, she was always hanging around when Jozef and I would visit. She was also a lead member in Jozef's group and she became one of my best friends, teaching me many of the old songs. Wiesia was patient with my language skills and would go over and over the words until I learned them.

Every day I would start my routine with a cup of tea, and a roll with jam, and then head over to the school for my lessons with Jozef. Jozef was also the gym teacher so while he was in class I spent hours working on the technique of the different Polish folk instruments. The children loved to sneak into Jozef's classroom and watch me practice. Often times the young ones would stand next to me and imitate my arms pumping the bellows and squeaking the big goat bag of my gajdy. After school Jozef would have a rehearsal with his folk group and the youngsters would practice songs, dances and skits for their many performances. Jozef encouraged me to join the group and soon I was stumbling around trying to dance and sing along. In many cases, it was the kids in the group who would end up teaching me the most. Jozef would teach me the basic melody and show me how to play the notes, but the children were the ones who would play and sing these songs with me for hours on end 'til they were sure I could do them.

THE FUJARKA

The basic instrument of the area is a wooden handmade flute called a fujarka, which has been used for hundreds of years by shepherds tending their flocks. In fact, there are many styles of flutes played specifically for the type of animals you are watching. They have one style for goats another for cows and still another for sheep. They use a very long flute with a deep bass note for when the old men would gather to tell stories and a tiny one called the sowa, or owl, as a signal for young lovers.

Jozef gave me a fujarka to practice on, but said that soon I would be making my own. One day while walking through the forest, Jozef gathered a pile of fruitwood and then asked me to look for a piece for myself. We placed the sticks in the basement to dry out and a few weeks later Jozef told me to go get my stick as we were now ready to make it into a flute. We spent the whole day working side by side peeling off the bark and then cutting it to size. Jozef handed me a long hand drill and told me to start hollowing out the center of my flute. It took a few hours as my hands twisted the long drill down through the hard wood. Finally, I told him, "I made it through." Jozef looked down and saw that my hands had blistered and were bleeding. He laughed and said, "You Americans lead such a soft life." Now, we heated up a thick nail and Jozef slowly bored the nail into the wood to create the finger holes. Then he took a sharp knife and cut a slot into the back side of the flute. He then plugged up the top leaving only a tiny sliver to blow into and handed me the flute, saying, "Now play." I put the flute up to my lips and blew out a strong note. "Good," Jozef said, "now we must get it in tune with the other flutes of the village." Very slowly Jozef carved each hole until it matched his master pattern. Then we heated some smaller nails and decorated the flute with burnt wood designs.

After I had my own fujarka it became my constant companion. Jozef taught me the songs and melodies of the fujarka in the most interesting fashion and we would re-create and live the song. If the song was about the sound of the water as it flows through the valley, we would walk out to the river bank and learn the melody with the river flowing behind us. One time he woke me up in the middle of a very dark night. As we walked through the dark forest, I asked him, "Why did you wake me up in the middle of the night?" Jozef replied, "To learn this song, 'Ciymna nocka idym niom,- Through The Dark Night We Go Walking'." There in the pitch black night, as we walked along the midnight mountain trails playing our flutes, he told me the story of the song. "It's a love song about a young girl waiting for her lover to come visit her in the dark night," said Jozef. He then pointed to one lonely window on the hill top and said, "Look, Ryki, that might be her window." We both laughed as we walked up and down the mountains while I learned the song. One day I was practicing a few melodies as I walked along the river and, after a while tiring of the exercise, I stopped in mid tune. To my surprise, and delight, I heard the far off echoing of another flute ringing through the mountains, finishing the rest of the melody. I then placed my flute to my lips and blew another song, once again stopping before finishing the tune. A few seconds later the mysterious flute player completed my song.

We continued the game until the flute player suddenly played a melody of his own. It was the old African-American Song "Kum-by-ya" that I taught the young students in Jozef's group. The player knew it was I all along. As the melody disappeared in the mountain air I knew that this place and this time was truly magic.

Sometimes Jozef would get his group involved and they would play act out a song, such as the haunting ballad of the love-sick girl of the valleys called "Dolina."

DOLINA

The story they play acted went something like this: somewhere in the southern mountains of Poland, a young girl is about to go through an old ritual. She is madly in love with her boyfriend. She can't eat, she can't sleep, or do anything but think of him, night and day, day and night. Of course, the boy's father knows that no work would be done with her around so he kept the boy busy. "Go chop some wood! Go fetch my tools! Go get some water!"

The young girl went to her grandmother, the only person who understood such things. The old woman laughed and told the girl just what she should do. The young girl follows her advice and she descends the mountain. As she goes she picks a bouquet of wild flowers and when she reaches the meadow (in Polish it is called dolina) she begins to gather some wood to make a small campfire. As the fire burns she takes the flowers and one by one lays them into the flames. As the flower petals burst into flames they start sending a magical smoke into the air. Then the young girl starts concentrating on how in love she is with the young boy and how she can't live without him. Suddenly her desires are transferred into the smoke, which becomes like magical love potion, wafting high over the mountain. The young boy is still hard at work chopping wood when all at once the smoke with the power of her love fills his head. The boy inhales the smoke, drops his tools and runs into her arms.

Of course not all of my lessons went smoothly. There was one day that Jozef told me that we were going to learn an old wedding song. We spent a few hours learning the song then went back to his house. Around six o'clock Jozef spotted me fully dressed in my costume, with my instruments by my side. He looked at me with a puzzled face and asked, "Ryki, why are you dressed up?" I replied, "Why, to go to the wedding." Jozef, dumfounded, said, "Wedding? What wedding?" Once again, I optimistically replied,

"Why, the one we are going to tonight. The wedding we learned the new song for." Jozef shook his head and laughed. Then he said, "I was just teaching you a song. There is a wedding tonight but we were not invited." I just sat there realizing once again that with my limited Polish skills, I only understood half of what was said and shame-faced walked back into my room.

THE COTTAGE OF JAN KAWULOK

Not far from Jozef's house is the old wooden cottage of the Kawulok Family. When Jozef first came to Istebna it was the master Jan Kawulok who taught him some of the songs and instrumental techniques that he is known for today. Jozef learned how to play the gajdy when he was twenty nine years old. He would often visit the Kawulok home and spend time watching Jan play his gajdy and make wooden flutes and the long wooden trumpet. Jozef became an expert on these folk instruments and in Kawulok's declining years often filled in for him in films and on TV shows.

Kawulok's daughter, Suzanna, has continued in her father's footsteps and opened her father's old style cottage to the public as a type of regional museum, where she explains and demonstrates the old songs and culture of Istebna. The inside of the large wooden, log building is filled with artifacts and memorabilia of her late father's work. There are two large wooden trumpets, two gajdy bagpipes, each in a different tuning, a long stand up flute and a large collection of wooden flutes. In the center of the room is a large ceramic stove. Years ago in Poland there was a tax on chimneys and, as many peasants couldn't afford chimneys, they just opened the windows and let the black smoke fly out. The entire ceiling of Jan's cottage is stained with black soot. Suzanna will often remark to visitors that this is real soot, not something we put up for the tourist. Suzanna is an expert musician and although today her health is failing, she can still play all the instruments with ease and is an expert on performing signals on the long wooden trumpeta. These trumpets were often used to call in the shepherds, or as a warning of invaders. On a good day you can hear the sound of the long trumpeta for almost two miles.

ALL SAINT'S DAY

On the day after what we know as Halloween, the Poles remember their lost loved ones on All Souls Day and it is the day that the Poles remember all the dead. An old custom was to decorate graves with flowers and, as so many people died during the war, there were flowers placed where every soldier fell or a battle was fought. Walking with Jozef to church that morning, I saw flowers scattered throughout the woods. After church we went home and watched a film on Polish television about the bombing of Warsaw and how the

Poles rebuilt the city almost exactly from old drawings and paintings. Next, we watched the news as cameras took us all over Poland showing the thousands of flowers covering the streets of every city town and village. Later that night the whole village came to the graveyard to decorate the graves and sing songs in memory of their loved ones. I never realized how many people were lost to the Nazis, and as I stood there among my friends, tears rolled down my cheeks as I tossed red flowers onto an old warrior's grave.

DOWN IN THE MINES

It was in the beginning of December that I was invited to perform at a most unusual event. A teacher, who taught English in the nearby city of Katowice, had a husband named Frank, who worked as a health and safety inspector for the region's coal mines. He had arranged for me to spend a day at a local coal mine and then later to perform at a holiday party to raise money for the orphan's Christmas fund. I was very excited about the idea as it was not only a great honor for me to sing for the miners, but also was a return to my roots as my great grandfather worked in both the coal mines of Poland and western Pennsylvania in the USA.

When my friend Frank and I arrived, they brought us into the locker room where we changed into the heavy white overalls, flannel shirt, rubber boots, hard hat and lantern worn by the miners. Once dressed, we shot down a fast elevator down deep into the bottom of the mine. Polish coal mines are much deeper than the ones that we have in America, with some of the shafts reaching below 800 meters. In this region of Poland, which is called Silesia, the coal mines make a labyrinth of tunnels that are larger than some cities. Down in the mine, a cool damp breeze blew through the shafts. It was so calm and peaceful that it was hard to imagine how extremely dangerous these mines are. We spent a few hours walking through the mines meeting the workers and watching them dig the hard coal from the earth. Later we went back to the elevator and went back up to the top of the mine to meet the president who ran the mine. After a few symbolic shots of strong Polish vodka I was told about this evening's festivity.

Once a year the coal miners get together a party to raise money for the orphans and widows of coal miners. It is not only a party but a kind of kangaroo court, where fines are given and special tasks are ordered for any infraction of the rules. I was issued a jacket and tie and was told to report to the union hall by 7:30.

That evening, I walked into a large room filled with tables, chairs and a large stage. On the stage was a weird assortment of objects: there was an outhouse, a fenced-in jail, a see saw, a table with a hammer and a bag of bent nails, a wooden stock, like they used in the old days to lock prisoners in, a huge log with a two-man saw and a huge icon of a Polish woman with two large plastic breasts, filled with beer complete with drinking straws.

At the head of the room sat the judges, splendidly dressed in the traditional black uniform with a plumed feather cap of the Polish coal miner's union. As the men walked in the room, a gargantuan pitcher of beer was filling every beer glass in the room. The men sat down and the rules were read by one of the Union officials; "Welcome to our annual fund raiser for the orphans. If you have not been here before, please be aware that you can be fined by our committee for any breach of our rules. For instance, all those who came with out a blue jacket and tie, please stand." About twenty-five men jumped to their feet, and were immediately fined. Then the official went on, "We will be observing you throughout the evening. If you drink out of turn, you will be fined, if you don't sing, or sing too loudly, you will be fined, if you eat too fast, you will be fined, and every time you leave the room to use the bathroom you will be fined so the more you go, the more you pay." As every one sat down, one of the judges called for a toast and, at once, every one stood and sang an old Polish coal miner song, picked up the full glass of beer and drank it straight down.

As the evening progressed, more and more fines were handed out and soon the stage was filled with activity, for not only were you fined with money, but were sentenced to a penalty. My friend Frank was caught for placing his glass down before he was told and was brought before the judges. They fined him a few zloty, and then locked his head and hands into the wooden stocks. Soon others were fined and were sentenced. Within an hour, the stage had two men sawing wood, a man pounding nails straight, men locked inside the outhouse and jailhouse, two men weighing their clothes on the see saw, and the most humorous of all, two men of completely different sizes exchanging clothes. When I saw this huge overweight man jumping up and down in his underwear, trying to squeeze into the trousers and shoes of a man less then half his size, while his comrade was swimming in over-sized shoes, with pants reaching all the way to his chin, I lost my control and let out a huge belly laugh.

All of a sudden the room was silent as the judges turned and faced my direction. "So, Mr. Polish Folklore, you think that this is funny? We will see how good you really are, and if we are not satisfied, you will be issued a fine, so go ahead, sing us a song." I stood up, faced the judges, and sang one of the mountain ballads that I learned from Jozef Broda, singing in the characteristic high voice range of the mountaineers called "The White Voice."

After my song, there was great applause and the judges smiled and handed me a coupon for free unlimited use of the bathroom. The party went on with endless rounds of strong Polish beer and food. The money was collected and the workers were thanked. I was then asked to sing. I did a short program of American Union songs and told them, with the help of my friend Frank, what the words meant. Soon the whole room was reverberating with Woody Guthrie's "Union Maid," as hundreds of Polish coal miners joined in on the chorus "Oh, You Can't Scare Me, I'm Sticking To The Union" followed by "Which Side Are You On," "We Shall Not Be Moved" and then the Merle Travis classic "Dark as a Dungeon."

After my union songs, I played some country songs and a whole line of men joined me and danced round and round as I played Hank William's "Jambalaya." The men closed the evening with songs of the Polish miners. I never heard such strong beautiful singing in all my life, and then the men cried out "Piwo!" and drank another round of beer. It was now early in the morning and the party was coming to a close. The president of the coal mine came over to Frank and me and said, "This was such a fun evening. Ryki's music was great and the men really enjoyed the banjo. As you have a long way to go, I want you to be my guest and have my driver take you home. I'll walk."

We laughed, as we loaded my instruments into the sleek black car, and waved to the president of the mine as he began walking back to his house.

CHRISTMAS 1984

Christmas 1984 was a very dark time for the Polish people. It was just at the end of Marshal Law, with food scarce and many material goods almost nonexistent. Living in Istebna, was almost like taking a step back in time. Very few people had cars so most still walked or used horse and wagon. In the wintertime they used a horse-drawn sleigh. Every morning I could hear the sleigh bells ringing as the horses plowed through the deep snowy hills. Many people used cross country skiing to get around in the mountains and the kids even skied or used their sleds to get to school. Even though this was a time of hardship it was also a time when people gained their strength through community music and dance parties. The holiday season began on December 6th, The Feastday of St. Nicholas. In Poland with a 90% Catholic population, almost everyone is named after a Saint and instead of birthday parties, the big event is your nameday, or the feastday of your saint. Of all the namedays, none brings more joy to the children of Poland than that of St. Nicholas or "Mikolaje" (pronounced em-eek-o-why-ya).

MIKOLAJE

An interesting custom that also takes place on this day is the old pagan tradition of driving away the evil spirits to keep them from entering the New Year. Somehow these two customs combined to make a fascinating experience. The children, who take part in this Halloween-like pageant, wear costumes representing all kinds of strange creatures. There are devils, goblins, storks, bears, mice, angels, a chimneys sweep, a priest, a gypsy, a doctor, old man time and a host of others including Old Saint Nick.

My teacher, Jozef, had the children rehearsing a street play based on this old tradition for weeks. The night before, Jozef's workshop was buzzing with activity. All the children were having a great time repairing their costumes and making all the props necessary for the big event. It was decided that I was to play the stork, and would be dressed in long white sheet while holding a large wooden stork's head attached to a long pole. There was a pull string that caused a clapping sound to be made as the wooden beak opened and shut.

The following morning was beautiful and sunny with just a dusting of white snow dotting the hills and covering the ground. When we did our first presentation, in the schoolhouse, the children were very excited as the gym room was filled with students, teachers and community members.

Our short, improvisational play opened with two altarboys fighting. Soon another young boy, dressed as a priest came along, to break up the fight. The priest ordered the boys to do some push-ups to punish them for their misbehavior at committing such a disruption during this holy time of the year. The children in the room laughed with glee as they watched the priest's scowling face as the two boys exhausted themselves in their punishment. From the corner of the room a tall figure came walking to the center of the room. He carried a long wooden staff and was dressed in a long robe, topped off with a tall miter hat. It was of course the hero of the play, none other than Mikolaje or, as we say, Saint Nick or Santa Claus. The old Saint laughed, as he saw the boys working away, and at once reminded the stern old priest that, "Boys will be boys" and persuaded the priest to stop the punishment. As the priest hugged the young boys a strange sound rang out from the corner of the room. An old woman, dressed in a ragged outfit, was being chased by a huge clacking stork holding a baby. The stork corners her and, while clacking his beak, hands her the newborn child.

The old woman takes the child but cries in despair as she does not have a husband. Once again, Saint Mikolaje comes to the rescue. This time he is leading in a lonely chimney sweep who is in need of a wife. The old sweep cries, "Oh, what am I to do? My family has all emigrated to America and left me all alone for Christmas." Mikolaje pats the old man's hand and says, "Fear not, for there is an old woman who is also lonely and who needs a husband." The astonished chimney sweep brushes off the black chimney soot from his clothes and hands and then takes the hand of the old woman who is clutching her baby.

The priest takes the couples' hands and gathers everyone together for the wedding. As the crowd gathers, a visitor, who arrived on horseback, forgets to close the door and the excited horse jumps around the room and kicks the chimney sweep. The chimney sweep falls to the ground as every one calls out for help. At this point the audience is stunned and shouts out, "Oh my." While everyone stares in horror, the devil, dressed in a black cape and a red horned wooden mask with bulging eyes, enters the room rubbing his rubbery red hands together. He is followed close behind by Death, dressed in a skeleton mask, and a gang of green faced goblins all rattling chains and snapping their whips around the room. (Here the crowd boos as the devil smirks and grins with delight)

The audience screams and as the mourners hoist the chimney sweep's dead body in the air, the devil and his henchmen try to snatch the corpse. Soon a big fight follows, with a cacophony of yells, bellows and chains hitting the floor. At this moment Saint Mikolaje kneels to the floor and begins to pray. A white winged angel flies into the room and kneels by him and the corpse. Now a doctor with his nurse arrives and examines the body. Saint Mikolaje and the angel pray for the chimney sweep's life and through the power of their prayer he comes to life. The doctor exclaims, "His heart is beating. He will not die." The devil and his band realizing that they were beaten retreat to the corner of the room whipping their chains at the audience as they pass by. The chimney sweep gets up from the ground and hugs his new wife. Everyone cheers as the couple is married and then they sing out an old Polish Christmas song and the audience roars out their approval as once again good triumphs over evil. As the play comes to an end the young children rush up to Saint Mikolaje as he hands out little presents.

After the school program, we walked all through the village, knocking on doors and repeating the short play. Everyone opened their doors as our ghoulish procession walked in. Sometimes the boys who played the devil and his goblins would whip chains around the room, steal fruit or even try to steal a kiss, if there was a young girl in the room. The owners of the houses would reward us with apples and candy then send us off, through the snow, to the next house. We walked to almost every house in the village, laughing and singing until dark.

WEGILA

After dark we made our way to the mountain church where we did our last Mikolaje performance of the year. After the show, the children gathered around as the priest handed out presents, for in Poland this is the day to hand out most presents, not on Christmas. The days that follow Mikolaje, all lead up to the big moment of Christmas Eve. There are many things to do to prepare for the holidays. The house must be cleaned, all debts must be attended to, and all the food for the meatless meal must be rounded up while the children spend most of their free time singing Christmas carols. The Poles believe that on Christmas Eve, all animals become human-like, so even in this country where meat is highly valued no meat is eaten on this day

On Christmas Eve, everyone fasts while the big meal is being prepared. In some households the old tradition of laying wheat sheaves in the corners of the room and under the table are still observed. This goes back to the idea of Christ being born in a manger. Another old custom that still survives in some old villages, is the hanging of wheat from the ceilings, or just the top of an evergreen tree hung up side down and festooned with candy and fruit.

The table is set so that there is an extra place setting for any stranger, but it should never be set for an odd number of seats, in the belief that, if it is, someone might die within the year. The meatless meal is made of fish (carp) and all the good things from field and forest like mushrooms, berries, vegetables, and plenty of soups.

STAR WATCHER

As evening falls on Christmas Eve, the youngest child is called on to be The Star Watcher. He or she waits and gazes at the sky, waiting for the first star to appear. Once it is sighted they run into the house yelling, "It is here." And then the family gathers round for the Christmas feast. The head of the house takes a piece of blessed holy wafer and breaks it into tiny pieces. On this day, when Poles share the wafers called "oplatek," they believe that everyone is your brother or sister. They exchange the bread and make wishes for the New Year and express words of thanks for the good times of the past. After the meal, the family exchanges a few small gifts. This is when I was given my traditional outfit by the village.

PASTERKA

Soon the family joins the rest of the village for the slippery climb up the mountain to get to church. Years ago people used torches to find their way through the woods. Today we use flashlights. Many of the people and children are dressed in the traditional outfit of the region, with heavy white wool pants, a bright red vest and a huge brown cape for men, black dresses with colorful aprons and beautifully embroidered blouses, all buttoned up in warm goat skin leather coats for the women. Inside the church, it is packed with standing room only. The service begins with the singing of some old Christmas carols led by my teacher Jozef Broda and his dance group. Then I was called on to sing a song from America. There, dressed in the new clothes that were given to me by this tiny poor village as a symbol of friendship and my acceptance by the community, I swung my long-necked banjo over my woolen vest and played "Silent Night."

Without a moment's break, the whole community sang back the next verse in Polish. It was as if time stood still, one of those magical moments where the song takes you to new highs. Here we were, two different cultures, separated by distance, language and at the time, political differences, all untied in complete harmony.

But by January, there was trouble brewing inside the country and I soon got caught up in it. I had just come back from a short tour with Jozef and his group over in France, when I received a letter telling me that I had to report to the police office. Every month I would go to the same building and hand over my passport and visa and get another extension. This time was different. When they handed back my passport I noticed that my visa was missing. I asked them if there was a problem and the policeman looked at me and said, "Why, yes." I looked at him with disbelief and asked him, "Well, what is it?" The policemen looked straight into my eyes and said, "There was a Soviet man in your country who was accused of spying and ordered to leave at once. In retaliation we are not renewing any American visas at the moment." I was stunned. He then smiled and said, "Oh, it has nothing to do with you personally. You will be welcomed back anytime but now you have only two weeks and you must leave." I stammered, "But ... But ... my studies." He, again, looked straight at me and said, "There is nothing I can do for you, and now you must leave my office." I was devastated. My friends back in Istebna felt bad but this was Poland, not America, and they were just as helpless as I when it came to government issues.

SAYING GOODBYE

I only had two weeks to cram in a lot of last minute details. A few weeks back, Jozef had planned a restoration of my bagpipes and as we never got around to the job, my bagpipes now lay in pieces. I also had not learned to make my own reeds, yet, and had never made a visit to my family. There was a lot to do with very little time left to do it. Some of my younger friends realizing my plight went to work building me a special bagpipe. I had no knowledge of their plans but I noticed them sneaking away gathering together bits and pieces of bagpipe material. Back at home, I talked to Jozef and he, with little free time, suggested that I should pay a visit to the man who made my bagpipe, to get my instrument sorted out.

Mr. Suhi was a kind gentleman who lived a short bus ride away. He lived with his wife and family in the village of Ustron and had the reputation of being one of the best instrument makers in Poland. On my first visit I came together with Jozef Broda but now with a better understanding of the Polish language I was able to visit him by myself.

I started making frequent visits and learned from Suhi how to make and tune my own reeds. He had developed a simple technique by using a used clarinet reed. He would take the reed and carefully split it into four pieces and he would then cut one of the pieces to fit the reed inside my bagpipe. After the size and shape of the reed was determined, he would shave it carefully until the reed could be lashed onto a brass reed holder and placed inside the pipes chanter or melody pipe to produce a note. Once the reed sounded, there came the lengthy process of getting it in tune. This was done by shaving off more wood until the main note sounded freely without stopping. Once the reed was working, a final process of tuning was employed by either placing bits of beeswax to lower the pitch or tying a strand of waxed string around the reed if the note was too low. It took hours to make a good reed. Even when they worked, many reeds were discarded while looking for the one that would play best in your instrument.

Mr. Suhi was a patient teacher for he knew that with out an understanding of reed making all my lessons on the instrument were pointless. Mr. Suhi surprised me by telling me that he had fixed my set of bagpipes with no charge. He wanted to give me a little going away present, as he said, to "Remember our friendship." On my last visit we sat in his kitchen sipping hot chicken soup together as he shared his bits of wisdom, knowing that we might never see each other again.

After my visit with Mr. Suhi, I knew it was time to go to see my relatives in Cmolas. It was a long train and bus trip to reach the village of my family. It had been years since my last visit and now I was going there, not as a tourist but as a fellow Pole. It was just a short ride from the town of Rzeszow to the small village of my mother's birth. When I got off the bus I found a few men waiting near the bus stop and asked them for directions to my family's house. The old men looked me over and said, "The taxi stand is across the street." I told them that I did not want to take a taxi. I wanted to walk." They said, "It's too far to walk. Take a taxi." I told them that I had been living in the mountains of Istebna and that I was used to walking. One man said, "Istebna? Then but of course you walk, it's only five miles." He pointed out the directions and off I went. It was a bright, sunny day with hardly any wind as I walked briskly past the rows of wooden houses.

Cmolas is farming land with large areas of flat pastures filled with cows. As I walked along I found myself trying to imagine how many of the houses that I saw were here when my mother was a child. The time passed quickly and, in a short time, I was standing at the entrance of my family's home. When I knocked on the door an old man with a gray woolen hat stood on the porch wondering, "Who is this strange man?" I reached in my pocket and pulled out a piece of paper where my friends from Istebna had written a short introduction. He read the paper and then said with a smile, "Riki, from America." At once, the family gathered around me as I was ushered into the living room and my aunts and uncles had tears running down their cheeks when they heard me speaking in their native tongue. "You speak so well," they said with amazement. "Now we will be able to share stories and ask questions without the aid of an interpreter."

We spent hours eating little sandwiches, with endless cups of hot tea, as we exchanged the news of weddings, births and funerals. All the while, I glanced over to the tiny bed in the next room, where great grandma was sleeping. At the age of ninety-three she had lost most of her hearing and was slowly losing her vision. Her face was wrinkled with just two teeth left in her mouth. She was a survivor, a warrior of old, now slowly fading away. As I looked at her my eyes filled with tears. My family, looking on, shook their heads saying, "She is so old and helpless she can hardly get up from that bed. We are afraid that she won't live much longer." The more I looked at her the more emotional I became. As my tears flowed down my face I wasn't sure if I was crying because I was so sad to see her in such terrible condition or if it was out of happiness that we had yet one more moment to spend together. That night as I slept in the guest bedroom, underneath an old goose feather blanket, I knew that I only had a short time left and I would have to leave in the morning.

Early the next day I went and sat by my great grandma. As I sat next to her tiny bed I held her hand and looked down onto her weathered face. As she felt the warmth of my hand she turned and looked at my face. My tears were now wetting her pillow as I said to her in Polish, "Grandma, this is the son of your granddaughter, Stephanie. I have come all the way from America to be with you." She opened her eyes and looked up to my face, slightly bewildered. Then the family shouted into her ear, "It is Stephanie's son from America." She then opened her mouth and said, "Did he eat with us?" The family cried out, "Yes, grandma, yes." "And did he sleep with us?" Again the family shouted, "Yes." Then the old woman smiled and said, "Then my family has truly come home," and she drifted back to sleep. I left my family by late afternoon and they insisted on driving me back to Rzeszow to meet my friend Janek, who was my host back at the Rzeszow festival in 1980.

JANEK'S BIG NIGHT ON THE TOWN

Janek explained that tonight was a special night, for it was the last day before Lent and we must go out and party. I have never been a heavy drinker, but living in Poland made it hard not to have a taste for vodka, so I was happy to go for the experience. The bar we went to was packed and every one was feeling pretty happy by the time our party of young women and men were seated. Janek said, "We must play this game," and set up eight shots of vodka in the shape of a V. Now he said, "When it's your turn, you must drink all eight shots, one after another, with out stopping." Janek demonstrated his skill and in minutes had drained every glass. The game went on until it was my turn. All eyes where on me for not only was I drinking for myself but, in a way, I was drinking for my country and I could not let America down. Swish, one by one I drank down the shots. The party makers kept up until hardly anyone could lift another glass. By this time the music was getting loud and unbearable, as was the clientele. Janek decided that we should take our party on the road and, after a few futile attempts to flag down a taxi he stopped a big street cleaner. Janek's friends all climbed in the driver's cab as we opened another bottle of vodka. As the vodka made the rounds one of the girls climbed on the driver's lap and drove his big machine in circles around the narrow city streets. The driver knew he had better park his vehicle before we all got arrested so Janek invited our whole entourage to continue the party at his apartment. Once inside Janek handed me his guitar and picked up his violin and we played merrily as the group of very intoxicated dancers stumbled round the room. Soon we put down the instruments and opened the last of the vodka and danced till the light of dawn. The next morning looked like Armageddon, with piles of young men and women in various stages of dress and undress, crumpled up in a big heap on the floor. Everyone was still sacked out when I slipped out the door. It was another day's ride, by train, to get back to Istebna and pack up all my belongings for my last concert in Warsaw.

THE LAST ROUND-UP

Jozef had arranged that I would have a final concert in the capital city at the University Club. It was now my sad duty to say farewell to these people who once were strangers and now seemed like my own family. I spent my last day retracing my early lessons. I knew that I had to get all of the songs that I was working on down on tape for future study back home. With the help of my friend Wiesia I spent the afternoon hiking through the snowy mountains to invite Janko over to a dinner at Weisia's parent's house. It was cold with the snow reaching past our knees. Janko was so happy we had come to visit that he ran and got out his accordion. He danced around the house, playing his big squeeze box, while we gathered together his instruments and placed them in a big sack for the journey over the mountain. It was a slippery climb up over the hills then down into the valley where Wiesia and her family lived. Janko was a good friend of the family so, was a much welcomed guest.

Everyone knew that if Janko was near there would be good music and fun not far behind. Weisia's grandmother cooked up a scrumptious meal of cabbage and sausage in Janko's honor, and being the kind and humble person he was, he almost refused the meal as he wanted the children to eat it. After our dinner, Janko brought out his squeezebox and sang every song he knew into my small tape recorder. Wiesia and her grandmother joined in singing in two-part harmony and then Wiesia herself sang unaccompanied. Her voice was so beautiful that Janko had to hold back his tears. Next, Wiesia went over each song slowly, word by word, until she was sure I could understand them. If it weren't for Weisia's help, and recordings, I doubt that I would have been able to learn as many songs as I did. Later that night all my friends gathered at Edek's. My friends Zbigniew Walach and Jozef Kawulok, surprised me when they handed me their special gift. They had worked for months gathering bits of wood, metal and leather, and had made a replica of one of the oldest bagpipes in the village. It was gorgeous and it even had a hand-punched, metal plate inscribed with their names and the date. I was overwhelmed. After a big meal and A few toasts of vodka, the party was over and everyone sang their way out the door and up the mountains and as they disappeared into the snowy hills I could still hear their voices echoing back, "Groniczki, Groniczki."

LAST NIGHT IN WARSAW

One of Jozef's group members decided to accompany me up to Warsaw. Stash, a big strapping boy, was barely seventeen but was strong as an ox. He had always looked out for me and decided that he wanted to make sure my last shows went well and, thankfully, I did not run into any trouble. When we pulled into Warsaw and saw, to our surprise, a big billboard announcing my performance at the student's club, I knew that we were already off to a good start.

When we arrived at the university, a young student greeted us and gave us the information on where we would be staying and eating. With a great deal of pride, the student told us that we would be their guest and would be well taken care of. He then mentioned a deal that they had with the local restaurant and told me that all my meals would be on the house. Then he introduced me to another student who would be taking us to visit an art gallery. I couldn't help but notice but this young man had a bandage as big as a golf ball covering his right eye. After touring the exhibit I asked him, "What happened to you?" At first he just smiled but then he led me into a quiet hallway and told me his story. "I was at a demonstration that was against the communists and supporting the outlawed union we call Solidarity. The secret police, known as Zomo, came with their rubber hoses and beat us. My eye was beaten with one of their hoses." He paused before he continued, "They want to crush us. They think they can stop us, but they are wrong. I might lose this eye, but if we win back our freedom, and our union, it will be worth it." My eyes swelled up with tears as I listened to the strength of his young voice. How many times had I stood on picket lines or marched in protests knowing that the worst that could happen was to be arrested? Here was a young man willing to risk his eye, or his very life, to gain freedom. I walked away with a new appreciation for Polish willpower and determination and any time I have a question of my own beliefs all I have to do is to think back to that young Pole's words.

The night of my final concert drew a huge crowd to the University Club. I shared the evening with a Polish Bluegrass band called Country Roads and we even did an encore together. After the show a student who ran a radio show wanted to do an interview so we went to his apartment and spent an hour retracing my stay in Poland and sharing a bit of the music of my own country. After the interview I went back into the student hostel for a good nights sleep. In the middle of the night my stomach had a bad reaction to the food that I had eaten at the restaurant. I made a mad dash down the hall to the bathroom. I realized that I was very sick and spent the entire night sleeping behind the stall in the men's room. That night I was so sick that I thought I was going to die. As it turned out I had food poisoning and just might have. By morning I was still sick as a dog but had to climb aboard my train to make my long journey back to Brussels and then back home. As I waited in the airport I wrote a few final thoughts;

"My trip is almost at its end and I have experienced more, during these short months in Poland, than I have words to express. It was like another lifetime. I learned that you have to be strong both in body and sprit and most important I learned that I can be anywhere in the world and as long as I have my music, I will survive."

This experience also taught me what the life of a musician really is. It's a lonely life, locked in crummy hotels, traveling in all kinds of weather, just for that one moment on the stage. It's not an easy life, but I wouldn't trade it. It's the life that I chose and love, my very own passport to the world.

WAY BACK IN THE HILLS OF OLD VERMONT

When I came back from Poland, I really felt lost. I missed my friends in Istebna and most of all I missed the musical community that I had become a part of. Being back home in Vermont, I had to face up to the fact that my relationship with Claudia was changing. Even before I left for Poland, I could feel that we were drifting apart. We had many problems that we just were not dealing with. We both vowed to try to start over again but after the first few weeks of excitement of coming home, we were returning to our old habits and spending more time in our separate rooms.

I found myself staring out side my window dreaming of the life that I left behind and wondering how to put myself back together. Vermont shared so many similarities with my Polish home that I began to incorporate many of the things that I loved about Poland, right in my own community. In Istebna, I had learned to cross country ski with the help of Broda and after our daily music lessons, we would put on our skis and spend hours skiing under the moonlight sky so I wondered, why not try that here.

I bought an old set of wooden cross-country skis for three dollars at a yard sale and, with my skis waxed and clamped to my feet, I spent hours relearning the basic skiing lessons that Broda had taught me. I quickly realized that learning to ski in Poland had a big disadvantage as I had learned everything in Polish and I did not even know the simple terms and techniques in the English language. I went to the library, found a basic book to get me started and then spent hours alone trying out the instructions.

Living in Vermont, in the wintertime, is like living in a picture postcard world. The winter sun dances on the snow covered mountains and the snowflakes glisten like bright diamonds against the blue sky. Skiing on the old logging trails, I found that I had developed a new love for the Green Mountain State. Where once I felt trapped in Vermont's icy grip, I now felt a new sense of freedom and love for the outdoors. I even wrote a song for my love of Vermont, though it would take years before I ever sang it. The song's first verse was inspired by an old Vermont folk song,

Way Back In the Hills of Old Vermont

I'm remembering the days before I went away
Back in the hills of old Vermont
And the orchard on the hill, I think I see it still
Way back in the hills of old Vermont

Chorus:
For tonight I long to be where the catamount run free
And the rattlesnake can lie out in the sun
Near the voices of the loon, when the apple blossoms bloom
Way back in the hills of old Vermont.

There used to be a barn, near the old fishing pond
Way back in the hills of old Vermont.
More empty fields of hay are vanishing each day
Way back in the hills of old Vermont.

Everything has changed, nothing stays the same
Way back in the hills of old Vermont.
Like the old brown panther's roar, you won't hear that no more
Way back in the hills of old Vermont.

I knew that music was my tonic, and the only way to get myself back on my feet again was to live and breathe it. My song writing was still in its infancy, so at that time I was committed to trying to become a Polish bagpiper. I had my work cut out for me as I had to commit to memory all of the new songs and techniques that I had learned in Poland. In order to accomplish this I needed to learn how to play a whole batch of new instruments. My days were spent sweating over my bagpipe bellows, making reeds, blowing into a ten-foot long trumpeta and playing melodies of the fujarka. I began to approach this new music with the same fervor I did when I was first learning my banjo only this time, instead of bleeding fingers, I was drowning in a pool of sweat while squeezing a dead goat.

While I was lost in my lessons, a new idea came into my mind. Back in Poland, many of my friends had tape recorders but had only a few blank tapes. They would often ask me to record a few songs for them and then say, "I will keep this tape forever." Knowing how hard it was for them to replace their cassette tapes, I thought that I would make up a few home recordings, and then send them to my friends. Soon another idea struck; why not make a real recording in a studio instead of just a tabletop tape. At first, it seemed like a far out idea for someone who did not have two pennies to rub together, but the more I thought about it the more I felt that it was the right route to go. For one thing, the timing was right. Up until the mid-80's, the only way to be heard was to be recorded by a record company. Many record companies were picking only a select few to record, and left the majority of struggling musicians out of the picture but by the mid 80s vinyl was falling by the wayside in favor of the cassette tapes. Every one had a tape player in their car so, more and more, tapes were what people were buying. Even radio stations were willing to play tapes on their programs and that fact alone meant that a new door was opening for the small local musician to get into the real music world

With the price of professional recording equipment going down, many musicians began buying their own recording equipment, setting up small recording studios and opening their services up to the local music scene. I found out about a heavy metal drummer named Terry, who had his own studio just down the road from where I lived. After a few meetings, I could see that it was possible to do a recording and started to strategize the project. My first obstacle was getting together the money. I thought that perhaps I could send out a few advance order forms to my friends to get the project off the ground. To my great surprise, everyone that I wrote to sent in a check, with many friends ordering a few extra copies. With my friends' support, I was off and running. In the studio, I talked over the project with Terry and told him my vision was to have an album that was sort of a mixed bag of my originals, some traditional folk and even a couple of songs in Polish. I thought that I would call the project "Last of the Gypsies" named after one of my best compositions of the time. Terry, who soon became the producer, as well as the engineer, just scratched his head and said, "Let's do it!"

I spent the next few weeks learning my way around the studio and began to record my tracks and then I asked a few friends to come down and join in the fun. With their help I was able to add a cello, rhythm guitar, bass and a few background vocals into the mix. A few songs needed some special treatment, so I brought in my Polish bagpipes, flutes and even my ten-foot long wooden trumpeta. My producer was amazed with the strange exotic sounds coming from his studio and was flabbergasted when I asked him if we could record the sound of falling water to the recently composed song I had written about a local water falls, known as the Comtu Falls.

I first became inspired by the falls when a friend from New Jersey came to visit and we stumbled upon it while taking a little stroll downtown. Later, I found a placemat in a local Springfield diner that outlined the important places in town that contained a few facts about the falls. Armed with that information, and few trips to the Springfield Library, I wrote a little song. I knew that it was not a poetic masterpiece, but it did have a catchy little tune based on the old folk song "Jesse James" with my own melody for the chorus.

Once we recorded the song, the next step was to actually record the sound of the falls. We loaded up Terry's car with microphones and tape recorders and went over to the falls. We then found out that it was almost impossible to record the falls with getting the noise of the traffic that was passing over the bridge. Then we went another route. Right above the falls was a small bowling alley that had a window that faced the falls. We went into the building and convinced the owner that if he let us drag our equipment near the window we might be able to lower a microphone into the falls.

The owner thought that we were a bit crazy but, with the promise of a credit on the cassette said, "Go ahead boys." We secured the microphone and carefully lowered it right into the mouth of the falls. As the long pole appeared out the bowling alley a curious crowd had gathered trying to figure out what in the hell we were doing. After the recording was made, we went down to speak to the crowd. The local folks thought it was wonderful that we were honoring the waterfalls in this special way and asked if they could buy a copy when it was done. Soon all the little stores in Springfield were asking if they too could have a few tapes to sell.

It was that same kind of community spirit that flowed through the entire project. When The Last of the Gypsies was released, it marked a major step in my life. Newspapers came to do interviews and even the local radio station used my song "Comtu Falls" as filler during their station identification segment. Not that my little tape was a big seller, (it sold way under a million copies), but it did pay for itself in the first few weeks that it was released. Best of all, my album gave me a chance to reach people and put me on the musical map, as now I was "A Recording Artist."

Along with the bit of local fame, another major stumbling block came down. For a few years I had been trying to get into the State Arts Council and was rejected each time. With my new tape ready for the next deadline, I thought it was time to try it again. When the letter from the council came I was preparing myself for yet another let down, when to my surprise, found out that they loved my new tape! With the acceptance of the Vermont Arts Council, I was now eligible to perform at a completely new host of venues including festivals, concerts and schools. My life was changing and heading in a new direction - and this was just the beginning!

WHERE THE BUFFALO ROAM

One day I got a call from an agent asking me if I could do a week- long tour in the state of Kansas. I just could not believe what I was hearing, she was asking me if I wanted to go out on the road and they would pay me. I was so excited. I was going to do my very first long distance road tour but then I realized that I had a big problem. I did not have a credit card so I could not rent a car, and I needed to rent a car to do the gig. Being the impractical, romantic fool that I am, I scraped up the cash to buy my plane ticket and just thought that I would deal with it when I got there. When I got on the plane bound for Wichita, I was freaking out saying to my self, "How in the world are you going to pull this off!"

Landing in Kansas, I boarded a bus pointing to my destination, Pratt, a small midwestern town in the center of the state. Arriving in town I took a room in a cheap hotel, then called the college to tell them that I made it. As they were telling me all the directions to the shows and best travel routes, I broke the news that I did not have a car or a credit card to rent one. The college said that I should call the local car dealer, tell them that I was doing the Humanities concert series and they would take care of me. Sure enough in a few minutes, I was on my way driving a rented car through the tall wheat fields and winding my way through the dirt back roads to do my shows.

Most of my time was taken up with performances at the college, schools and nursing homes. Pratt Community College had set up this tour as a way of bringing the arts into the community. The tour took place in a multitude of venues and was a like a training camp for young performers. The audiences varied from being totally involved with the show to listeners falling fast asleep or even yelling and vomiting. Through it all you had to keep the show moving. While the college likes to think of the tour as a Community Outreach an old friend of mine best described it by calling it "the jabber, stammer and drool tour."

The person who was in charge of the program was a local musician and farmer, named Leni, who lived a few miles outside of town with her husband Gordon, a soft-spoken milo farmer. Leni and Gordon invited me out to dinner at their farm and we had a great time, sharing stories and swapping a few tunes, with Leni playing on her dulcimer and me on my old banjo. After our musical jam, Gordon took me over to see the grain elevator where he brings his crops. We shot up to the top of the tall cement elevator and looked around at the inside of elevator.

It was amazing to see how grain is processed and hear Gordon speak about the many months of hard labor it takes to grow and harvest his crop. It is times like this that I realize how blessed I am. To not only be able to travel and sing my songs, but to also be able to experience the wonder of peoples, everyday lives and get to know what America is really all about.

FROM RIK'S JOURNAL

As I ride through small town America, I can understand why so many of these folks never left for the temptation of the bright city lights. They know they belong here rooted close to the land. Every one grows old together and accepts each other warts and all. In one small diner, I noticed a bunch of old gents having a bit of fun when one of the fellows knocked an ashtray on the floor. "Well, that's old Joe," an old farmer shouts, and then the waitress bellows out, "You can't take him anywhere without him just making a mess." The guilty party just turns to his friends and says, "You better watch it or I'll knock over the salt shaker too." The waitress shakes her finger while the old farmers cackle and grin. One old farmer just slaps Joe on the back and says, "We better get moving or we'll all be in trouble."

On my last free day in Kansas I made a trip west out into the old cow town of Dodge City. It seems that the town's early roots sprang up around the old Santa Fe Trail, with thousands of wagon trains carrying settlers west. As the settlers were threatening the Indian's way of life, the Native Americans were not exactly laying out the welcome mat, thus began a feud between the two cultures often ending in wagon burnings and sometimes scalping.

To protect the wagon trains, a fort was built in 1865, which provided food, lodging and a mail station for both the troops and the settlers. About five miles from the fort a ranger named Henry Sitler built a little sod shanty that became a good stopping place for buffalo hunters and travelers. After Sitler built his home, other homes and shops sprang up and soon Dodge City was born. Around the year of 1872, the Atchison-Topeka and the Santa Fe Railroad pulled into town and attracted every two-bit drifter, farmer, buffalo skinner, railroader, soldier and whore for miles around. This filthy bunch of nomads all came to town to raise hell in the saloons, hotels and brothels that lined up along Front Street. The buffalo skinners were often so in need of a bath from being out for weeks on the buffalo road, that they earned the nickname of Stinkers because of their foul smelling clothes. They often found a warm welcome in the red light district, whose "Soiled Doves" were more than happy to relieve them of their dirt, lonesomeness and pocket cash.

As the town became crammed with hastily built storefronts it rapidly became a Mecca for gun-crazed outlaws and as the towns free-for-all status grew, so did the number of graves out on a make shift cemetery known as Boot Hill. With the outlaws came the host of legendary sheriffs like Bat Masterson and Wyatt Earp who patrolled the two sides of Front Street. Each side of the main street was separated by the long steel rail of the railroad tracks. On one side of the street it was declared a safe, gun free area, while on the other side of the tracks it was "anything goes." Dodge City was quickly earning the reputation of a place where men lived hard, fought, died and were buried with their boots on.

By 1875 most of the buffalo were killed off with an estimated 850,000 of the hairy hides shipped to the east, to make coats, while their bones were ground up for fertilizer and china. Now that the buffalo were gone, the long horn cattle trade was beginning. Over five million head of these long horn galoots were being driven up from Texas through New Mexico on the Cimmaron trail to Dodge.

With the cattle also came a new breed of men called Cowboys. The origin of the cowboy goes back to our southern neighbors in Mexico and South America. While most Europeans were happily tending sheep with dogs, the Spanish vaquero was developing a charismatic way with horses and cattle. The image of the vaquero and even the name, which in Spanish means cowmen, would be an inspiration for generations to come. Americans soon adopted not only the vaquero's skill with horses, but also imitated their way of dress, by wearing high leather boots and wide brimmed hats. Contrary to folk's idea of the bedazzled, clean, white faced hero riding a stallion off into the sunset, the American cowboy was often a Hispanic, black or southern rebel who took to ranching after the Civil War. The glamorous life often portrayed in the cinema was very different from the lonely and often dangerous life that these tough men led. Many were drifters who did not own their own horse and just carried their saddle from town to town.

Today most of the old west is just a cheap facsimile of what it once was, built for the tourist trade. Unfortunately, that is also true of the old town of Dodge City. The original Front Street was destroyed by fire and the new front street was rebuilt in the same location, using old photographs for authenticity. It has a museum, and features a shoot-'em-up extravaganza with actors playing the parts of gunslingers and merchants while performing a daily gun fight complete with smoking revolvers. Alongside of the tracks, you can still see the old general store, dentist, black smith, print shop and even have a drink at the Long Branch Saloon. The saloon is built and decorated to fit with the time period and on the weekends, they feature an all girl review filled with songs and dances of the old west. Inside the old style saloon is an original wooden bar and hung above it, the customary painting that was often found at many of the watering holes of the west. The painting displays a voluptuous, naked woman riding in a carriage, pulled by two white stallions. The painting is appropriately called "The Cowboy's Dream."

As I looked around the old bar I noticed an elderly man dressed from head to toe in black, with two shiny silver revolvers hanging from hand carved, black leather holsters. He was sitting near a piano with an old guitar balanced on the piano top. I walked over, smiled, and tried to engage the old fellow in a bit of conversation, but he was not in the mood for talking. Then I asked him if he would mind if I played his guitar. He looked me over and then said, "Suit yourself," and went back to staring into space. When I picked up the old guitar and started playing an old version of a cowboy ballad called "Bury Me Not on the Lone Prairie," his wrinkled old face broke into a grin and he said, "Now where in earth did you learn that version of the song?" I told him that I first saw it in an old collection of cowboy songs by folklorist John Lomax and heard this version sung by Joe Hickerson. The old fellow said, "You know that was the theme song that we used in one of the old western movies that I made called The Lone Rider. Hey, what's your name?" I said, "I'm Rik, a traveling singer, out here to sing a few shows at the college over in Pratt."

The old man stood up and thrust out his hand, saying, "Well, I am the great grandson of Pat Garrett, so they call me Pat. I do a little singing, a few rope tricks as well as some trick shooting. I don't make a lot of money but it helps to make my Social Security check go a lot further."

"Well now, Rik," the old fellow said as he lightly touched my shoulder, "Would you be willing to help me out in the next show I'm doing for the tourists?" I noticed there was a line of eager faces waiting to come in and see the show and I said, "Well, it's my day off, but I'd be glad to help you." Then he handed me a few props from his show as he let in the crowd. As everyone grabbed a seat I picked out the melody of the old cowboy ballad and said, "Now, please welcome The Lone Rider." With that, the old cowpoke came out with his revolvers blazing and laying out a cloud of smoke. He moved like a jaguar, twirling his pistols in and out of his holsters while firing at the coins that I threw in the air.

Old Pat then handed me a deck of playing cards. As I tossed the cards, Pat snapped his leathery bullwhip at each card before they reached the bar room floor. Then I handed him his old guitar back and he sang a few of his favorite songs as the enthusiastic crowd filled his tip jar and clamored for more. After his show, he asked me to join him for a cup of coffee and eagerly asked if I was going to be in town for a while. "No, I have a plane to catch tomorrow, but I do hope our paths will cross again," I said. With a wink, he replied, "Well, you are welcome any time." At this point I knew it was "time to get out of Dodge," so I tipped my hat to Pat, and drove away.

THE GREEN MOUNTAIN VOLUNTEERS

In the late 1980's, one of my guitar students asked me if I wanted to go with him to France and Spain. When I asked him for more details, he told me that he had joined a dance group called the Green Mountain Volunteers who specialized in New England-style contra dancing. He also said that the group was looking for a few musicians to accompany the dances and thought that I might be a good choice. I decided to check it out and drove up with Tom, my student, to meet with the group.

The Green Mountain Volunteers had been doing these international tours for quite some time and on each trip put together a band to not only play for the dancers but also engage in a few skits and play between the sets. Even though I did not really know any of the other musicians we seemed to hit it off and the group for the summer tour accepted me. At least once a week Tom and I made the long drive up to a little town called Hinesburg, not far from Burlington, Vermont, for a rehearsal.

The group itself was a mixed assemblage of young and old, skilled and unskilled dancers. The group leader was a bearded be-speckled fellow named Ben Bergstein who had formed the group back in the late 1970's. At first the group was made up of a batch of dancers who got together to dance international style dances, especially from Bulgaria, Rumania and other parts of Eastern Europe. When Ben was invited to perform at a festival in Bulgaria, he knew that dancing European style was like bringing coals to Newcastle, so he decided to create an American New England style dance ensemble. To make the group stand out, he and his partner April, researched and sought for original period clothing. In its early years, the dance group was a huge success performing everywhere from local dances, schools, and festivals, and then going on to perform at the state house and the winter Olympics. They even appeared on an Andy Williams TV Christmas Special. Besides concerts in the states, they also did several International tours, and this year the tour would be based around the Festival of the Pyrenees in Jaca Spain.

GOLDEN BOOKS

When I was still a child, I had several recurring dreams. The first one had to do with the atomic bomb falling through my bedroom ceiling and the second was a very strange fantasy about a room filled with gold bound books. Little did I realize that these two themes would play a great part in my later years.

One day, when I showed up for rehearsal, the musicians were asked to go to the home of one of the members to work out the details of the tour set list. When we arrived at the house, I got a strange feeling. I had never been there before but there was something familiar about the place. Then, as I walked into the living room, I saw something that made my hair stand on end. It was a bookcase filled with gold-tooled books, just like the ones I saw in my dreams years ago. At that time, I did not even know whose house we were in but I was soon to find out. When we got back to the rehearsal, a long-haired woman, in her early thirties, came over and asked April for the keys. I had noticed her before. I mean, how could you not notice Marianna? She was strikingly beautiful and the best dancer in the group.   At the time, I do not think that she even noticed me at all and, in fact, I do not think that she even liked me.

TEA, COFFEE AND SANDWICHES

About the same time as the dance tour, I was also planning my own tour of going back to Poland and I knew that I needed to get more material for my Polish program. As always, money was a problem but, as in the past, I had a hunch that I could get over that hurdle if I could only find a sponsor. I started racking my brain thinking of how I could get over to Poland, and then it struck, but of course, an airline could be my sponsor. I looked through a few magazines until I found the telephone number of Poland's largest airline, LOT Airlines, and gave them a call. I reached the sales manager, Mr. Ziebinski, and tried to tell him my idea, but he said, "We don't give away free tickets." Perhaps it was my background, of living in Poland that kept me from giving up but before our conversation was over, it was agreed that I would send him a video. It was a real long shot.

A few weeks later I was surprised to get a phone call from Mr. Ziebinski, telling me that after looking over my video he was willing to meet with me, and asked me to come to the main office in New York. A few weeks later Claudia and I were standing on fashionable Fifth Avenue, staring up at the huge building that housed the LOT Airlines office. I had prepared a written proposal of what I would do in Poland and Claudia brought along a sample of the Polish Folk arts that she was creating. As we passed through the large hallway and boarded the elevator I took a deep breath and said, "Well, here we go."

We went up to the office and were asked to have a seat. I sat there staring at the promotional posters while my mind was preparing for the interview. I knew from my days in Poland, that during a business meeting you could almost tell how things were going to go depending on the hospitality of the host. If there was tea on the table, it meant that you were not very important, but if you were offered coffee, then a deal was possible and, if there were cookies or sandwiches on the table, it was a done deal. As Mr. Ziebinski walked in the room he called out, "Ryki, so glad to meet you. I recognize you from the video." My heart almost stopped at that moment and then I heard him say magic words, "I have already ordered some coffee." Now, I knew that we were ready to make a deal. As Mr. Ziebinski drank his coffee, he told me that he was very impressed with my work and wanted to help me. We went over my proposal and then he smiled and said, "Here are your tickets. All that we want is for you to mention LOT Polish Airlines before you perform and, of course, to send us any newspaper articles from your trip." I could not believe it. One of Poland's largest corporations was sponsoring me, and, best of all, I was going to be able to go back to the country that I loved.

BACK TO POLAND!

The next few months rolled by in a flash, and before I knew it, Claudia and I were getting on a plane bound for Warsaw. The plan was that we would spend two weeks in Poland and then I would continue on to my next tour with the Green Mountain Volunteers while Claudia flew back home.

We got off on the wrong foot right from the start of the trip. When we arrived, we were told to report to the festival where I was invited to play. Our timing was off and we had arrived almost a week before the festivities began. We decided that we had enough time to go to southern Poland, visit my friends, and then return to play the festival. It was then I made another mistake. I was in too much of a hurry to get on the train and left most of my clothes at my room at the festival, only taking a pair of shorts and my Polish outfit.

Of course, I did not realize my folly until hours later. During this mayhem, Claudia was getting irritable. On the way to Istebna we ran into my old friend Jan, who had helped me during my first trip. Jan said that he wanted me to perform at a large gathering, for young people, in a nearby town. I agreed, and off we went to do the show. As we drove towards the mountains, the weather was changing and it was getting cold. As I was still wearing my shorts, I looked through my knapsack and realized the only other pants I had to wear were the heavy woolen white pants from my Polish outfit. Oh yes, these pants were made in the old traditional style without buttons or zippers. The mountaineers wear a long white shirt that fits underneath the large opening in the front and covers up the parts of you that are best not seen.

To my frustration, I realized that I had also left my long shirt back in the festival room and the only shirt I had, with me was a rather short Ben and Jerry's T-shirt. As I waited back stage I saw thousands of young teenagers sitting out on a hillside, and I knew that it was almost my time to go on. It was too cold to wear the shorts, but my T ?shirt did not really cover the big gaping hole, so I did not know just what to do. After I few minutes I opted for the T ?shirt and woolen trousers, and decided that if I sat down to perform, everything would be fine. A chair was brought out to the center of the stage and I quickly sat down and started singing. After a few songs, I quickly left the stage, however, as I reached the back stage area, I heard the crowd yelling for more. Jan said, "Ryki, you must go back and give them and some more music." As I turned around, I noticed that the chair was gone but, as I walked back to the stage, I decided, oh what the hell, let it all hang out. It was a great show in many ways.

After the show, we made our way through the high mountains over to my second home in Istebna. It did not take long for the news to break that I was back in town and when I met with some of my friends, it was decided that there would have to be a big party. Knowing that I had to return to the festival the next day, they sent a young boy to run around the town and tell everyone, "Ryki is back and there is a party going on." By evening, my old friends came in by the dozens. My host, Edek, lit the campfire, and put out rows of Polish sausage. I heard a familiar sound echoing through the woods. Coming down the hillside, dressed in the traditional clothes, was my old teacher Jozef Broda and his band. Jozef greeted me by singing my favorite song "Groniczki" or, translated, "How I Long for My Small Mountains." Tears of joy filled my eyes as I heard Jozef singing in the high white voice. By the second verse, I joined him singing in a lower harmony. It was almost five years since we last met and we had much to talk about. After a fun evening of drinking, dancing, eating and singing it was time for me to go.

Jozef and his band said goodbye, and then sang as they walked through the hills, until their voices faded away in the distance. Even though I was thrilled to see my old friends, Claudia was not happy. She felt out of place and wanted to leave. I could not understand her reasoning but the longer we were in Poland the more we fought until, one day, I just had enough. There had been many problems throughout the years and, to be honest, many of them stemmed from our difficult lifestyle and the fact that I needed to travel. To complicate matters, Claudia was also not feeling well and was beginning to have some health problems. It was a few days later that we had an enormous fight and I vowed that our relationship was over. She did not really believe me, but it turned out to be true. After the festival, Claudia went to the airport while I boarded a train for Paris.

IN AN OLD FRENCH CATHEDRAL

When my train pulled into the Paris station, it was late and the exchange office was already closed. I did not have any French currency, so it was going to be a little tough without the right money, or language skills, but I somehow convinced a cab driver to have pity on me and take me to my hotel for American dollars. When my cab pulled in, Ben and Marianna were waiting in the lobby and were relieved that I had made it. The next was another free day, so I hung out with the musicians and realized that none of us had any money. While the rest of the group was out eating at a posh restaurant our little band had just enough money to scrape together to buy a round of beers.

The next morning we all boarded our tour bus and started our long journey to southern France. While all the dancers filled the front seats of the bus, we musicians held court at the back. To pass the time, we played tunes as we rode through the French countryside. That night the bus stopped at a little French villa, where we spent the night. Early in the morning, Marianna came into the band's room and asked if she could take a photo of us standing out in the nearby sunflower field. After a few photos, she looked at me with her tantalizing deep blue eyes and said, "You know I hurt my shoulder when I had to carry your suitcase." Then with a laugh, she walked over and climbed into the bus. As the bus rolled on, the band noticed that every time we tried to leave our seat we would bump our heads on the luggage rack. In a short time, the dancers started making their way to the back of the bus to listen to our music and just hang with the band. When they too bumped their heads, they became initiated into our little club. As the miles grew, so did the number of people at the back of the bus, to the point that it was almost impossible to stand in the aisle. When Marianna made her way to the back of the bus she too bumped her head and we voted unanimously that she was now part of our club. Marianna was certainly having an effect on me and the longer that she hung out at the back of the bus, the more I wanted to be with her. The days went by going from one small town to the next, one show after another. All the while I was making friends with everyone in the dance group, but one dancer in particular captured my thoughts, it was the blue-eyed, girl with the long braided pigtails. It was Marianna. Our friendship was deepening and then something almost surreal happened.

It was our day off and the group was free to wander around the small town of Saint Marie Oleron. It was a beautiful little town, with a very old cathedral in the center of town. A small group of us walked into the church and, at first, we all stayed together. Then most of the group went ahead, walking towards the main altar. Marianna and I were left standing alone at the back of the church. Someone up above began playing a huge old pipe organ. As I took her hand, and walked through the church, it was as if we were both transported back in time. We felt like two soul mates joined back together, returning to our own wedding from ages ago. The pews of the vacant church filled with ghostly figures dressed in their finest clothes and there were flowers everywhere.

At that point, Marianna looked at me and said, "I've never been down the aisle before." As I looked into her eyes, I could tell that she too was experiencing this paranormal wedding and also felt the presence of these lost soul mates. The feeling was so intense that neither of us knew just what to do. When we left the church, Marianna said, "Did you feel it, too?" I looked at her pretty face and said, "Yes." Then we walked back to our tour bus, but we knew that something was happening. Something that was both beautiful and out of control. We were falling in love.

The Omen

In an old French cathedral, in the middle of the day,
we went walking down the aisle when the organ began to play.

Though all the pews were empty, old spirits filled the room.
It was just like a wedding, you were the bride, I was your groom.

So, as we walked to the altar, with hands entwined,
we both knew, in an instant, the thoughts that flickered though our minds.

But what we just imagined, we thought could never be.
It was just an omen that you were meant for me.

When the organ stopped it's playing, and we stood side by side,
we looked up at the ceiling while love was filling up our eyes.

Though not a word was spoken, when we left that church behind,
the feelings that touched us both, will forever be painted in our minds.

In an old French cathedral, so many miles from home
Two lost souls joined together in the town of Oloron
Two lost souls joined together in the town of Oloron

One day Marianna and I found ourselves sitting together on a park lawn. We had just finished performing at a parade and had a few free hours to kill before the next show. Finally, having a few precious hours together we started to really talk. At first, I started talking about my life as a musician and artist, but then Marianna said, "I don't want to hear your stories. I want to get to know you." At that point I had to drop my performer's mask and start to tell her who I really was, my background, my hopes and dreams.

Marianna too let down her guard and began to tell me her own story. She told me, "My father was a bookbinder and he married my mother, Christel, when he was in his seventies. They met at my dad's bookbindery in Boston. My mother, an immigrant from Germany, was the daughter of a well known German minister named Emil Fuchs." Her brother, Klaus, was a brilliant scientist who, with a group of other scientists, helped build the atomic bomb.

As Marianna sat on the green grass of Jaca, Spain, spinning out her long family history, I was thinking back to those strange dreams I had as I child, of gold tooled books and the atomic bomb. Had I really, in some strange way, met the girl of my dreams? When the tour ended, Marianna and I went our separate ways, with her going back to Burlington and me heading back to Claudia. When I got back home I realized that whatever Claudia and I had built together had been lost in time. We had come to the end of our relationship

Marianna was also trying to get her life and head back together after our trip. Even though nothing really romantic happened between the two of us in Jaca, there was still a strange force that was pulling us together.

It was if the old souls we met at the church in Oloron were pulling at our heart-strings, and driving us both crazy for, try as we might, we just could not stop thinking about each other. In the end we both realized that we wanted to be together and decided to give away everything to make our dream a reality. It was not easy to break up as there were many strings to sever. My marriage was over and I had to let go of the past and move forward into the unknown.

STEPPING THROUGH THE LOOKING GLASS

Stepping through the looking glass, leave it all behind.
Don't know where I'm heading to or what I'm bound to find.
I gave away an iris to smell a yellow rose, Opened all the windows, my story to expose
But the Iris was fragile, flowers never last long
Stepping through the looking glass though I don't know where I'm going.

In life's long journey, lots of curves in the road
Sometimes you're uncertain which direction you're to go

Stepping through the looking glass, People acting so strange,
Even those who once loved you, Won't call you by your name
But the past drags behind you, like some old ball and chain
Stepping through the looking glass, things will never be the same

In life's long journey, lots of curves in the road
Sometimes you're uncertain which direction you're to go
Stepping through the looking glass, one small step at a time
I'll just step forward for you can't go back in time.

Gasoline Gypsy

ROAD WARRIOR

After my break up with Claudia, I was not sure just what to do. I knew that I wanted to be with Marianna, but we each thought that we should not rush into anything as we both needed some time to think things out and get our lives back together.

My dilemma was answered when I received a call from a school assemblies program that I had applied for a few years earlier. It seems that an artist who was scheduled for the tour had to cancel and they wanted me to take over the tour. The timing was perfect; it was January 1991, the beginning of a New Year and time to make a change. I found that the tour would start off in Kansas, in the town of Coffeyville, then make its way out to Idaho, Oregon, Washington, Wyoming, Illinois, Tennessee, and end up in Michigan. I would be gone till late May and I'd really start living my life as a gasoline gypsy and road warrior.

I only had a few weeks to get everything together but it was plenty of time to tune up my old VW Rabbit. That old Rabbit had almost 100,000 miles on it already but it still ran pretty darn good. The car itself had an interesting story. I bought it from a friend back in Springfield for a dollar. He had just purchased a new car and as his old Rabbit had high mileage they were not going to give him much for it so he sold it to me for a buck. It really wasn't much to look at, just a dull dirt brown body with a bit of rust here and there. The seats and roof lining were torn and the dash box never closed, but it did have one attribute that made it very special. It was a diesel and would get about fifty miles to a gallon. When you plan a tour that works its way through the American heartland, out to the west coast and back, that kind of mileage can save you a heap of gasoline.

Marianna was sad to see me leave but we both knew that this tour was an important test of our relationship. If we could get through all these months apart, and still want to be together, then perhaps we could really start building a life together. So with more than a few tears and good wishes, we packed up my little Rabbit in mid-January, and I hit the road.

CHALK CAT

It only took me a few days to reach the town of Coffeyville, Kansas, the first stop on my long tour. I did not know it when I first arrived but soon found out that this town was famous for being the place of where the Dalton gang was gunned down. Right in the center of town still stands the bank they tried to rob, complete with the bullet holes in the large glass window. The old story of Daltons attempt to rob the bank is kept alive by the citizens of Coffeyville at a little museum that was built honoring the lives of the Dalton Defenders. Inside the museum you can read of how when the Daltons came into town the local merchants set up a booby trap and gunned them down in the Alley of Death, just across the street from the old bank. If you walk down the alley you can see the old jail where the dead bodies of the Dalton gang were displayed. In a kind of ghoulish way the town keeps the gangs memory alive with a hokey exhibit. You pop a quarter in this little speaker machine and the lights of the jail flash onto a group of wax figures laid out as if they were just shot. While you stare at this gruesome site, a little crackly voice from the tinny speaker tells you the whole dang story.

The town itself is just a typical Kansas town with a railroad line, grain elevators, big courthouse, and a little town square. Sadly the town center was made up of too many empty store fronts that lost out to the Wal-Mart and Box Stores that had opened on the outskirts of town a few years ago.

I was set up to stay at the home of one of the local arts patrons who rented out rooms at a very affordable price to the artists who played the nearby community college Humanities Out-reach program that I was a part of. The landlady, Selda, was a striking woman with her gray hair pulled up into a 1960's french twist that sat up at the top of her head. She was very into the theater and was a costume designer and actress for the local theater group. She lived with her friend Allen, another retiree who loved to dabble on his viola. Together they made quite a pair and kept me well entertained with their fantastic stories after my daily school shows. One night, as Selda was cleaning off the dinner dishes, she told me a story that really caught my attention. She was talking about her growing up in Coffeyville; "When I was a young girl here in Coffeyville, we lived in a house off the highway near the train tracks. At the time there was a big roundhouse where the trains would come in and often on the trains rode old hobos. The hobos would get off the trains and then would walk a half a mile to our street, looking for any kind of job they could do to get some food. My mother would always feed them even though they didn't have to work for the food. I can remember getting up in the morning and noticing a drawing of a chalk cat on the sidewalk in front of our house. I never knew what it meant or where it came from, as none of us kids had chalk like that. Years later I found out that the hobos used to mark houses that they ate at with chalk. They used the sign of the chalk cat to mark the house of a kind-hearted woman.

Selda's story stayed with me all that night and through the next afternoon. While I was riding back to her house I had an idea for a song and finished the song before I reached her house. Later that day I told Selda, "I have something I want to share with you." I then picked up my guitar and started singing;

Chalk Cat

The life of a singer is a hard row to hoe
Driving in the wind, the rain and the snow
All night on the highway with miles left to go
Towns you never heard of, people you don't know

Chorus:
Chalk cat on a doorstep, smile across her face
Stew pot overflowing with her warmth and grace
Like her mother before her, she's gentle and kind
Way down in Kansas, on the Oklahoma line

The hobos of yesterday would always make a sign
On the doorway of someone who was so very kind
They'd draw a cat on the sidewalk, where it wasn't hard to find
To help the next traveler, ease their troubled mind
Chorus

Friends in town or cites, help lighten up the load
A beacon of sunshine on the dark and lonely road
We sing and talk till midnight, awaken at dawn
With sad eyes and good byes, sing our farewell song
Chorus

By the time I finished singing the song I noticed that Selda was in tears. She said, "I never told anyone that story before, not even my son, and now you turned it into a song." I could tell that she was moved and watched as she called her son to tell him of the birth of this new song. In a few days, my shows in town were over and I had to say goodbye. I loaded up the Rabbit with my instruments and, just before I left, snuck away from Selda and Allan to draw a small chalk cat on the corner of her doorstep.

It was a long lonesome trip out to Idaho. It was my first real taste of what road life was like and the one thing that I seemed to have left out when I had my romantic fantasy of touring was just how damn lonely it can be. While I was doing my shows it was fine but as soon as I had an open weekend I had to deal with the fact that I had a whole lot of time on my hands!

FROM RIK'S JOURNAL

It's tough being out here on the road. Living in a hundred towns every week, not knowing a friendly soul to laugh with or cry with. Night time is worst of all as you really feel truly alone. Passing through the small towns, you see that some houses have their living room or bedroom drapes pulled wide open. Riding by, you can get a peek into the lives of the people inside. Lit by a naked light bulb, or the television, you can see furniture and sometimes a few pictures on the wall. You hardly ever see the people for they are hidden behind glass and wood and their bodies are just mere shadows dancing on the wall.

It's long after midnight. All the lights are out and you, the voyeur, are bathed in the blackness and loneliness of the dark highway. In the towns, everyone has gone to bed. Children sleep restfully after that last loving good night kiss on their forehead, while their parents rock in each others arms till they too, fall gently asleep. For you, the traveler, there is no kiss, no fond embrace, only the humming of the vibrating engine and the sound of the wind whipping across your windshield as you travel down an endless road.

LIFE UNDER THE BIG TOP

I guess it is time to fill you in on just how these school tours work. First thing you must know is that when you take on a tour like this you have to be responsible for almost everything. The agency office sets up the tours and sends you a list of your performances, but after that you are on your own. You have to provide your own transportation, expenses, food, and lodging. Most importantly you have to find your way to all the shows on time, every time despite weather, car problems, health problems whatever, "The Show must go on!"

In the beginning of the tour I am given a big schedule of all the schools that I have performances at but, as schools always change their mind, I have to make sure there are no changes about the times or dates of the shows. To get these little weekly updates I have to find the closet post office to my last gig of the week and pick up my mail by general delivery. If I am lucky, I will be able to pick up a letter with any changes of my next week's programs. I say lucky, because there is many a time that the agency's letter does not makes it in time or the post office can't find it. Needless to say, when you are a stranger, getting your mail by General Delivery you are not of the highest priority.

You will notice that I did not say anything about directions to the schools. Often the schools were in such small towns that all I had to do was search out the town water tower and the school would not be far away but sometimes this wasn't the case. In times like this I would be madly dashing around town dressed in my full Polish regalia pleading for someone, anyone to point out where the school was.

Now to the real fun part; each day consisted of shows taking place in at least four schools per day. I sometime had barely enough time to get from one school to the next without being late. After the last show of the day, I had to drive sometimes into the night to reach the next school as they were occasionally even in the next state.

When I got to the town I would try to park next to the school. When the weather was real nasty I tried hooking up a small car heater into the schools electrical outlet. As soon as I pulled in to the schoolyard, I would wait until the police showed up. They would never disappoint me as they would often arrive, "Johnny on the spot," flashing their big blue lights as soon as I entered the schoolyard. Other times they would not get to me till about three or four o'clock in the morning. At this ungodly hour they would knock on my window, wake me and then poke their flashlights all around my car. While I was still half asleep, I would have to produce a series of documents and answer a litany of dim witted questions, telling them that I was supposed to be here and would be doing a concert in the morning.

As these small town cops had lots of time on their hands they would often wake me a couple of times during the night just to make sure I was OK. A few even offered such excitement as going to work out at the Police gym together. Needless to say at three o'clock in the morning, even though their friendly offer would sound mighty tempting, I would tell them that I had to be up early in the morning but maybe next time.

When the sun came up I would wait 'til the janitor arrived and unlocked the building. I would usually get along pretty well with the janitor by telling him that he is the most important person in the building, as he holds all the keys. Many times, if I was early enough, he would let me grab a quick shower. This, to me, was one of the true pleasures of my life as I could not always find a shower on the road and I would work up quite a sweat doing my shows. Showered or not I would find a place to change to my Polish Mountaineers outfit and once again become Mr. Poland. Soon the principal would come to meet me. After getting over the shock of looking at some weird long-haired galoot that looks like he just fell off the planet Pluto, we would discuss my program. As I needed the help of a few teachers and students it was up to him to pick out the right ones to fit the job.

As my program was about the old Polish folk culture it had a few places for audience participation. Back in Poland, my teacher, Jozef Broda, would always tell me "You can not separate the Polish bagpipes from the other parts of our folk culture for you must present it as it is, with music, dance and stories." I was following his methods but some of them seemed a little strange to many American school principals. Often our conversation would go something like this:

Principal: So you need the help of a few teachers and students, well, can you tell me what they will be doing?

Rik: Well, in order to really give them a true representation I will be doing a few simple dances. The first one is easy just a simple hand clapping dance, but the second one is a little different. It's a courting dance.

Principal: Well, what is that?

Rik: It's a dance where every one joins in a big circle, while I walk around with a handkerchief. Then, when I say stop, I pick the closet female teacher, bring her to the center of the circle, lay down my handkerchief and ask her to kneel down. While we are both kneeling on the handkerchief I kiss her on the cheek then jump up and dance with her.

Principal: You KISS her?

Rik: It's just a little kiss. Could be an air kiss. But anyway, then I pick up my bagpipes, I hand her the handkerchief, and she repeats the dance with a student.

Principal: She kisses a student?

Rik: Well, as I said, she really doesn't have to kiss them, just pretend. Of course, if we were in Poland it would be a real kiss, but it's a different culture. Anyway, after the teacher kisses the student, that student picks and kisses another student.

Principal: Wait. First you want to kiss one of my teachers, then have them kiss a student and then have them kiss each other. Is that correct?

Rik: Well, it's tradition but don't worry. You'll really like the last dance, as it is a kind of athletic competition between the boys. We just have to watch out when I swing my axe.

Principal: You're bringing in an axe?

Even though my shows sounded a bit exotic they were one of the highest rated assembly shows of that year. The show had a magic all of its own and really brought the school and community together. It was a universal message that worked with every age group and culture and this show had an amazing effect on almost every audience. Even in schools where they spoke mostly Spanish, the costumes and tradition in my presentation crossed over the language barrier and made every one feel good. At the end of my show I would leave them with this message, "We are all Americans, whether we are born here on this land as Native Americans or whether our ancestors traveled from many lands to make this their home. Each one of us carries songs, dances and folklore from our own ethnic backgrounds that make us unique and special, and no matter where your family came from, always be proud of who you are."

SINGING FOR THE COOK

Although my weekdays were full, I had a lot of time on my hands on the weekends. Often, I would try to find a museum or park to hang out at but many times I just pulled over on the side of the road and spent the days reading, writing and playing music.

Sometimes, I would get so lonely that I would go over to a small cafe and have a nice meal. After I finished my food I would tell the waitress, "My, that was a good meal. You know, I'm out here on the road doing programs of Polish folk culture at the nearby school." This would perk up a conversation and they would often say, "Oh, yes, we heard that there was a program like that going on." Then I would say, "Back when I lived in Poland we had an old tradition that when we liked the food we would sing for the cook." This would really get things going. "In fact, if you don't mind I would like to sing for your cook." The waitress would be laughing and say, "You're putting me on. You want to sing for our cook?" I'd reply, "Yep." This one waitress said, "Well, this I just got to see." Then I would go back into my van, quickly put on my Polish outfit, pick up my pipes and walk back into the cafe with the pipes blaring away.

On one occasion in a small cafe near Bismarck, the whole restaurant stood still while I piped my way back into the kitchen. There I was standing and piping away while this big fellow was flipping hot cakes in his greasy apron with me singing in his ear. After I finished the whole cafe applauded, the owner ripped my check in half and said, "If you are ever back here again, dinner is also on the house!"

When I wasn't hanging around singing at cafe's for my supper, going to museums or national parks, my next favorite thing to do was go to hat stores. I just love cowboy hats, especially Stetsons. I found that most of the hat shops employed great storytellers. They would talk your ear off if you gave them even half a chance. Most of them loved to talk about, what else? Hats. They would start off with something like this:

"Stetsons are, in my mind, the king of hats. J. B. Stetson founded the company back in Philadelphia in 1865 and for a long time it was considered the best in the world. They were made out one hundred percent beaver fur and were practically indestructible. The cowboys used them for just about everything, as shade from the sun, or a fan to keep cool. They used them like a bellows to start fires, made them into a dipper to fetch water, waved them in the air as a distress signal and as even used their hats to say good bye as they rode off into the sunset. You can't be a cowboy without a hat and back in the old days the worst thing that could be said was, 'He's all hat and no cowboy'."

Sometimes you can hear a pretty good story as these craftsmen steam and shape their hats. While I was in one shop in Wyoming a hat maker was busy fitting another old gent into a new sombrero when I heard this one. The old fellow who was getting his new hat was from Texas and, as Texans will do, was bragging about how great the Lone Star state is. At this point, the hat maker said, "You remind me of a fellow who I was in the army with, he was from Texas, too. One day when we were stationed over in Hawaii and flying over the islands he started bragging about Texas. Oh, the cows are so much bigger in Texas, the water cleaner, the air purer, why everything you could name was better in Texas. Just then we flew over a huge volcano and I said, 'I bet you have bigger volcanoes in Texas'." My pal was stopped in his tracks and for a few minutes didn't utter a word. Then he looked me straight in the face and said, 'Well, you know, our Texas Volunteer Fire department could put out that volcano is less than an hour'!" After the hat maker finished his story the old Texan said, "You know, come to think of it, our hometown fire department is one of the best around." The hat maker winked at me and said, "He's hopeless!"

As I said, "You can always find a few good stories at a hat shop."

COWBOYS ON THE PRAIRIE

My first real encounter with cowboys took place in a Chinese restaurant. I was in between shows when I decided to stop in a little shop to pick up a quick oriental meal. As I still had another show to do I was still dressed in my Polish outfit complete with my heavy woolen pants, leather belt, wide brimmed hat, red vest and old heavy woolen black cape. I knew that I was looking pretty strange but had no plans of making any conversation. Just a few feet from me were three guys with big cowboy hats having a fantastic talk about bluegrass music. Being so hungry for both a bit of conversation and the idea of playing anything but Polish folk music I just had to stick my neck out and join in. I shyly piped in, "What kind of music are you talking about?" As my words floated through the air the cowboys stopped mid sentence and turned in my direction. A big mustachioed fellow who seemed to be the kingpin of the outfit replied, "Bluegrass." I slowly replied "I play a bit of banjo," while handing them my flyer, knowing that the way I was dressed was not that of a banjo picker and I really wanted them to believe me. The leader took my flyer and gathered round his flock as they pored over the words and photos of my little hand out. Then one of the fellows came up to me and said, "Do you really play banjo? I'm just trying to learn the instrument and having a devil of a time with it." Then the leader said, "Yeah, Mike could sure use some help. By the way, what are you doing this weekend?" I told him that I had a school show on Friday but after that I was free till Monday morning. After a little more talk about where it was that I was playing on Friday, it was decided that they would come to my show and then take me up to their ranch in Prairie. With that ,we all sat down to eat and then everyone went back to work.

Later that day, I looked over the map and found a place marked Prairie on the road map. I also noticed that there were no real roads to get there and it was at that moment that I realized that I was off to another adventure.

The rest of the week slowly crept by with the only excitement being the sightings of a few bald eagles. By Friday I was wondering if these cowpokes had been pulling my leg and really were having a joke about taking me up to the ranch. Just in case I told the principal of the last school that there may be a few guest coming to see me and to please make them welcome. I was just getting ready to start the show when some of the wildest looking cowboys I ever saw walked into the auditorium. They were decked out in huge cowboy hats and high boots.

After my show, the leader, whose name turned out to be Nielus, told me that I should follow them up to Prairie. We started out on the highway but soon turned, near a big dam, and followed the river through a series of narrow twisty roads. Then we flew straight up one of the dirt roads twisting and turning up a huge side of a canyon. Finally at the top of the rocky hill was a flat Prairie framed by the panorama of the Saw Tooth Mountains with a view that was so beautiful I was almost speechless.

Nielus parked his old pickup near a modern looking ranch-style house and invited me in to meet his folks. His family were ranchers and had been living this way since God knows when. Nielus did not live with his folks, but had a modest cabin nearby. After meeting and eating with his folks, some of the other cowboys from our restaurant meeting popped in with their instruments and we all went up to the loft, where there was more room to play music. We spent the rest of the night playing together, with Nielus on guitar, Mike on banjo and Steve on the mandolin.

The next morning we all had breakfast at the ranch and I spent the rest of the day giving banjo lessons into a tape recorder. By the evening a little party was thrown where we played till way after midnight. On Sunday morning I was told that they had a surprise planned just for me. Nielus said, "Rik you gave us a great time with your music and lessons that we thought that we would give you a real Idaho experience. We are going to let you help us feed the cattle, but we are going to do it the old fashioned way, using a team of horses pulling a sled."

He then led me out side to a big hay wagon mounted on two metal sleds and hooked up to a team of horses. Nielus handed me the reins and instructed me how to maneuver the wagon. "Did you ever do anything like this before?" one of the youngsters called out, but before I could answer, Nielus gave the command and the horses started pulling the sled across the snowy prairie lands. The next few hours were like something out of a western novel. Our sled bounced over the snow as we rolled off about one hundred bales of hay to the hungry cows. We laughed our way through the entire trip with one of my new friends adding, "Just wait till you tell your friends back home, they won't believe you!"

In a short time I knew I had to leave but plans were already in the making for my next visit and I couldn't wait!

The next week seemed a lot easier to handle now that I had found some new friends to hang out with. The schools were in a lot of small towns and the kind of places that usually don't get much entertainment. At a school in Twin Falls I met up with a schoolteacher who was also very into my kind of music. Her name was Donna and she was almost as crazy about folk music as I am. When I told her about my new friends in Prairie she was intrigued. As I was already planning another trip that weekend I made arrangements for Donna to come along. Donna had a beautiful voice and she also played mountain dulcimer and Irish penny whistle, just the right kind of person to join in the fun up in Prairie. Friday I drove back to Twin Falls and picked up Donna for the long ride up to Prairie. As we were driving up the large canyon up to the main road Donna remarked that this place was unbelievable. The weekend turned into another fun time of sharing songs and learning a few new tunes. My visit from the previous week was the talk of the town, so on Saturday we decided to put on a little show at the school house, where even more folks could join in the fun. On Sunday we once again fed the cattle this time as the snow had melted, we hooked up the horses on an old wagon. Donna was thrilled to have a taste of the Prairie experience and would join us for a few more jams.

On my last weekend in Prairie, Nielus saddled up a few horses and said we should just spend the day out on the trail. Steve and Mike also saddled up and off we went up through hills. After taking a short break for a little food we were just about to head off when Nielus said to Steve, "You might think about checking out your cinch as it's looking a bit loose." At that very moment Steve's saddle slid down the horse's back and dropped him on the ground and, in an instant, that horse bolted like lighting. Lucky for Steve his foot slipped out of the stirrup before the horse ran off with him. Nielus jumped on his horse and rode hell bent for leather after the marauder. With the runaway horse in sight, Nielus whipped his lasso rope high over his head and roped that critter around its sweaty neck. After all the excitement he took the horse back up to Steve, saying "Folks just don't understand horses, and treat them like some kind of pet. They just don't realize that sitting on a horse is like sitting on a keg of dynamite for you never know when they are going to explode."

I spent that last night over at Nielus' cabin. We played and sang till we ran out of songs and our voices were just plumb sung out. Since the first time I met Nielus I had admired his fringed buckskin coat. When I asked him where he got it he told me that one of his hobbies was in making old style buckskin shirts. I found out, not only did he make the shirts but he also would shoot, skin and tan the deer himself. He used the old brain tan method to make the leather feel soft as butter. The Indians used the same technique by using the animal's brains and then smoking the skin over a fire. Nielus laughed, "See, every animal has enough brains to tan its own hide." He told me if I wanted he could make me a shirt, but it would take a while. We shook hands and I told him I can wait. Sadly, we both knew it was time for me to move on and shared a bunch of fare thee wells, I drove my little Rabbit back down the long windy road back to the interstate and headed off down the highway.

YOU'RE JUST A CAR

One of the neat things about having my old diesel Rabbit was that I had to go to truck stops to get my fuel. Back then the only pump for diesel was right alongside the big tractor-trailers. I found that I loved these places as I was able to get know a lot of truckers, hear their stories and get the best directions to anywhere on this planet. It was while I was in a truck stop in Montana that I was inspired to write a song.

I had pulled up to a big row of semis and filled up my tank. When I walked in the store to pay my bill the tough woman who ran the cash box asked me, "Hey, Bud, which rig is yours?" When she looked at where I was pointing and saw my tiny little Volkswagen Rabbit standing alongside a row of monster trucks, she just broke out laughing and said, "Honey, you're just a car, but you'll be a truck someday." That line hit me like a ton of bricks and later that night while camped out near a snowy river I wrote down the words to a fun little children's song.

You're Just A Car

Chorus:
You're just a car, you'll be a truck someday,
Then you'll be driving down your own highway.
You won't be listening to what I say,
You're just a car, you'll be a truck someday.
There was a time, I was just like you.
I could hardly fill my own shoes.
Those were days I was bound to lose,
When I all I did was cry the blues,

Then I got older, and life got worse,
Like I was under some mean old curse,
A lonely frog, near a wishing well,
Waiting for a kiss to break my spell

Chorus;

Then one day, I got the gift of song.
My eyes opened, when I sang along.
The clouds had lifted, the night had gone,
The first time I sang my own song.
Chorus;

Well, I can't tell you and I don't know,
Which is the right road for you to go.
Just live by the school, that you were taught,
and sing with the love that is in your heart
Chorus

GOING TO THE DOGS!

The rest of the tour was pretty uneventful except for a trip out to Spokane, Washington to see a lady about a dog. Well, when I was living in Poland a lot of my friends had these big white dogs that looked like the Great Pyrenees but had a much narrower face and before I left for this school tour I had the idea that I should get one of these dogs.

Marianna liked the idea but neither she nor I even knew what kind of dogs we were talking about. Then one day while looking through a dog encyclopedia I found a picture of a white dog called a Polish Tatra Sheep Dog. The book went on to tell that it is a very rare breed found in the high Tatra Mountains of Poland often used by the mountaineers to guard their sheep. At the very end of the article it talked of a Polish Tatra Sheep Dog Club but gave no more information than that. Being the detective that I am, I wrote a letter to the author of the article and to my good fortune they wrote back and told me whom to contact. I found that there was a woman living in Maryland who had two of these dogs and was a member of the club. As Marianna and I were already planning a trip to Florida we thought that we could try to visit this woman, Betty Augustowski, on the way home. When we stopped we found Betty and her husband to be delightful people. I was so excited to see the dogs that I asked her if she would like me to play the Polish pipes for her and went through the who ritual of putting on my full Polish outfit. The dogs in real life were amazing. They are huge and they also are a bit on the wild side as they were bred to defend the flock. Even though it was a bit risky I came over and let these big dogs sniff me and at once fell in love with the idea of getting one.

Betty said that she did not breed them but she had a friend in Spokane who did. Then she asked me why I wanted one. When I told her that I would be doing a national school tour about Poland and I thought I would like to work a dog like this into the show her face lit up. She said that she would see what she could do. The next day, when we got back to Vermont, there was a message on Marianna's phone from Betty. She said that we did not know it but the day of our visit was her birthday and by playing her my wonderful music I gave her the best birthday present that she'd had in years. Then she went on to say that she had already talked it over with the president of the Polish Tatra Sheep Dog Club, Carol Wood, and that they both liked the idea of what we wanted to do in the schools by teaching children about Poland. "Carol has a litter of puppies on the way and would like to give you one for your program as it will be a great way to introduce people to the breed."

A few months later, I heard from Carol that the dog had delivered her puppies. The very next day I was in Spokane peering over the little wooden crate and gazing over a big pile of fluffy white puppies. Carol gave me all kinds of warnings about the breed. "Too many people look at these precious little puppies and forget they are going to grow up to be from 100 to almost 150 pounds. Not only that, they were bred to guard sheep and they can be pretty vicious if they are not handled with care." Just looking at her dogs she did not have to warn me twice as they were both huge and, let's say, guarded. After the warnings she went into a bit of history; "The breed is very much like some of the other white sheep dogs like the Great Pyrenees, and the Hungarian Kuvasz. But if you really look closely, you can see that they do have their own individual characteristics. Their head is not as boxy as some of the breeds, they don't drool and they clean themselves." Carol laughed and continued, "It's true. They have oil in their fur that sheds dirt!" She went on further; "For years, they were used by the Polish highlanders to guard the sheep. When they are first born they are actually placed with the sheep so that there is a bond between the two animals. As they grow in to their roles in life they both herd and guard and will protect the sheep against any predators. There are stories of how these dogs not only have attacked wolves but also have been able to frighten away bears up in the high Tatra Mountains."

These dogs almost did not survive the Second World War because the Nazi were terrified of them and they were often just shot on sight. After the war, Dr. Derezinski, a veterinarian who lived in the town of Zakopane in the Tatras, carefully selected a few breeding pairs from the handful that were left and brought the breed back. Well, some-what. There are only about two hundred and fifty of these dogs in the United States and, perhaps, only a thousand of true full breed Tatras left in the world.

After our talk Carol was confident that I knew what I was getting into and was ready to take on that responsibility. We then went back to the litter and she showed me the one that she had picked for us. She said, "This one seems right for the job. She is not too aggressive but has character. She is still too young to travel so I will keep her until she is ready." "Do you have an old shirt that has not been washed?" she asked. "Something with your scent on it?" She went on to say that she would give her the shirt to play with and the puppy will bond with the scent and, hopefully, to me by the time she sent her to me.

I went into my bag of clothes and found a bright red festival T-shirt that really needed to be washed. Carol laughed and said that it would do fine. That night we had another little music party for Carol's family and friends. Everyone enjoyed hearing all my instruments and even moved the furniture so we could have a dance in the middle of her living room. The next morning I said my goodbyes to both Carol and my little puppy. Carol asked, "Did you pick out a name?" I replied, "Yes, I think we are going to call her Koza." Carol looked at me like I was a bit off my rocker, "Rik, you do know that Koza means goat in Polish don't you?" "Yes, Carol," I replied, "it also is a slang term that the mountaineers use for their bagpipes." She laughed and said, "Now, I understand."

The success of my first tour opened the door to another school assembly agency. This one was for the full school year with just a few weeks off in December and, as it seemed to fit my needs I jumped on it and signed on. Only after I signed on did I realize that the whole tour would take place in North and South Dakota, Minnesota and Nebraska, with most of the winter being spent in North Dakota. I knew that I could not stand to do another tour of hotels so I decided to buy an old blue and white Volkswagen van and rig it up as a camper.

DOG TALES

By September I was off on the road in my VW van and traveling with my new road manger, a cute little Polish Tatra Sheepdog named Koza. This fury white bundle of fluff had arrived at the end of the year when I was out on the road and was taken care of by Marianna, till I returned.

By September she was ready to do her first road trip and we hit the road together. Our first show together was in a small elementary school in Minnesota. When we reached the school, the young principal fell in love with Koza immediately and, while Koza was busy climbing all over her, I set about the task of getting my instruments tuned and ready for the show. When the room was ready I took Koza and held her chain as the kids screamed down the hallway and ran into the gym. As this was Koza's very first experience with a large number of kids and being up on a stage, she did what any frightened baby might do - she peed.

I was stunned and mortified and frankly did not know what to do but the kind principal looked at me with a warm smile and said, "Don't worry, the kids do this all the time." Then she quickly grabbed a mop, wiped up Koza's spill and said, "Now, on with the show!"

It did not take Koza long to adjust to the world of the stage and, in fact, in no time at all she was the star of the show. Within minutes after pulling into the schoolyard the kids would rush my van and scream, "Look at that dog. Hey, there's a dog in the school. Hey, mister, what's your dog's name?" When I would tell them her name, it would ring out like a siren across the school. "Koza. Hey, Koza. Come here, Koza."

Little did they realize that one reason I had named her Koza was to teach them a Polish word. My plan was working and Koza was a great ambassador of not only her breed but of Polish folk culture. Once you met her you would never forget Koza. Even though Koza was very protective of her van, she was as gentle as a lamb when it came to her flock of children. The kids loved her as she loved them. They would often take her out for a walk and then return with both them and Koza covered in mud. They even taught her how to drink from the school water fountain a trick that much to my dismay she always remembered every time she went into a school.

When we were on the Sioux Indian reservation she made quite an impression. To the kids she looked as spiritual as their sacred white buffalo and they were in awe of her size and pure white fur. The Indian teachers teased me saying, "We are going to honor you by not eating your dog." In the old Sioux tradition they would often eat dogs in a religious ceremony. This was one time that I was very happy to not follow tradition.

Now, that is not to say that we did not have other problems. The worst was the day that she decided to drive. The show was in Minnesota, back in the early weeks of the tour. Koza and I were driving hundreds of miles each week living together in my tiny van. She was getting very comfortable in her new home and sometimes felt like it was in fact more her van than mine and refused to get out of the drivers seat. Whenever I left the VW, Koza immediately was in the front seat protecting and guarding her home.

On this particular day, we pulled into the schoolyard and I left Koza in the van while I went to set up the show. What I did not remember to do is to put on the emergency brake. When I came back out of the school I noticed that my van was gone. As I panicked I heard a man screaming "Hey, fellow is that your blue and white van?" He pointed to my van as it dashed down the road, then he added. "Look there's a big white dog driving it away." Sure enough Koza had somehow knocked the van into neutral and now it was rolling out of control with Koza at the wheel. I ran as fast as I could, trying to catch the van before it caused an accident. All of a sudden, I saw it hit the curb and fly up on the sidewalk. Fortunately, I had enough time to reach the handle, pull open the door and stomp on the brake before it rolled away.

There was another time that I can remember when Koza really got my goat. We had just pulled in to a truck stop after a little snowstorm. I went into the cafe to grab a cup of coffee and left Koza in the driver's seat, leaving the van unlocked and the keys still in the ignition. When I came back and went to start the van, I noticed that the keys were missing. In a panic I started searching the entire van. Meanwhile Koza had moved to the back of the bus and watched as I frantically searched every inch of that van. The snow was now covering the roof and the truckers were peeking out the windows as they watched me unload the contents of my van into the parking lot. After everything I owned was out of the van and snow covered, Koza looked at me, yawned and jumped off the seat, exposing the missing keys. The keys must have caught on to her collar then fell on to the seat when she sat down. While I was going out of my mind searching for the keys, she had been quietly sitting on them all the while.

WINTER IN THE DAKOTAS

Living in Vermont you get used to cold and most of us think we know how bad a winter can be. Even though I have experienced many a bad Vermont storm, nothing I had experienced could prepare me for a whole winter in North Dakota. My winter adventure really started when I was still on my way out to the midwest, just crossing the Iowa state line. It was right there that I ran into a hell of an ice storm. I was listening to the radio warnings but had no idea that the very road they were warning about was the one that I was driving on. As I turned my van into another interstate lane, I could feel my tires slipping. What was even worse was that all the cars around me were losing control, with some even skidding off the highway. I knew I was in trouble when the car next to me crashed into a large signpost and my own van was sliding across the icy road. The force of the skid threw poor Koza and slammed her into the back of the bus, then threw the van into a spin that left me facing in the wrong direction with a huge tractor trailer bearing down on me. I could barely see the driver's face, but I could tell that he, too, was out of control.

Now the big rig was almost upon me. In desperation I grabbed my steering wheel, turned hard and floored the engine till my tires squealed, jerked and pulled me out of the snow. I was just able to move in the nick of time out of the way of the skidding truck. I was pretty shaken. Koza, too, was upset and we both did not know what on earth to do next. I once again stomped my foot on the gas and was able to move us back on the road. All traffic was stopped, as you could not move an inch without sliding. As I stepped onto the road my feet gave way and brought me down on the hard pavement. The road was a solid piece of ice. By this time the trucks had blocked off the road not letting anyone through. Soon the police came and told us that we had to get off the road. They were sanding a few miles back and as soon as we could we should move directly to the next exit and find a hotel as this road was too dangerous for travel. Hours had passed, my gas gauge was getting low, so I had to turn off the engine and wrap myself in my sleeping bag just to stay warm. It took over six hours before the roads were sanded and we were able to crawl off at the next exit. Even though I hated hotels this was one night where I just had to give in and was glad that I did for the snow and ice blew all night long.

In the morning, as I headed to North Dakota, I could see the highway was littered with tractor-trailers. There were so many off the road that it reminded me of playing with match box cars when I was a kid but, unlike my games, there were real people in those bashed up trucks and I shudder to think how many got hurt or even killed that night.

On one of my first shows near Bismarck, North Dakota, I met up with a school-teacher whose husband raised buffalo. She invited me to visit the family for dinner after my show. The rancher and his family enjoyed my company and especially some of the old cowboy songs that I knew. After dinner the old rancher asked me, "So, you are in these parts for a while?" I replied, "Yep, the whole school year." He shot back, "So, I guess you are staying mainly in hotels?" To his surprise I said, "Nope, I am just staying with my dog in my van." "In your van? This is North Dakota. People die if they get caught in a storm. Do you have any heat in that van of yours?" I told him, "Well, not really but I do have a warm sleeping bag." Once again, the rancher could not believe my ignorance. "A sleeping bag? You are staying out in your van in a sleeping bag?"

At this he got up and walked out of the room. In a few minutes he was back holding a large buffalo hide under his arm. "Here," he said, "The Indians have survived many a cold winter wrapped up in one of these. Take it and wrap it around you and hopefully you won't freeze to death!" So thanks to that rancher's generosity, I now had half a buffalo to sleep in, and, believe me, I used it every night.

Up in the Dakotas the cold takes on an almost mystical form and it feels like you are in some kind of bubble. It is almost surreal because you don't think it is as cold as it really is. People in North Dakota are used to cold but every once in a while comes a storm that even the most seasoned Dakotan has to be weary of. One hit me just outside of Fargo. I was playing at an Indian school, and just getting ready to leave when a teacher said to me, "There is a bad storm heading this way are you sure you can make it?" I reassured him that I was used to driving in the snow and I would be fine. He just shook his head and wished me luck. As I rode down this little country highway I saw something unlike anything I ever saw in my life. It was a little white ball of swirling snow. As I drove a little closer I realized that I was driving smack dab into the biggest snowstorm of my life. I tried like mad to turn around and race back to the school but it was no use as the storm was upon me. I then turned around and tried to drive my way through the storm and found out that I was in big trouble. Really Big trouble! The snow was blowing so hard that I could not see the road and the ice was forming so thick on my windshield that the heater was useless. I was trapped. In a few minutes the police came and rescued me. They helped guide my van down the road to a nearby 7-11 store, where all the motorists were held up. The storm was not letting up and one of the policemen said, "Well, no one is going to make it home tonight." They asked the stranded drivers where they lived and as most were local folks, they drove them home. When it came to me they said, "And where are you staying?" I told them that I had a bed in my van. The cops said, "If you stay in your van we are going to have pull your dead body out in the morning." They told that there was a cheap hotel across the street and they were sure the owners would let me spend the night for just a couple of bucks. They also reminded me take my dog in as it was going to be a real bad night.

With that bit of advice I walked over and booked my room and that night all hell broke loose. The wind howled like a pack of wild hyenas, the ice clawed up the windows and there was this eerie moaning sound that scared poor Koza out of her wits. The storm was so violent that it shook the entire building. In the middle of this great storm I had an idea of what would later become a humorous song about life in the midwest.

FREEZING IN NORTH DAKOTA

Chorus;
Freezing in North Dakota feelsl
as cold as an ice cream soda,
teeth are rattling like an old pianola,
while the wind blows through my ears.
Not too far from Minnesota,
where a polar bear can catch pneumonia,
and the buffalo dream of Arizona
cause it's sure gets cold around here
Yo-del -lay ee-aaee oo
Driving up and down these country roads
wind chill up to forty five below
can't see nothing except for snow
as the roads all disappear
car heaters on, but my knees are shaking,
old timers say stop your belly aching
you think this is cold, why you're mistaken for
you shoulda been here last year.
Chorus

The land is cold but the people are warm,
Friendliest folks every been born
Tip their hat and blow their horn,
As they go driving by
they fix you some coffee and taken you in,
Then tell you a story to make you grin
of old man winter and of how life's been
underneath the prairie sky
Chorus

The morning following the storm was one of those picture perfect days. As I drove to the next show I was enchanted with the ice covered prairie lands outside of my window. Every blade of grass was encrusted with a glimmering shield of sparkling ice. With the bright sun shining down on the ice covered grasslands it made the highway light up like the Yellow Brick Road of Emerald City.

The longer I stayed in the Dakotas, the more it intrigued me. One of my hang-outs was the old town of Deadwood in the Black Hills of South Dakota where I would often risk life and limb, by driving back and forth across the state in all kinds of weather, just to spend my weekends there.

The old town of Deadwood started out as a gold boomtown back in 1874. A group of scientists called the Jenny Campaign confirmed that there was indeed "Gold in them-there hills," after a few random claims from early prospectors known as Argonauts. As a sprawl of tents and shanties sprang up around the mines this narrow canyon soon became a little boom town of saloons, card houses, and houses of ill repute. By 1876, it was officially incorporated as Deadwood named after the dead trees that lined the canyons. Of all the characters that ever walked the streets of Deadwood, and there were many, only a few have remained as famous as the fast shooting, gun slinging, card playing, reckless, long-haired, sharpshooter known as Wild Bill Hickok.

He was originally born as James Butler Hickok in Illinois back in 1837 and even as a young boy he had a mean stubborn streak in him and a passion for guns. He did not get on very well with his parents so by the time he turned eighteen he left his folks and head-ed out to find adventure in the untamed west. James (Bill) landed his first job in Monticello, Kansas working as a stage coach driver on the Oregon and Santa Fe trails. These stagecoaches were constantly losing axles, being raided by outlaws and Indians, and breaking down in the middle of the wilderness. Their unreliability really put young Hickok's sharp shooting skills to the test.

On one trip out to Colorado, James's stage ran into a bit of trouble and he had to spend the night camped out on the ground, leaving his guns inside the stage with his stranded passengers. While he lay sleeping an overly famished bear came down to check out what was on today's menu. James, like most drivers, had not bathed in weeks and his clothes were rank from sweat and bacon drippings after the night's dinner. The bear found James body perfume simply irresistible and enthusiastically took a big bite out of Hickok's rear end. While the shocked stage passengers looked on, aided by their lanterns, they saw James grab a hunting knife and began to wrestle the big bear to the ground. As the bear's sharp teeth and claws ripped at his body he repeatedly stabbed the beast. When the dust cleared James was badly injured but the bear lay stone dead. After this legendary feat of bravery his reputation grew. He was no longer being called James but was given a nickname that stuck like glue, and from then on was known as "Wild Bill." It took a while to recover from the bear attack but after his wounds healed, Bill quit working for the stage companies and found himself a new career as a small town deputy in the dusty streets of Nebraska.

As a deputy, Bill once again proved his mettle by cunningly entrapping the McCanles gang, a bunch of no-count, train robbing, horse and cattle thieves. Bill wanted to teach these pesky boys a lesson and catch them with their pants down. He persuaded the local town drunk to hand deliver a personal forged invitation from the local madam to invite the boys to a free night at the local cat house. The drunk was so convincing in his description of these voluptuous young naked women that the whole gang swallowed the bait. The outlaws were so enticed by just the thought of spending a night with a flock of Soiled Doves that they even accepted the drunk's advice to "Just leave your guns at home." The drunk lured the desperadoes to a parlor just at the end of town and told them that the girls would leave the light on to welcome them.

Bill arrived a few hours earlier to set his trap. He knew that the madam and the girls had left town and he had plenty of time to arrange a grand welcome for the McCanles. To start off his little reception party, he blew off the door lock with his pistol, opened a bottle of whiskey, turned on the lights and then waited for his prey. By the time the gang entered the whorehouse they were ripe and ready for a night of fun and frolic. As they rushed through the doorway, looking for the girls, Bill popped up from behind a table met them with a flash of smoking silver bullets from his blazing revolvers. Single-handedly Bill gunned down almost the whole gang. The few who were left still breathing he led down into town and locked them up in the jail.

With each new notch on his pistol, Bill's status as a gunman grew. Soon every dime store publisher was sending out young reporters to hunt him down, and write about the notorious man known as Wild Bill Hickok. Reporters were so overwhelmed by Bill's legendary presence that even when he was obviously stretching the truth they wrote it down like it was the gospel. When one young reporter asked him how many men he had killed, he flippantly replied, "Without counting the Mexicans and Indians, I'd say over a hundred."

Despite his outrageous claims Bill did have a strong reputation that was hard to beat. He did serve as a scout against the Indians, was a heroic soldier during the Civil War, played a two-bit actor with Buffalo Bill and could play a mean game of poker.

At the age of thirty-nine, the years of gunfights, booze and wild living were beginning to take their toll. Bill's sharp shooting days were over and he decided to try his luck as a professional gambler. He had just married a pretty circus entertainer and was hoping to settle down, when he wandered out to Deadwood, South Dakota to play out his hand at a game of poker at the Number 10 Saloon. Wild Bill was sitting with his back to the door, holding his cards (a pair of eights and aces) when Jack McCall snuck up behind him and fired his pistol into the back of Wild Bill's head. As Bill fell to the floor his cards fell on the table revealing, forever what would from this time forward be known as The Dead Man's Hand.   After the townfolk chased and caught McCall, they took Bill's body up to the nearby graveyard on a little hillside over looking the town.

When I first came to Deadwood I was intrigued by its old western flavor. Even though the main streets are lined with tacky tourist shops, overpriced saloons and casinos, you can still breathe in the history of the town. One of the best places to get a taste of the Old Deadwood is at the Mount Moriah Graveyard near the graves of Wild Bill Hickok and Calamity Jane. There was one Sunday morning that I made a pilgrimage up to their tombstones and had an almost a mystical experience. I later wrote about it in this little poem.

WILD BILL'S GIFT

Out in Deadwood city, in the South Dakota Hills,
I went to find some memories of the old west and Wild Bill.

There beneath the autumn pin's sleeping safe and sound,
Laid old Bill in a winter's coat, of frost upon the ground.

If these old stones could talk, oh the stories they could tell,
of poker games and dance hall dames and the outlaws who burn in hell.

But the graveyard is silent, sleeping tongues lie still,
and the old west is fading like the legend of Wild Bill.

As I paid my last respects and started back to town,
just a few feet from Old Bill's grave was a bullet on the ground.

I picked it up, and thought a bit, then a smile fell on my face,
I figured it was a present, from old Bill, in his resting place.

Old Bill wanted to remind me of how the West was won,
by miners, drifters and Cowboys with bullets, guts and guns.

For not much of the old west is standing anymore,
so all we have left are the legends, myths and lore.

So thanks to you Old Wild Bill, I said my last good bye.
May we meet again,' way up yonder, in that old poker game in the sky.

GHOSTS ON THE HIGHWAY

I was out in Oklahoma at a truck stop getting my van filled with gas when I spotted a young woman, in her twenties, panhandling near the entrance to the coffee shop. Even though there were a lot of customers walking in and out, no one seem to notice her and, in fact, they would not even acknowledge that she was there and looked right through her as if she were some kind of ghost. As I watched her I noticed that she made frequent checks over to a beat up station wagon. Inside that old jalopy were three young children and with them were all of their worldly belongings, clothes, toys, and boxes of cereal. It was at that point that I realized that both this young woman and her children were homeless and living inside of that old car. I walked over to her and pulled a few dollars from my jeans and placed them in her hand. She smiled and thanked me and then I went off down the road. That night I pulled into another little truck stop near Okemah, the home of Woody Guthrie. While I sat there parked under a streetlight I remembered the young girl and her children and wrote down a few lines. I wanted to remind myself that the homeless are out there and they need our help and that they are not ghosts on the highway.

GHOSTS ON THE HIGHWAY

Chorus:
Ghosts on the highways, forgotten souls so it seems,
Ghosts on the highways, lost in American Dreams.

Sleeping with the trucks in Oklahoma,
Sleeping 'neath the trees in Tennessee
Wishing on a star in California,
Dreaming of a home that used to be.
Chorus

Please can you help me won't you mister,
I need some gas for my car.
My children are hungry and they're crying,
With love you can only get so far.
Chorus

In the daytime, I'll be working,
Just trying to make a little bread.
In the nighttime, I'll be walking,
Ain't got no place to rest my head.
Chorus

My grandpa was a miner
My daddy worked in the factory.
Me, I'm just a rover
But it's not the life I planned for me.
Chorus

COTTON PICKING TIME IN MISSISSIPPI

Silly as it sounds; while I was driving through Mississippi I had the strange urge to pick some cotton. As I drove down through the Delta, the land was covered with a blanket of white cotton balls as far as the eye could see. Every morning as I headed out to my school gigs I would see farmers out in fields of high cotton and I just knew that sooner or later I would just have to try it. One night I pulled my van off the road and disappeared

Pete Seeger & Rik 1980
(Photo by Bob Yahn)

Riding the Camden-Amboy Line

The Sloop Singers - 1980

The Palieri Kids - Rik - David - Tina - Lisa

Rik's first PR Photo

Rik & Sis Cunningham

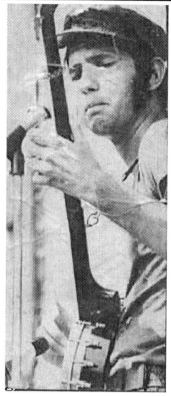

Rik Performing in 1976

Rik & Gareth late 1970s

On the Clearwater

Harry Chapin & Rik

Rik at the Rzeszow World Festival

The Saint Nicholas play

On French TV

Istebna Poland

Jozef Broda & Group

Beata, Wiesia & Ryki (1984

With old friends Rick Nestler and Guy Davis

On the boardwalk at Pelican Alaska.

Playing the Didgeridoo.

"Apache" on Route 66.

Out on the trail in Idaho.

Holding a Roo in Alice Springs.

U.K.Traveler, Rik and Sheila Stewart,
in Scotland at the Glasgow, Scotland
Open Road Festival

At the 100th Annual Hobo Convention in
Britt, Iowa.

Rik & Utah Phillips back stage at the 40th
Philadelphia Folk Festival

Rik with Bruce Springsteen
(Photo by Mark Lamhut)

Rik, Ramblin' Jack & Rick Robins
(photo by Craig Harris)

Rik & Jimmy Driftwood

The Green Mountain Volunteers parade in Jaca, Spain. 1989

Being dubbed "The International Hobo
Troubadour" by Hobo Queen Lady
Nightingale and King Redbird Express.

Rik & Kevin Locke
(Photo by B. Yarwood)

Rik hosting his TV show with guest
Clive Barnes of Ireland.

Rik playing a Native American flute.

Mom & Dad Palieri in the 50s

Wilfried & Rik at the
Wartburg Castle,
in Germany
(Photo by Iris
Mengs)

Making sausages with Wilfried &
friends in Germany
(Photo by Iris Mengs)

Video taping the
Song Writers Notebook
special, on the Aston
Martin car, in England.

Road Warrior Rik
in the 90s
(Photo by
Marianna Holzer)

Rik playing a bar gig in
Vermont 1980s

A visit to C. F. Martin Guitars

Interview with Colin in OZ

Wilfred and Rik in Rudolstadt

Rose Tattoo on the Rails!

Rik with Banjo

Rik with Uke

Russian Gypsies and Rik

Chris & Merideth Thompson (photo by Craig Harris)

...on the road again

into the cotton fields. It was pitch black and there was not a house in sight so I thought, well, it's now or never. As I put my hands on the cotton balls I could feel a pricking sensation. In no time at all my fingers were sore and I had hardly done any work at all. In my short cotton picking experience it gave me a better understanding of just how hard it must be to pick cotton all day.

Too, often when we sing old folk songs we have very little understanding of what we are really singing about. For years, I really thought that I had understood the meaning of the words folk music. I had read plenty of books, gone to festivals and even knew some of the legendary performers. I was shocked when, while living the rural country life, I had missed the central idea of what the music is really all about. I discovered that folk music has nothing to do with performing, being on a stage, making records or any of the other trappings of the music business world. It is really about the music of the community and how that music reflects their lives. I found a good example of this was when a friend asked me to help fix dinner by helping to chop the head off a live goose. I said, "I have never killed a goose before." She said just hold the goose while I nip off its head. I stood there holding the bird while with one whack she finished the job.   Then we carried the headless goose into the basement and started pulling of the feathers. As I sat there plucking feathers I thought of a song I had sung for years, by the old bluesman, Leadbelly, "The Grey Goose."

The song went on to tell of how a preacher went hunting and spied a gray goose, killed it, then plucked it and when he tried to eat it found that it was so tough the fork wouldn't stick in it and the knife wouldn't cut it. I had sung the song for years but had never plucked a goose. Now, with feathers in my hands the song took on a whole new meaning, for something you can't explain happens when you start living your music.. Like my friend Utah Phillips says, *"You can either be a folklorist and study folklore or, be folklore and be studied."*

I ended up spending three and half years on the road playing for over 1000 schools. I wore out two cars and saw more of the back roads of America than most people see in a lifetime. Here are just a few more road tales of those School Tour years.

SINGING AT THE CATFISH HOUSE

I was driving on to my next show out in central Oklahoma when I went into a gas station to fill up my van. When I walked in to pay for my fuel I noticed a whole line of musical instruments hanging on the wall and I asked the gas station attendant if he played all these instruments. The young man said, "Well, I do play a few of them, and we run a jam session over at the restaurant next door." I told him that I was a traveling singer just passing through but would love to meet some local musicians. The fellow asked me what kind of music I played and when he heard that I played the banjo, his face lit up like a light bulb. "Well," he said, "How long will you be in the area?" I told him that I had to do a show this afternoon then I was free till the morning. "Well," he said, "I'll make a few calls and see who we can get together. If you can make it back, I'll give you all the catfish you can eat."

The deal sounded too tempting so after I finished the day's shows, I made my way back to the little town and parked in the restaurant parking lot. I could tell that the folks in this town were either hungry for music or the catfish was truly out of this world as the lot was so full that I could hardly find a place to park. Inside the room was filled with guitar pickers and fiddlers not to mention the wafting smell of catfish floating in from the kitchen. Once we started jamming, the catfish started piling up on my dinner plate. By the end of the night I had eaten more of the tasty fish then I could fit in my belly. After I shook hands with all the pickers I made my way back to my van with a greasy sack of fish for Koza. That night we camped next to a river and under the moonlight both Koza and I had a feast with the leftovers. When you are singing for your supper, life does not get much better.

BUFFALO BILL'S HAT

Another one of my favorite haunts is the town of Cody, Wyoming. The town sprang up around the colorful character Buffalo Bill and has a fantastic museum that houses his memorabilia. On one visit I spotted a large brimmed cowboy hat styled in the manor of the hat that Buffalo Bill wore. As I'm a real sucker when it comes to hats I peered at the tiny card that revealed the price tag of $500. "Whoa," I said to myself, "That is a whopping big price tag." Looking closer I saw that the card also listed the name and number of the local hat maker. I copied down the number and called the shop. The owner of the shop almost fell off his chair when I asked him, "Do you make hats for real people?" The astonished hat maker asked, "What do you mean real people?" I replied that I was a traveling musician who was just passing through and just saw his hat over at the Buffalo Bill museum with a $500 price tag, and just wanted to know if he made hats for ordinary folks, too. With that he said, "Hey, where are you now?" When I told him I was just down the street, he invited me to take a look at his hat shop.

When I walked in the door of the Wind River Hat Company, I saw a big display of hats and a dusty old cowpoke sitting drinking a cup of coffee next to an old guitar. We spent a while talking and then he said so what kind of music do you play. When I told him he said, "Well then, go get that banjo and we'll pick a bit." The hours rolled by with friends of the shop popping in for a bit of conversation, coffee and music with Jim always having plenty of everything to share. After I spent the whole day at the shop Jim asked me if I really wanted one of his hats, that he would swap me one for a few guitar lessons and $50. We shook on the deal then went about picking out the right hat style. He laughed and said, "Well, you know that hat you saw in the museum is pretty much like this one here. I think that with a little bit of steam and shaping yours will look pretty much like the one in the showcase." We spent the next three days together swapping songs and stories and he even brought me out to his ranch to watch him break in a few horses. At the end of the weekend I walked out with a new hat and my new friend learned a few new tricks to add to his guitar playing and both agreed that it was a good trade.

THE OKIE IN CALIFORNIA

I was kicking back in my van at a truck stop, somewhere near Modesto, playing my song, Ghost on The Highway, when a stringy looking fellow stepped up to my van and knocked on the window. He looked like a man who just stepped out of a John Steinback story with his wrinkled clothes and sweaty brow. As I put down my guitar, he said, "Hey, mister can you help me? I have been having trouble with my car. You see I'm from Oklahoma and I and my family came here to find us some work. They sent a paper saying they needed workers to pick the fruit, so we headed out to California. When we got there, there was no work and now our car is broke down."

I was stunned. This fellow sounded like he was quoting from the Grapes of Wrath. I had to wonder if he was putting me on, or maybe I was dreaming the whole thing up. It was no dream and he did not look like he was a liar. He said, "I only need about thirty dollars to fix my fuel pump and then we are going back home." I looked into his sad eyes, and reached into my pocket and handed him a ball of folded dollars. "Well," I said, "I hope this helps. Now just promise me that you'll fix up that car and go back home." The old man said, "Oh, thank you! Thank you so much. I have been here at this truck stop all day and no one would even listen to me. Yes, thank you, I will fix the car and go back home."

With that the man disappeared into the blowing dust. I guess he could have been a con artist and just took my money to have another drink, but I don't think so. I knew I was the last guy who could afford to give away thirty dollars, but I felt if I was going to sing songs about the homeless then I should be the first one in line to give a bit of help when it is needed. After all, as my Indian friends have told me, "You have to walk your talk!"

THE MUSIC IN ME

After over three and a half years of playing schools I realized that there were bigger fish to fry and moved myself away from doing this kind of tour. Well, I'd better clarify that; I still did some schools but my main focus was trying to get into more of a concert situation by playing folk festivals, folk clubs and performance centers.

I was even preparing for this shift in my so-called career when I was still out doing the school shows, by gathering enough songs to make a CD. The years of travel had filled my mind with stories and images that ended up as songs. With so many new songs and a bit of pocket cash, I was able to go into the recording studio and produce my first CD, The Music in Me.

When I thought about a title for the project, I chose a song that I had written about my musical path called The Music in Me. The song came to me as I was struggling with the idea of changing my life with Claudia and becoming a full-time musician.

The Music in Me

My life's just an endless song,
New verses are written with each dawn
The music in me won't let me free;
I just have to keep on, moving on

Chorus; (After each verse)
I'm moving down the highway, clouds floating above me
This old guitar and these lonely roads are the only life
That I know.

Driving in from Kansas in the spring.
Snows so heavy I can't see a thing
I'm driving three days, my mind in a haze,
To get back in your arms again

Sleeping on a European train,
the night is gone and the sun peaks through again
My eyes are so weak, from not enough sleep,
But I always sing for a friend

Don't you shed a tear for me.
I'm just as blind as can be
The music in me won't let me be,
I just have to be who I am.

The Road Is My Mistress

The songs on the album were a collection of ideas that I had written about love and loss and a few songs reflecting some of my experiences out on the road. When I first thought about this recording, I just wanted to give my songs a home but it turned out to be much more than that. I found out about a little record company called "Straight Arrow," run by a tall, John Lennon-looking fellow named Michael Billingsly. Michael wanted his label to be able to give new artists a chance to be heard, and my project seemed to be right on target with his philosophy. In this project, Michael not only acted as my producer but was head engineer, CD designer and even singing coach. In the beginning of the project we decided that each song should have a life of its own and not be bound by genre or style. With that thought in mind we brought in a whole batch of musicians and friends to bring our vision to life.

We recorded most of my songs in just a few long days in the studio, but Michael wanted more than just the old songs that I had written he wanted me to flesh out some of the ideas for songs that I had not yet finished.

Such was the case with an unfinished song that I had in my notebook about a Vietnam vet named Monroe. I met Monroe at an open stage night, at a little bar, while I was on the road in North Dakota. He was a big funny fellow, with thin blond hair and a big sweeping mustache. He played a few songs on a beat up old guitar. After he heard me sing, he offered for me to join him at his table. After a few drinks he asked me what I was doing out in this part of the country. When I told him about my school shows and living out in my van, he laughed and said, "You mean you have been sleeping out in the cold, in that old van?" As we looked out the window the snow was coming down in sheets, "Well," Monroe said, "I am not going to let you sleep outside in this storm." With that he asked me to follow him back to his place to spend the night. Monroe lived just a mile or so from the bar in a small trailer camp. His little trailer was tidy but sparse. After a few beers he turned on the television and then we watched the late night news. The main story was about the heroes of desert storm returning from the war. As he watched the joyful parades welcoming the soldier's home, tears swelled up in his eyes. "They didn't have any parades for us, when we come from 'Nam," he bellowed. " No, when we came home, they threw rocks at us."

Then he asked me if I had been in the service. I told him that I had just missed it, as the draft ended the year that I was eligible to go, "But," I said, "I thought it was an unjust war, and I was one of those who protested against it." Monroe laughed and said, "Hell, the war sucked. You think we wanted to be there? No, we didn't have much of a choice did we?" Then Monroe talked of his years of fighting. He talked of his friends who were blown away right before his eyes. As tears rolled down his cheeks he cried, "Sometimes I wish that I had died with them." Then he rolled up his shirt to revel a massive bullet wound left behind as a reminder of his duty. As the night went on he talked of how he had killed so many men that sometimes he still sees their faces crying in agony as he tries to fall asleep. Monroe's story seemed almost like a horror tale from a TV mini series, but unfortunately, it was sadly all true. By the end of our conversation the bottle of Jack Daniels was empty and he nodded off to sleep. I made myself a bed on the couch in the next room and then I too went to sleep. In the morning I heard the TV still blasting away while our old war hero was fast asleep in his Lazy-Boy chair. I tried to say so long, but he was out like a light. As I drove off to the next show, Monroe's story was still ringing in my ear. By nighttime I just had to write it down.

MONROE

In the muddy rice paddies, of the long bloody war
He carried his rifle like his brother before
He fought like the devil, earned the stripes on his arms
In the hot steamy jungles of South Vietnam
CHORUS:
A bitter-proud solider with old battle wounds
With a war he's still waging in eveyr dark room
He's hitting the bottle and filling his pipe
Still dodging the bullets when he turns out the lights

An enemy bullet took him deep in his chest
But some of his buddies, they caught their last breath
When they flew him back home, his friends went for the ride
In a cold metal casket with a flag for each bride
CHORUS

Sleepy morning pint of whiskey by his knee
Watching war movies on a pawn shop TV
In his broken down trailer, adrift and alone
Still waiting for orders to send him on home.
CHORUS

After I told Michael this story, he knew that it just had to be on the album. He was so intrigued by the song that he spent hours inserting sound effects to add to the imagery of the words. When he was done, you could almost feel like you were back in that trailer with Monroe. Michael took the same kind interest in every song on the CD and when it finally came out we were more than pleased with the results.

When The Music In Me was first released it came out at the beginning of a new interest in singer/songwriters. I did not know it at the time but my new CD kind of fit into this new category. Much to my surprise, after I sent a few copies out to radio stations, more and more requests came in. Soon my little CD was being played all over the country on small community and folk stations. Along with the airplay my CD was also getting a few favorable reviews in well-known folk magazines like Sing Out!

Not long after my first CD, I followed it up with two more recordings on a little home spun label out of Canaan, Vermont called Promise Land. The first album was called Ryki: Song of the Elk and featured all the music I learned in Poland. Much to our surprise it was cataloged in the archives of the Library of Congress.

We followed that with a live children's album. While I was recording these two albums I was stockpiling enough songs for a new CD of my original songs. As it was a bigger project, I hired noted folk producer, Pete Sutherland to help me with the album.

Working with Pete was another good learning experience and, with his help, I was able to put out my next album called Panning for Gold. Most of the material on this project reflected my years on the highways but also touched on my political pulse. The title track came from my first trip to the Kerrville Songwriter's Festival in Texas. As I felt that this album was stepping into the singer/song writer's world, it was appropriate that the title reflect that idea. The song was written while driving back from the festival and thinking about the songwriters that I met while sitting around the song swap campfires.

Panning for Gold
Words & music by Rik Palieri 8 1994 (written on trip from Texas to NJ after my first trip to the Kerrville Folk Festival)

Eyes filled with wonder, hair spun to silver, He keeps on courting the muse.
With his lady beside him, bindle-stiff troubadours dancing in vagabond shoes.
With a banjo and a fiddle, squeeze a joke in the middle They'll sing 'til the last story's told.
Visions of wanderlust, lives built on love and trust singing a song down a long Texas road.

Chorus: (After each verse)
Like miners of old, they're panning for gold, Hoping for fortune and fame.
Searching the night for a bright neon light, Like a moth flies in to a flickering flame.
In the daytime she stands at the head of the courtroom, At night she sings for the bar.
She closes her eyes as the spirit inside, Takes flight on an old Guild guitar.
Shackled by law books, files and papers, Imprisoned by wardens of time.
She gets her pardon from a musical garden, Stolen moments in a kingdom of rhyme.

He just blew in on the winds of Chicago, Hobo-ing a fast airplane
His day job went south now he's filling his drought, Selling the songs that he sings.
Gamblers, crap shooters who'll take all or nothing, Why, it's hard to explain.
This gypsy king poet will try don't you know it, Win, lose or draw, just to stay in the game.

Another important song on this CD, was a song I had written about my early childhood growing up in the 1960s. While I was writing the song I flashed back on photographs that were embedded in my mind from that time period. Even though I was quite young when most of the incidents occurred, they still had a profound effect on me.

Child of the 60s

Child of the 60s, you watched that sputnik fly,
Just a latchkey baby, watching TV, Learning to survive,
Sharing your house with Captain Kangaroo, Soupy Sales, John and Paul, George and Ring too
When you first went to school, and heard the air raid sound,
Khrushchev said he bury you, beneath the cold, cold ground.
You bowed your head, underneath your desk and then began to pray,
Hoping that the Atom Bomb wouldn't fall on you today.

Child of the 60s, you saw your heroes die, murdered by assassins right before your eyes.
Jackie in her bloody dress, Martin lying on his side,
Bobbies face close to death, made you weep and cry
Bloodstains on the TV set, the Flag raised at half mast.
Your hopes for future were buried with the past
Camelot is burning, the walls are tumbling down
dreams are forsaken, when bullets steal the crown

Child of the 60s with your long flowing hair,
You believed in love and peace and freedom everywhere.
Marching to Washington, you held your head up high,
Telling Richard Nixon, Vietnam's no place to die.
The newsreels told the story, but Nixon had no shame,
Sending young lives to die for a war we fought in vain.
Now you cry with the Veterans and morn for the dead
And hope we learned a lesson for the rough times ahead...

Child of the 60s, head lost in the clouds, Smoking dope, now take a toke to be one of the crowd
losing your perspective in a marijuana haze, not living for tomorrow, still lost in yesterday
the line's drawn on the table your life's is up your nose
you watched your friends disappear, with the poison that they chose
new flowers in the grave yard, the candle's burning dim
you jumped into the ocean, but never learn to swim

Child of the 60s, not living in the past, Trying to hold on to a world that's spinning fast.
Cyber dreams in outer space, with both feet on the ground.
Talking to the universe, while the world spins round and round,
Talking to the universe while the world spins round and round

One of the more political songs on my album, is one that I wrote with the help of Marianna's activist mother Christel Fuchs Holzer. Because of Christel's unusual story, I thought I would take a few minutes to give a brief look at her life and why we wrote this song together.

Christel has spent most of her life trying to end the proliferation of nuclear weapons. Activism is in her blood. She was raised by a very progressive family in Germany. Her family was often called the Red Foxes as the name Fuchs means Fox in German and they all held strong socialist convictions. Her father Emil Fuchs was a Lutheran theologian, while her mother came from an aristocratic family.

At a young age, Christel learned about keeping her family's principles. She recalls when Hitler was first coming into power; "At first, we did not realize what a mad man he was. Then one day my father received a notice that his books were to be picked up. My father thought that there were going to pick them up for the library, so my father instructed us children to dust and clean the covers and then polish our best suitcase and place the books inside. When the Nazis came to our door they took the books and burned them right on our front lawn. That is the moment that we first realized that there was trouble ahead."

Darkness was sweeping over Germany but her family did not flinch and instead tried in their own way to fight the Nazis. Her siblings got involved in the fledgling German resistance and Emil planned out a more astonishing way to combat his foes. He started a late night taxi company. The drivers and cabs would rest during the day, but when night time came, they would help smuggle Jews and other high risk friends out of the country. Her family soon played a heavy price for their actions. Her sister mysteriously was killed in a train accident, and one brother was sent to a concentration camp. Her father was arrested and spent most of the war in and out of prison. Christel's mother could not stand up to the fact that her family was breaking apart and out of desperation committed suicide.

When the news of her mother's death reached her, Christel was a young student studying under Carl Jung. After returning home she reconnected with what was left of her family. After her trip, she realized that becoming a physiologist might at this time might not be the best career for it would be all too easy to fall into the hands of the government and she did not want to be a puppet in Nazi Germany. She switched her major to teaching Arts and Crafts, a trade where she felt she could do more good then harm. When it came time for her graduation she realized that she would have to give the customary "Heil Hitler" before she could accept her diploma. Her friends at the time encouraged her "to just do it" as it was only words. But coming from a family of high ideals and principles, when the time came to say the words, they just would not come out. Christel remembers, "It was as if time stood still, there I was on the platform and I just could not say those words. The room became silent and I had to rush out the back door. As I left the building, a relative who was in the room, handed me some money to leave the country." She hitchhiked her way to the docks and boarded the USS Harding, using her uncle's money to get her across the ocean bound for America.

When Christel went to America, most of her family was either dead, in concentration camps or in prison, but she did have one brother who had escaped Germany before the madness broke out. Her older brother Klaus had left Germany to work in England as a scientist. Klaus was like the rest of his family, not only highly educated but also very politically aware. At the time Klaus was working with a group of British scientists in "The Tubes Alloys Project," using his scientific knowledge to help develop a bomb using atomic energy before Hitler beat them to it. As the war with Germany heightened, many German immigrants, including Klaus, were sent to resettlement camps in Canada. While he was in the camp he received an invitation to join his old group of British scientists to work on a new project in Los Alamos, New Mexico.

Klaus was sent over to America with a bunch of his British colleagues to begin work on "The Manhattan Project," a code name for a secretive project that would later become one of the most important and controversial projects of this century - the building of the first atomic bomb.

Even though all the scientists knew that Klaus was German, and had strong socialist ties, they realized he was a gifted physicist and was worth the risk. In England he made contributions in the "Of implosion and gaseous diffusion cascades theory." This kind of knowledge made him very valuable as he was one of only a handful of scientists who could figure out how to detonate the bomb, a problem the scientists in America had yet to solve.

When Klaus moved to America he contacted his sister and, through her letters, he found that Christel was getting settled in her new home. She learned English at Swarthmore, found a husband and now was starting to raise a family in Cambridge,

Massachusetts. Christel invited Klaus to join her and her family over the Christmas holidays and during his visit he told his sister a little bit about the project he was working on in Los Alamos. When Christel heard of the terrible bomb that her brother was working on she said, "How can you work on a project like this?" Klaus replied "If I don't do it, someone else will, but at least if I am involved I will see to it that it will never be used again."

On August 6, 1945 the first atomic bomb was exploded over the Japanese city of Hiroshima. After the scientists witnessed the terrible destruction and devastation of the bomb, many wanted to find a way to control it's power by sharing the information with other nations but the American government wanted to keep the bomb and its mighty power for its own and refused the scientists request. Klaus knew that if only one country had the bomb it could be used over and over again. He felt deep in his heart that the only way he could prevent the use of the bomb was to have a counterbalance. At the time Russia was still one of our allies and even considered a "friendly nation." As the war against Germany and Japan was now over, Russia, with its Stalinist communism, seemed to be next in line.

Klaus knew what he was doing and was willing to risk his life in order to contain the nuclear nightmare that he had helped to create. Klaus had contacts with the Soviet Union and slipped them some information to aid them in creating a bomb of their own. The American government was worried about spies and soon tightened its security but before their security net was drawn Klaus managed to get enough information to the Russians to put them three to five years ahead of schedule. When Klaus finished his work in Los Alamos, he went back to England to continue his work at the Energy Research Center at Harwell.

Soon the FBI found out about Klaus and a few other people through the Verona Cables, the code used to crack the KGB's secret communications and sent agents to England. In 1949 Klaus was under suspicion because of his pre war communist background. As Klaus knew that he had been spotted, he decided to face the fire and gave himself up on March first 1950 to the British authorities. Though Klaus confessed about his own involvement, he refused to name anyone else.

Back in Washington, the FBI was furious and wanted to get Klaus and send him to the electric chair but as Klaus was a British citizen, the FBI could not get their hands on him. On March 2nd, Klaus was put on trail. His case was over in less than two hours and he was sentenced to serve fourteen years in prison for passing atomic secrets to a friendly nation.

When the FBI heard the news they said, "If we can't get Klaus, we can still get his sister." By this time the Police and FBI were swarming around Christel's house like bees around honey. The heat was on, as both Christel and her husband were both in the progressive movement. Under the pressure both Christel and her husband cracked and caved in. No one really knows what or even how it happened but soon Christel found herself, divorced and in an insane asylum. While she was there, she was put through a series of drug treatments and even shock therapy. Christel remembers men coming to see her and showing her hundreds of photos trying to get her to identify Klaus's contact.

After a few years, a young conscientious objector came to the hospital to serve out his military duty. The two became friends and after a while this young man realized that she was far from insane. He carefully took notes on Christel and when he had enough proof of her sanity he brought her case up. After a short a while, thanks to the young man's help, she was released. Leaving the hospital with only the clothes on her back and just enough money for cab fair she went to apply for a job at a local book bindery, a skill she had learned back in Germany. The owner of the bindery, Albert Holzer, was an older, fair haired gentleman who lived with his sisters. Albert took pity on Christel, hired her and set up lodging for her in a spare room with one of his sisters. After a while, Albert became quite fond of his young German employee, and asked Christel to marry him. They soon were not only working together but also starting a little family.

They had two little girls, Marianna and Heidi. The girls grew up around the bindery and would often play there while Albert and his employees were busy binding books. As Christel returned to family life, she also renewed her interest in politics. Albert was an open-minded fellow and did not mind going to Quaker meetings or even spending time at silent vigils. The young girls were also exposed to political gatherings at a young age and would often accompany their mother as she held a sign protesting the use of nuclear weapons.

The first time I met Christel, I was performing at a march for Peace and Justice near Rutland, Vermont and as I walked along with the marchers I noticed Christel. She was there helping organize the gathering and stood out from the other marchers with her silvery gray hair tied in a neat bun and her strong facial features. I could tell, by how the others treated her, that she was someone very special. By this time, her involvement with peace work was almost legendary. She helped spearhead the Nuclear Freeze Movement in Vermont, had organized a women's book bindery in Nicaragua and in Germany, and was awarded the Vermont Peace prize in 1981, awarded by the Physicians for Nuclear Responsibility.

It came as quite a surprise when I first started dating Marianna when I found out that she was Christel's daughter. It took awhile for Christel to warm up to me but after a while we found that politically we shared some similarities. As the years passed, we often found ourselves standing side by side holding a big sign, standing together as a family. When I was asked to write a song about the abolition of nuclear weapons, I asked Christel for some advice and, after hearing her words, thought that it would be better if we wrote the last verse together.

PANDORA'S BOX

Words and Music by Rik Palieri. Last chorus by Christel Fuchs Holzer.
This song was written on behalf of all those who lost their lives from the American bombing of Japan and in the hope for continued nuclear disarmament.

The war's end was near at hand, when the news was heard world wide.
We had a secret weapon, with a big surprise inside
We learned to split the atom, it was the latest rage
When we opened up, Pandora's Box, And let the monster from his cage.

Our leaders and some scientists were happy with their toy.
And sent a plane named Enola Gay, to deliver, Little Boy
Those lousy Japs, with their sneak attack, it's time to make them pay.
So they opened up Pandora's Box, sent little boy on his way

The Atom Bomb exploded, in a fireball of flames
It scorched the earth and shook the ground, while buildings fell like rain.
Men and Women screamed and yelled, their bodies burned to dust
We opened up Pandora's Box now the war belonged to us.

Since that day, the world has changed, with bombs in many hands
And every time a war breaks out, the fear returns again
Will someone push the button? And point the bomb at us
We opened up Pandora's Box, there's no one left to trust.

Brighter than a thousand suns, this power house of flame
Its angry winds of hate and fear disguised in freedom's name
The lust for power, land and wealth, just feed it's holy flame
We opened up Pandora's Box and the monster still remains

There are no real winners, when a nuclear war is waged
For all of life's living, will return back to clay.
There's no quick solution, but if we only could
We'd put the bomb back in the box, and lock it up for good.

Then we'll lay down our weapons, and learn to live as one
and then my Friends, our work for peace will finally be done!

The release of Panning for Gold opened up a batch of new opportunities working with more singer/songwriters. With this new kind of exposure I was able to start touring again but this time performing at more listening venues. This was just the start of many fantastic adventures.

WHALES, BEARS AND SINGING FOR THE HALIBUT IN ALASKA

In the fall of 1996 I had the interesting opportunity to tour Alaska. My tour was based around the Alaskan Marine Highway and the ferry that runs from Bellingham, Washington up to Juneau and Skagway, Alaska. The trip takes about three days with stops in Ketchikan, Petersburg, Sitka and Wanggel. The ferry can hold up to 600 people plus 150 cars and trucks. I worked on the Arts On Board program, doing two concerts per day. In return, I got space on the solarium, a big outdoor deck where you can set down your gear and roll out your sleeping bag. You have to buy your own food (It's even better to bring your own food) but from my point of view, it is a great way to travel and understand what Alaska is all about. The tour really started when I flew into Bellingham, Washington, where the ferry docks. While I was waiting to catch the ferry in Bellingham I was able to meet a new friend from the Folk DJ cyber community, singer/song writer, Tracy Spring. It was a lot of fun to exchange songs and road stories with Tracy. She sang me some of her favorite songs like "Love is a Round," "Woman on The Road" and her beautiful "Gabriel's Lullaby." We sat around for hours passing songs back and forth until we drove down to catch the huge white ferry that was waiting at the dock.

The ferry was enormous! You had to climb endless staircases to reach the top deck. When the ship's loud horn blew, everyone on board rushed to wave goodbye to their friends and family down below. I checked in with the ship's purser who told me my daily schedule. I was to perform two shows during the day and then do a nightly performance in the ship's lounge. I was also told that I could roll out my sleeping bag on the solarium deck and that I was entitled to free beverages. I walked up to the top deck and placed my gear in a deck chair right next to a happy young couple from Australia. Leanne and Dave were riding the ferry up to Skagway and from there planning to ride all the way to Cape Horn at the tip of South America on their motorcycle. They turned out to be great deck mates.

The solarium is where most of the young travelers stay. They camp out on deck and even heat up their home brought food on the long heaters that warm up the deck. The best part of camping on the deck is that you have an incredible view. Even though the ferry is really for shipping cargo and people, not a tourist boat, you can see pretty amazing scenery as the boat navigates the narrow inlets. It was common to see eagles, wolves and even grizzly bears right from your deck chair.

The ship makes many stops along the way which gave us a chance to stretch our legs and even do a bit of sight seeing. Our first stop was in Ketchikan and when we docked, there was a tourist bus waiting to take us into town. I rode out to see the infamous Creek Street and Saxman Totem Blight, arguably the largest collection of these monolithic wood carvings in the world. The totem poles were fascinating and they were often carved with elaborate designs of ravens, eagles, bears, salmon and whales. Each pole told a different tale. Some were carved memorials, while others told of family accomplishments and heraldry. To see so many totem poles standing in one place was just incredible and I would have stayed there for hours if I did not have to get back to the waiting ferry. The trip rolled on to Wranggel and the Norwegian styled town of Petersburg. We reached Sitka in the wee hours of the morning then on to our final stop at Haines.

On that last night we had a fantastic jam in the lounge. Earlier in the day, while walking around the deck, I had noticed that there were many travelers who were packing instruments along with their gear. I invited all the players to join me in my evening show. That evening, the lounge filled up quickly with guitars, hand drums and even a didgeridoo. The ship's lounge looked like something out of the 80's disco era, complete with a plush red leather seats and a glittering globe hanging above the dance floor. It is funny how music can change even the tackiest surroundings into a friendly atmosphere. As soon as everyone brought out their instruments any listener could have imagined that they were sitting on someone's front porch.

We were having a great time picking and grinning, 'til late in the evening when a storm hit. As all the other pickers went to their cabins to batten down the hatches I was left to carry on. The waves were rocking the boat 'til I felt like I was riding in a roller coaster. At the point where all the glasses were falling off the bar, I was told to pack it in for the night. This is the kind of tour that you would do even if you did not make a cent but, luckily, not only did I have the time of my life, but also brought home money to pay the bills.

My first Alaska show was up in Haines and, after saying goodbye to my new friends on board, I was whisked away in a small sedan by my host, Ray Meniker. Ray, with his curly beard and heavy woolen hat and shirt, fit the part of what the Alaskan's call an old Sourdough. Sourdoughs were those tough men who came up to Alaska to get away from society and live by the rules of nature. Ray and his wife, Vivian, settled here years ago, leaving behind the bright city lights of Manhattan, and built their own Shangri-La out of the trees in the forest.

Ray was once in involved with the folk scene, back when the Almanac Singers were hosting hootenannies in Greenwich Village. A relative of his from Boston told me that Ray would be glad to put together a few shows to help me out. Ray, who helps out at the local radio station, had no problem organizing a day at the school followed by a concert at the Chilkat Performing Arts Center. Whenever I'm staking out new territory I am never sure how many people are going to turn out. As I looked out from the beautiful stage, with a carved wooden backdrop of native Tinglets designs, I wondered if tonight's show was going to be a bust. As I sat back stage I heard the sound that makes all performers come to life, the sound of people entering the door. Because of Ray's good publicity and my school programs, we ended up with almost a full house. After the show, Ray and Vivian talked about taking me out to see the Eagle Reserve the next day. I have always found a kinship with the American Bald Eagle and just the thought of seeing them in their wild habit got my blood to pumping. Just a short drive from Haines is the largest natural eagle reserve in this country. In November, over 4000 of the white headed raptors congregate to feed on the yearly salmon run. As I was there in October there were a lesser number of big birds but it was still impressive. Ray and I spent a few hours snapping photos and watching as the massive eagles dove and circled over the mighty Chilkat River. As my ferry was leaving later that afternoon, we had just enough time to get back to the dock before the big ship pulled out for Juneau.

It was just a few hours 'til our ferry docked at the state capital of Juneau and as we were on our way a typhoon had hit town. The streets were flooded with rainwater, with many telephone poles knocked down. I got off the ferry and rode a bus into the center of town to meet with my next host Jeff Brown, a DJ on KTOO NPR radio. As I walked towards Jeff's house, I noticed a big brown bear also walking down the street just a block from the state house and I thought to myself, "Well, welcome to Alaska!"

I met up with Jeff at the radio station just in time to take part in the annual pledge drive and the big KTOO Halibut Feed. The Halibut fund raiser was held in a downtown building right near the docks. The fresh fish were cooked up by radio staff, and volunteers, and had an "All you can eat buffet" of all the freshly caught halibut you could fit in your stomach. Jeff asked me if I could play for the people while they were waiting in line. After singing for my supper I sat down and had a feast, filling up on fish, salad and cake. It was a great way to meet the Juneau community and support KTOO.

The next morning, while at Jeff's house, I heard Jeff's little daughter, Callie, scream, "There is a bear outside our house!" Sure enough, a big old black bear somehow got into Jeff's back yard and was trying his best to get out. Jeff's neighbors started calling telling him about the bear and Jeff's wife and son made a mad dash out the back door to get to work and school. Jeff, Callie and I watched as the poor bear walked round and round the house, while all neighbors peeked out their windows. Even a taxi cab came with a few tourists, to see the wandering bear. After some time the bear left and life went back too normal. Jeff invited me to do his kids' radio show, helped me line up a few more gigs and introduced me to more of the Juneau musical community. I stayed a few days with Jeff and his family, then moved over to visit his next door neighbor who was also into music.

The Road Is My Mistress

After my show I continued my tour out on the Island of Gustavus. My shows in Gustavus were hosted by another friend of the folk community, Heidi Robichaued. Heidi makes her living as an artist doing scrimshaw on fossilized mammoth ivory. I had heard about her concert series from Utah Phillips who was once snowed-in on this remote island. Hearing that I was a friend of Utah's, Heidi fit me right into her fall schedule. Getting to Gustavus was no easy matter and, in fact, the only way to get there was to fly over in a little bush plane. I took off from the Juneau airport and touched down in a tiny airfield. Heidi was driving a real ramshackle car with broken windows and doors that barely closed. With hardly any paved roads, or really any roads at all, it was understandable that even having a car here was a luxury. Heidi brought me over to the schoolhouse and introduced me to the teachers and staff who would be helping me out with both my school shows and evening concerts. Back at Heidi's house we shared a bear and wild game stew and made preparations for my shows. The shows went fine and soon I was heading back to Juneau on the plane.

When I got back to the airport there was quit a stir going on. The National Aerodynamics Board in Washington, DC had informed them that they were closing down the airport, as none of their flight simulators were able to land an airplane there on their test. This news outraged the public! "Who do they think they are," one old sourdough exclaimed, "Just because they can't land a plane in their test in Washington doesn't mean that we can't land up here. Why we've been flying and landing planes here in weather that they can't even dream of." But Washington had its way and not long after I flew in, the airport was closed. I had a few days back in Juneau to do a few more shows hoping that the airport would reopen in time for my next engagement out in the remote town of Pelican. Luck was with me and on the very day I was to fly, the airport reopened. Jeff's wife drove me down to the airport but this time, instead of flying in a bush plane, I was flying in a float plane. Not far from the runway were a few narrow channels of water. The planes, with big pontoons, sat tied to the dock as we loaded in the gear. As I was the only passenger going to Pelican that day I found myself strapped right into the co-pilot's seat. Once we were loaded the two huge propellers twirled around as our plane scurried down the waterway and launched into the cloudy blue Alaskan sky. Once we were airborne, I could understand why the bureaucrats in Washington were worried, as I could not see a bloody thing in the dense fog. The pilot sensed my insecurity and assured me that he knew every mountain range like the back of his hand. "Just because we can't see it, doesn't mean that I don't know it's there." We flew high into the sky 'til the clouds melted away. At one point, the pilot pointed to a spot in the rolling sea. "See that," he said, "There is a humpback getting ready to breach." With that the pilot swooped down from the sky flying right over it's head as the huge leviathan rose from the waves. Eventually we circled around a tiny fishing village.

As I looked down at Pelican, it was just the Alaskan town I had pictured in my mind whenever I though of going to Alaska. It had tall mountains, a fishing harbor and eagles flying through the huge evergreen trees. The whole town was not more than fifty houses up on stilts, connected by a long wooden boardwalk and a cannery at the far end.

Our plane splashed down from the sky and skimmed across the waves, stopping at a floating wooden dock. The school host was there to meet me on the dock and help me with my luggage. When I tried to get out of the plane I noticed that my right leg was in a lot of pain. The night before the flight I had tripped down the basement stairs. My ankle twisted in the fall but it had seemed all right. Now after sitting for hours in the plane, my ankle was red, swollen and in a great deal of pain. I hobbled my way onto the dock and watched as the plane roared out of the harbor. That night I spent the whole evening with my foot soaking in a big pail of water and by the next day I was feeling better but still sore. The school's schedule was that I would spend the day going from room to room. I tried to explain about my foot but the teachers decided it was easier to stick with the plan and so I spent the rest of the day hopping on one foot, carrying all of my instruments down the halls.

There is not much to do in Pelican other than to walk the boardwalk. After you spend a few hours walking up and down the boardwalk, you meet almost everyone who lives there. After a few trips walking up and down the wooden road there was only one place to go, to the local watering hole.

There is a famous bar right on the boardwalk, called Rosie's. Rosie sold the place and it is under new management now, but when Rosie ran the place it was really wild. There are hundreds of signatures written on the bar's ceiling. Rosie used to ask new people in town to climb up on the bar and sign the ceiling. As they looked up to write their name, Rosie would grab their pants and pulled them down. This became the bars trademark. Even T-shirts were printed up saying "Take off your pants and dance at Rosie's." It was while I was having a beer at Rosie's that I met up with a fisherman/guitar picker named Flash. Flash, who was always dressed in his rain slicker and tall rubber boots, was well known at Rosie's. He had a good reputation as both a singer and song writer. Flash and I hit it off, right off the bat, and were soon entertaining the crowd. In no time, the bar was lined up with complimentary drinks and we played some good old foot stomping music. The next day Flash asked me if I wanted to go and check out his house, so we climbed into his little row boat and headed out to his camp. He lived in a little shack just a short distance from the main village. As we motored along past swooping eagles and otters, Flash said that usually we'd see a whale or two, but not today. When we got inside his sparse lodge, Flash made up some coffee and we spent the rest of the afternoon swapping songs 'til we had to get back into the boat and head back to the dock. This was my last day as the ferryboat had just pulled into town.

My trip in Alaska was almost over with after another three day voyage on the ferry back to Bellingham. The trip back was pretty uneventful for most of my deck mates had moved on and I was left with a bunch of tourists.

I will share one story though. I was performing my afternoon show for the audience made up of about 70?100 people, of all different ages and backgrounds. I was standing right at the front of the bow, with windows all around me, looking out into sea. Everyone was singing along when all of a sudden, a huge humpback whale came up and breached out of the water, right behind me. The crowd shouted out, "Look, a whale." When I turned and saw the whale, I knew that I was no competition for such a majestic creature, so I moved aside and said, "Hey, let's all take a picture of the whale," and picked up my camera as the whole crowd rushed over and ran to look at the whale. After the whale had passed, the audience went back to their seats and I picked up my banjo and finished the song I was singing. After the song I said, "Well, I've shared the stage with many other performers, but this is the first time I've ever shared it with a whale."

THE MUSIC BUS

I was just getting back, from touring Alaska, and was ready to fly home out of Bellingham, Washington. Once I started checking in, I noticed there was a big problem. The counter person was throwing up her hands as she had to tell everyone that all the planes were having problems and they would not be able to fly today. You can just imagine the stress that was in that room. Then it was suggested that a bus would be provided that would take us to Seattle and perhaps some of us would be able to make our connections. Everyone was worried as we only had an hour and a half to make the connecting flight and the bus was not even at the airport yet. The bus pulled up and the driver says in a nasty tone, "They just pulled me out of bed, after an all night shift, and they expect me to perform a miracle and get you to Seattle in time to catch your flight. Good luck." Needless to say, everyone was in a real bad mood. I was loading my stuff into the bus, and had slung my banjo over my back when the bus driver said, "What? Are you going to play that in my bus?" "Well, I really did not plan on it," I replied. "I was only kidding," said the driver. But I started thinking and I reached inside my case and pulled out the banjo. A worried angry woman said, "Well, what if I don't like it?" "Then tell me and I'll stop," I replied. The bus drove off and the tension inside the bus was horrendous. Then I started plucking away at the old standard "Blue Skies" (a neat version a learned from Pete Seeger) and, in a few minutes, I noticed everyone was humming along. A few more minutes went by and I heard a few voices singing. I started to sing too and before long the whole bus burst out in song and even the bus driver himself sang along in his big bass baritone. One song led to another, and everyone seemed to have a request. "Do you know "You Are My Sunshine?" Soon photographs appeared, pictures of vacations, family members, little newborn babies and old friends.

Everyone laughed and sang, with food being passed around the bus, and before long the airport was in sight. The bus driver called, "We made it with time to spare," and everyone clapped their hands. Then he said, "We would never have done it with out the help of our banjo player" and shouts of approval rang through the bus. The bus stopped and, as we all got out, people exchanged address and invitations, a few exchanged hugs and we all went our separate ways. As I was leaving the bus driver said, "This was the best ride I ever had. Thanks for your music." A few weeks later, back in the hills of old Vermont, my mailbox was filled with letters of reminisces of that "musical bus ride."

THE OZ BARE BONES TOUR

I never thought of going to Australia 'til one night, about three A.M., I received a strange phone call, " Hey, mate I just received your new CD and there's no CD in the case." At this time of the morning you have to get your wits about you so I replied, "What?" The friendly voice at the other end was Colin Nightingale a DJ from the Folk DJ List Serve on the Internet. He said again, "There must be some mistake as you sent the CD shrink wrapped but when I opened it there was no CD inside." By this time I realized that the call really was from Australia and laughed telling Colin, "Do you know what time it is?" After a bit of laughter on both ends I agreed to re-send the CD. Colin ended his call with, "Did you ever think of touring here? If you do I can help you, mate!"

Thus began a flurry of e?mails and late night calls to my new friend Down Under. After a bit of research we found the right festival to be the anchor date and with the help of two other Australian DJs put together what we called Rik's Bare Bones Tour. The tour would take me to Sydney, Melbourne, Brisbane and a remote place in central Australia called Alice Springs. While the DJs worked on the details of the main cites I worked out my trip to The Alice.

As with many of my half baked ideas, my romantic notion of going to The Alice, started with reading a book called A Town Like Alice, a fantastic novel by Neville Shute. After reading about this out back bush town I knew I just had to go there. I realized, very quickly, that no one I knew had any contacts in Alice Springs and those who ever heard of the place said that it would not be easy to find any gigs out there. As I'm not one to give up on a challenge, I went right to work searching out any information I could find on the Internet. At the time, there was only one contact, a web site called "Alice Springs, Movies and More." It was really only a pet shop that listed some of the movies playing in town. I started writing to the poor woman who owned the web site trying to find a place to perform in town. She politely kept telling me that she only ran a pet shop and had no idea of who to ask about any kind of performance. I just could not let it go and kept on writing and writing until she brought my letters into one of the local bars. The bar owner was amused at this Yank wanting to play in town and booked me for a week at his club.

Now, knowing that I had a gig in Alice Springs, I went to work on my next idea. I have always wanted to learn how to play the didgeridoo, that ancient instrument played by the aboriginals and I thought that this trip might be just the right time to learn. Over the years, the Vermont Council of the Arts had always been supportive in helping me out and when I explained my idea they said, "That sounds wonderful, but what's a didgeridoo?"

After going through all the necessary paperwork and explaining just what a didgeri-doo was, the Council awarded me an Artist Independent Study Grant to learn to play this exotic instrument with the understanding that in return I would do a few workshops in Vermont and share what I had learned. Now, I was truly ready, with my tickets in hand, and banjo over my shoulder, I boarded the big airplane for the twenty something hour ride to the Land Down Under. As I sat aboard the plane, I began reading about my new adventure.

Australia was discovered by Portuguese and Dutch explorers and then, later, was claimed by the British. Then Captain Cook thought to use this vast continent as a penal colony, and England sent hordes of pickpockets, murderers and troublemakers to this god-forsaken place. Today, many an Aussie can trace their ancestral roots back to some scoundrel and most are quite proud of it. The wildlife in the Land of Oz, as it is some-times called, can also be considered very exotic. I mean where else can you find kanga-roos, wallabies, koala bears, kookaburra birds, egg-laying duck-billed platypus and more dangerous snakes, spiders, sharks and crocodiles than any other place in the world. Putting down my travel guide, I looked out the window to see my first glimpse of the rocky coast and knew that soon I would see it all with my own eyes.

My plane landed at Sydney where I went through customs. The Australians don't need any more insects then they already have so each visitor is checked carefully for any item that might contain some hidden beasts and then the entire plane is fumigated. After I cleared the customs' area, I boarded another plane to reach my first destination, the cos-mopolitan city of Melbourne.

THE FIRST LEG: MELBOURNE

I was filled with jet lag when I was met at the airport in Melbourne by my first tour sponsor, gray pony-tailed DJ, Roger Holdsworth of PBS FM. Roger whisked me off to his house where I met his partner, now wife, Pat and they filled me full of tea and then shipped me off to bed. Roger said, "Your first show is in four hours. Do you think you can handle it?" I replied with a favorable grunt and hit the sack. Even though it was only a few hours, the little nap revived my weary bones and I was ready for my first show of the tour.

As our car pulled into the driveway of the Boite World Music Club there was already a throng of people waiting to get in the door. As with all of my shows, I always shared the bill with an Australian artist. It was the country's way of making sure that they keep their artists working. For me personally, it was a great way to make new friends and share musical ideas and styles. For my first show, I would be sharing the stage with two artists, an Australian banjo playing storyteller, and a didgeridoo player named Bill Harney.

Bill grew up on a cattle station out in the bush and his program was filled with the stories of his aboriginal people. Bill was also a didgeridoo maker and it was a very happy coincidence that on my first show in the country I got to work with a master of the very instrument that I had come to learn.

I was transfixed as I listened to him blow into his long wooden didgeridoo. Its earthy, gritty sound was like an echo back to the past. During Bill's performance, he talked about his life growing up on a cattle station with an aboriginal mother and a white fellow for a dad. In his stories, he told how his mother would smear his body with mud so that when the inspectors came to town he would look like the rest of the aboriginals and not be taken away. He also talked of Dreamtime Stories, those old Aboriginal stories that tell of the creation of the earth by the great ancestors who slept deep under the ground. These ancestors looked like plants and animals but acted like man. After these great beings created the sun, the wind, rain, mountains and all of life on earth, they left the responsibility of stewardship of the planet to man and they themselves withdrew back into nature.

After Bill's program, I had to leap into action. Somehow, the sleepiness faded and my body filled up with light and energy. After my show, one woman commented, "It was as if you transported me to a Kentucky mountain top." After doing our separate shows, we all joined together ending the evening with two banjos and a didgeridoo playing "Shady Grove." After our show, I spent a bit of time talking with Bill about his didgeridoo. Bill was delighted to show me his "didg" and even offered to make one for me if he could find the time. One of Bill's friends pulled me aside and told me that Bill is a very sought-after maker and even if he does not make one for you it was an honor that he said he would. Bill smiled and repeated his offer. I thanked him and walked out the door. To my surprise and delight, Bill did make me a didg and sent it to me before the end of my trip.

THE SECRETS OF THE DIDGERIDOO

After the show with Bill, I was psyched to try the instrument. Roger had set up an intensive day with a master didg player named Raymond Mow. I took a train from Melbourne out to meet Ray on the outskirts of town. Ray came to pick me up in his old VW van and immediately handed me a feather from a cockatoo. Ray's plan was to have me spend the day with him so he could teach me the basics. In our first lesson, Ray had me pick out a didgeridoo that felt comfortable to the shape of my mouth. Next, he gave me a brief history.

The didgeridoo is certainly one of the oldest musical instruments on this planet. It is made from the hollows of native stringy bark, gum or blood wood tree found in the northern Amhen lands. The instrument is made from the work of termites. The termites build a nest alongside the trunk of the tree then eat their way through it hollowing out the center. The aborigine's knock on the trees to find out which ones have been hollowed out then cut them down. The didj maker then knocks out the insects inside of the log until it is cleared, and then paints them with natural okras and berry plants. Many times, these didg's become a work of art and are covered with aboriginal tribal designs.

Even through the instrument is just a simple hollowed out log, playing it is anything but simple. In order to play the didgeridoo properly, you have to attain a skill called circular breathing. Circular breathing means that the player has to store enough air in his cheeks that while he is blowing the didgeridoo he can sneak a bit of air while he is exhaling. Ray demonstrated this technique and then had me practice by blowing bubbles through a straw submerged in a half a glass of water. Ray said you will know when you are doing it right, as the bubbles will never stop. Even though I was having trouble, Ray told me to be patient then gave me more instructions. He said that it was important to remember that you don't need a lot of air to play this instrument and just a fine stream of steady air will suffice. He demonstrated this idea by lighting a candle then blowing across the flame. He said, "You must be able to blow the flame with out putting it out." The hours flew by with Ray instructing and encouraging me. When we took a few breaks, we watched a couple of videos about the didgeridoo and a special homemade video about the didg festival that Ray runs. One of the players in his video made a special visit to join us and show a few of his special didg tricks.

Neither Ray nor his guest, Chris Adnam, were aboriginal, but both were totally committed to both the instrument and culture of Australia's original people. Chris told an interesting tale about how he became interested in the didgeridoo.

Chris grew up not far from an Aboriginal tribe near Melbourne. "Even as a young boy, I was affected by their customs and began to have very vivid dreams about the tribe. The dreams were coming so often that I started to write them down and, after a short while, I discovered that the dreams were actually sending me information about the tribe's history. When I had collected enough material I went to visit the tribe to make some sense of my dreams. The elders were at first shocked to discover that I was channeling their history but later decided that I was an important link to their past and I was asked to become a member of the community. At first, I did not realize what they were saying, but soon found out. For me to become a member of this tribe I had to go through a sort of initiation and purification ceremony. They told me that there were toxicants inside my body that I needed to get rid of and they had arranged the perfect way to do just that. I was soon led by two of the young girls to the beach and was buried up to my neck in the sand facing the ocean. The tide was still out and the young girls told me that they would be back after I was clean. I first I thought this was some kind of a joke and waited for them to start laughing but they did not laugh, they just left.

As the time passed and the tide started to come in I thought that I had been tricked and started to struggle to get out of the hole, but it was no use I could not move as they had packed the sand tightly around my body. The more I struggled the more I sweated and the faster the water rushed around my head. Soon the waves were reaching my throat, then the bottom of my chin. As the water reached my bottom lip I thought I was a goner and just about everything in my body came out. Just when I was ready to give up all hope, the two young girls returned and dug me out of the sand. When I returned to the tribe they treated me like family and that is when I really started playing the didg."

After Chris' amazing story, he told me that he was also into using the vibrations of the didgeridoo as a healing tool. He demonstrated this by blowing the didj around my body. As he moved the didg to some of the healing centers, or chakras, I could feel an intense vibration pulsing from the end of Chris's instrument. Chris said that more and more didj players are using this Vibration Therapy to help people with their physical and mental state. He also pointed out that playing the didgeridoo also helps keep the player healthy, too.

I could have listened to both Ray and Chris for days on end but, as my train was due, we had to wrap things up. Ray packed up my didj in a smart looking cloth bag that I draped over my shoulder and then drove me out to meet my train. As the train pulled out of the station, Ray stood on the train platform shouting, "Don't give up, you'll get it - just keep trying!"

THE PORT FAIRY FOLK FESTIVAL

The next few days I spent at Roger's were a blur of radio shows, concerts and sightseeing. Roger did not have a car so he arranged a series of pick ups and drops offs to get me to all of my commitments. As I did not know any of these people, it seemed quite strange to be parceled around by complete strangers. Often I would stand on a corner and wait until a car pulled up with the driver asking if I was the American chap. Once inside I would be driven to the next drop stop. By this ingenious method, I was able to get around and meet with a lot of locals while seeing such places as the Great Ocean Road, a few nature parks and an amazing row of stone monoliths set into the ocean, called the Twelve Apostles. After a week of being parceled around, I was ready for my big trip out to the Port Fairy Folk festival.

Port Fairy is Australia's second largest folk festival and it hosts some of the world's best entertainers from Australia and beyond. The festival holds up to 30,000 people and the tickets sell like hot cakes. On the festival grounds are a string of large white tents, each one big enough to hold thousands of fans. In the center is another huge tent that is sponsored by Guinness. It is fair to say that this beer tent is one of the favorite hangouts for festival goers and performers.

On the first night there was to be a special concert by all the friend performers. As I stood back stage with my friend, Tracy Spring, getting ready to go on, a fellow song-writer from Canada, James Kellaghan was busy lighting up some Native American sweet grass and smudging each of us and our instruments, wishing us good luck on stage. With my new friend's help I was able to do a great show and had an audience of over 2000 singing along within minutes. While at the festival, I met with a huge array of performers, sang on the ABC national radio and also made a lot of new acquaintances.

Another new friend I met was English songwriter, Jez Lowe. Jez is a skilled song-writer with a great sense of humor. One night as we were hanging around the beer tent talking about some of the worst gigs we ever played Jez piped up with this: "I was in England playing with a friend and we were asked to start a new afternoon concert series at a church. I was a bit late getting to the show so I was surprised to see the entire audience, including my friend, standing out in the weather. When I asked my friend, "Well, what's going on," he wouldn't say a word and just pointed to the church door. I was amazed and asked him again, "What the hell is going on?" He just pointed to the church. Every one in the crowd was silent so I knew something was amiss. When I walked into the church, I almost died. There, right in front of the altar, was this bloody coffin! Walking a bit closer, I could see that the corpse was inside. I went back out to my friend and discussed the matter. The crowd was getting uneasy and we did not know what to do. Should we just go on with the show and set up around the coffin, or just play in the hallway, or outside. While we were discussing the proper way of performing for the deceased, the priest turned up and apologized, saying that they had scheduled a funeral for later this evening and had forgotten all about our concert. He then quickly removed the coffin to another building and we did the show. Well, perhaps we were hanging around the beer tent too long ... but strange things do happen!

Besides meeting new friends, I also happened upon a familiar face. I was checking in the instrument lock up when who did I run into but my pal from the Alaskan ferry trip, Dave. Dave had brought along his mate from work and his pal decided that as they didn't have tickets that maybe they would just hop the gate. Both of them seemed to have been well into commemorating our happy reunion with many rounds of beer hours before we met. They surprised me when I went to check in my instruments and jumped me from behind saying, "Aye, ya Mate, it's me (hiccup) Dave." As you can imagine I was shocked to meet Dave in the instrument tent, supposedly the most secure place on the grounds, and even more stunned to learn that they didn't have tickets. Not to mention that they were three, or even four sheets to the wind. Of course, I knew that this was not acceptable and made sure that they were given passes and treated like guests for the rest of the festival. Though I was able to get them passes into the festival on the condition they were in already, I could not sneak them into the hotel. Dave just said, "No worries mate," and they found a nice quiet place in the local cemetery to sleep off their hang over.

All too soon, it was time to head back to Melbourne to get back to Roger and Pat's for a farewell dinner before going up to my next shows up in Brisbane. As I did not have a ride, my friend Dave said that he would take me. Unfortunately, both Dave and his pal got into some more booze and were in no condition to drive. Dave told me that I should drive and handed me the keys. What Dave forgot to tell me was that he and his friend had "borrowed" the company car, and that many of his colleagues were here at the festival. Dave said, "Rik ?, (hiccup) you can drive so they won't recognize us." As my under-the-weather pals were worried about their own notoriety, I realized that I had just been on the main stage where the whole festival saw me, not to mention my trademark big cowboy hat that makes me stand out like an elephant in a parking lot. I knew that I had to help out, so I took off my hat, climbed in the car, turned the key and drove away in a car with the company's name boldly displayed on each door. As I drove off, Dave and his pal hid low behind the dashboard as I waved to the faces of the happy fans along the festival gate. Of course, I had little experience driving a car that was set up to drive on the other side of the road and had numerous stops just trying to brake and shift. Dave and his pal took great advantage of these little pit stops as a chance to have a few more rounds at the local pubs. Needless to say, it took the first explorers almost as long to discover this bloody country as it took for us to reach Melbourne.

BRISBANE

After our drunken party reached Roger's house, we all enjoyed a fantastic meal that Pat made, and then had a good nights rest. The next morning I was on a flight to Brisbane. As I left Melbourne, by plane, my host of the next leg of the tour, Colin, and his party left by car for Brisbane. Once again, fate stepped in and a huge blunder was about to occur.

Once I landed, I waited and waited and waited for someone to pick me up at the Brisbane airport. After a few hours went by, I realized perhaps there was some sort of mix-up so I did what any folk singer would do on an occasion like this, I pulled out my banjo, started playing, and in no time drew a crowd. One of my "select crowd" had a mobile phone and after hearing of my sad plight, started making phone calls. After a few calls to my host, radio station Bay FM, we were told that I was not supposed to be here yet. Colin and Dawn were still driving back from Port Fairy and Jan was told that I was coming tomorrow, not today. The business fellow asked about a cheap hotel near the station, but the woman who was at the station didn't have a clue, so this fellow made a few more calls to his friends to see if they were interested on having a banjo player for the night. I guess the thought of having a banjo in the house scared them off and I was left to jump into a taxi and head off to the Hotel Diana. Well, it was a bit pricey, but it did have a health spa, complete with a sauna and hot tub. After my long day I just hopped into the hot tub and forgot about all my worries!

The next day Jan, a tall red headed woman, who was my tour publicist, arrived in her old heap of a car and whisked me off to downtown Brisbane. It was not long before I met her young daughter, Becky, and enjoyed endless cups of tea, "boiling the Billy," and exchanging stories of life, and music.

We met up with Colin at the ABC radio station and after endless rounds of apologies, did a few interviews with my "bag of musical tricks," then went over to my gig at the Zoo Club. If ever there was a club that was not for folk music, The Zoo was it. The walls were painted with black and had 60's style day-glow paintings on them. The soundman only knew two levels, loud and LOUDER. The show had a "very select" audience, (this is a polite term we performers use for a very small crowd, often meaning you and the sound man.) but by the end, there were enough people to have a good time.

The next show was at the Yandina Club, a small folk club on the Gold Coast. I found out, just before I had arrived, that my show was going to be the final show at the club as it was shutting down. Even though there was a bit of sadness in the air, with the club's staff and friends sharing their precious memories of the club's long history, as the evening progressed, it turned out to be a jolly good night.

The evening started off with two women, who had heard me on the radio, joining

Jan and me at our table. One woman said, "We have never come to a folk club before, but you sounded so interesting over the radio, that we had to see you in person." Then she went on and on about, "Why do you American's always yell "Yahoo" at every concert?" I was just beginning to explain this cultural phenomenon, when her girlfriend, started turning blue from choking on a chicken bone. Jan followed her to the toilet, while another woman ran in to give assistance. Luckily, there was also a woman who had some training as a nurse and she popped the bone out. Now, with everyone back in their seats, I jumped onto the stage and went to work. It was a great night, with lots of singing and, you guessed it, the two women who we sat with were drinking and yelling "Yahoo" the whole night through.

The next show, at the"Paddington Workers Club, had to be the best show of the whole trip. We had a good crowd and the good part of the folk community to boot. I was able to sing a batch of the old Union songs and fit in more of my political songs, so it made the night very special. The next day Colin was planning to put together a little party with the folk community. During daylight hours Colin, and his brother Tony, drove me around the town while we picked up a few things for the party. We made a run to the local fish shop. It was at the little shop that I made the mistake of saying, "So, are we going to throw another shrimp on the barbie, mate?" imitating the Paul Hogan commercial for Foster's beer on American television. "Shrimp?" Tony yelled out with his turned-up nose. "We don't call them shrimp unless they are tiny. Now look at this one, mate," pointing to a colossal specimen. "That's what we call a prawn, mate!"

Anyway, the party was a real good one. About forty-five people filled Colin's back-yard for food, song and merriment. The music was momentous, with local singers, and even Colin's brother, Tony, leading songs. Of course, Colin was having such a wonderful time that he did not want it to ever end but he did pay for it the next morning.

My last night was being a part of a little jam session over with my new friends at the Kookaburra Club. Everyone who was involved with my tour showed up and brought lots of their pals plus a few listeners who had heard me on Colin's radio show. It was an extraordinary evening with singers singing songs both old and new. There was such joviality in the room that evening that we sang on until the lights went out.

THE ALICE

It was a long flight into The Alice, but looking out my window at the endless miles of red sand, I could tell it was going to be worth it. When I got off the plane, the official Alice Springs' Welcome Wagon, (flies) came to welcome me in full force. These pesky little flies were all over us and, as we walked off the plane, we were swatting in every direction. At the airport, the daughter of my host was waiting to pick me up and in minutes I was off riding through the McDonald MT range over to my host, Ron's, house. On the ride, we discussed my schedule and all the radio shows I had to do.

We pulled up a long dirt driveway, into a little camp of houses. I put my stuff into one of the small houses then walked over to meet the other 'guests' of the ranch. They were two kangaroos, some beautiful birds and a two-year old camel named Charley. It seems that Charley was rescued, just in time, from a hungry aboriginal family, and given to Ron who made him a part of the family.

After checking my hat at the ranch, we headed off to the center of Alice Springs and the club, "Bojangle's," that I would be playing at for the next few days. Ron ,the owner, greeted me with a big smile, and a hot plate of freshly caught Baramundi fish. Then his daughter and I roamed the endless tourist shops that line Todd St. Later that night, Ron and I talked the whole night away, with stories about Alice Springs and Australia. Ron reminded me that the town of Alice Springs grew up when the Overland Telegraph line, which stretched from Adelaide to Darwin, set up a station at a little spring, in the middle of the outback, in 1872. The building of the telegraph station brought more settlers, prospectors and shops. Today The Alice is a little boomtown with modern malls, tourist shops, restaurants and hotels. It is also the home of the Royal Flying Doctor's Service and the School Of The Air. The School of the Air transmits lessons to students who live in the remote cattle stations that dot the out back, where the only teacher is a voice on the radio and your classroom is a lesson book set on a kitchen table. One of the colorful events that take place in town is the annual Henley-on-the-Todd Regatta. This colorful spectacle stages a madcap race in the dry bed of the Todd River. Participants make bottomless boats and use their legs to race down the riverbanks.

Ron loved his town and the longer he spoke of his marvelous home in the out-back, the happier I was to come here and experience it.

In the morning, a loud crying followed by a big snort woke me. It was Charley, the camel wanting some friendship. I walked over to the large fenced in area and Charley reached his long neck over the pen. Soon the two "roos" also came by to say hello. I found a great delight in meeting all my furry little buddies and found my self spending hours watching their playful antics. Soon a car arrived and I was whisked off to my inter-views. The first one was a quick in and out interview at the local commercial station, then we went back into town for the show that Jan had set up with the ABC. This was to be a live feed from Darwin and would reach throughout the whole Northern Territories. The show went off without a hitch, and I ended up doing about 45 minutes. Another long interview followed at the local community radio station and at the end of the interviews, calls came pouring in, one saying, "This is what radio should be."

In between my shows, I tried to sneak in a bit of sightseeing. The first thing I did was sign up for a one?day course at the Didgeridoo University of Central Australia. In this intensive course, an aboriginal teacher named Paul Ah Chee-Ngala gives students a chance to learn how to play the didg. As I had already had a few private lessons, I thought it would be interesting to also take this group course. The teacher, Paul, was very friendly and had a little different spin to his teachings. I found this course both relaxing and informative. Paul started the lessons by looking around the room and seeing that half of his students were women. He laughed and explained that in his culture women were not allowed to play the didgeridoo, or yidaki as he called it in the native tongue. He explained that many of the tribal rituals surrounding the didg had to do with the males coming of age and it was for that reason, and the mysticism behind these rituals, that woman did not play these instruments. Of course, since none of you here are aboriginal, this does not apply to you. Paul took great pleasure in making sure that everyone in our group under-stood the correct playing technique and gave his own view on mastering the difficulties of curricular breathing. He said that this is a skill that we all once knew but through time for-got. He said, "As young babies we all used a form a curricular breathing while we were breast?feeding." He laughed and encouraged us to just visualize the image of us being able to relearn this old skill. After his speech, he handed out a variety of wooden didgeri-doos and prompted us to start buzzing our lips into the mouthpiece. It did not take long until the whole room was filled with good vibrations.

After my lessons, I headed for a few hours on a camel safari. Camels were brought from Afghanistan to move goods and materials across the vast red desert sand. Huge car-avans of up to eighty camels once trekked across the hot sand and were the only link from the outside world. In 1929, the camels were replaced by the Central Australia Railroad, aptly named the "Ghan," and today are mostly used for tourism, giving the many visitors a chance to ride a camel through the outback.

It was just a short walk over to where the camels where waiting for the next batch of riders. The camels were stretched out in a long caravan, each one connected by a rope attached to a plug in their nose. Supposedly, the camel's nose is very sensitive and that makes the best way to control this huge animal. The camels were all sitting close to the ground when the camel driver helped us mount the saddle. Once everyone was in his sad-dle and the driver gave the command, the whole line of camels jumped up to their feet and we were off. I have heard the old saying of "riding high in the saddle" but had never experienced anything like this. You were so high in the sky that you were almost in the treetops. The camels walked from the ranch, into a dry riverbed, and carried us through miles of white gum trees, and down the sandy trail through the mountains. As I sat riding the big camel, I felt like I was in a strange dream and had to keep telling myself repeatedly that this was for real. Occasionally, my camel turned to face me and brought me right back to reality with a big burst of camel's breath, and there are few things on earth, that I can think of, that are as foul as camel's breath. All too soon, the ride ended and I watched as the caravan disappeared out into the desert.

My shows at Bojangle's were typical bar gigs, not a performance, so I went with the flow but my last show was a community jam, and I had a great time jamming with some of the folk community. It got some of the folkies out again and after the show they said, "We used to get together all the time, thanks for giving us a good excuse to play again." I really loved The Alice. I loved driving around in the old Land Rover, through the bright red hills and through the narrow canyons. I also loved the afternoon I spent on the camel safari, roaming through the dry Todd River bed in the desert sun. I know that I just have to return, perhaps next time fly the Outback mail run.

SYDNEY

Back when I was at Port Fairy, my friend Dave reminded me that when I reached Sydney I would be staying with his old girlfriend Leann. When my plane landed, Leann and her girlfriend Dani, were there to greet me. Needless to say, this was a completely different experience than staying in my little shack out in The Alice. Dani, a long, slender, blue-eyed gal with a pageboy hair cut, works as a Corporate Librarian and has a habit of lodging foreign young men. When I got there, she had three: two from England, one from Ireland, and now me from America. I guess the best way to describe this lifestyle, is like a dorm in a college. As you can imagine, the beer flowed like water and the nights lasted way into the wee hours.

One night, I decided to give a little concert for the household. Perhaps it was the beer, but before long we moved into the kitchen and I taught them a traditional Polish dance. So there we were jumping up and down and dancing to the Polish bagpipes 'til 3 o'clock in the morning. Good thing that there were no neighbors to complain. I had just a few radio interviews and one show to do so it gave me plenty of time to just hang out. One afternoon, Leanne took a group of us out to see The Three Sisters, in the Blue Mountains. It's a long drive from Sydney, but when you finally get there it's like a whole other world. The lush vegetation gives the mountains a bluish hue ,hence the name, but there are also three fantastic stone pinnacles that astound you. These magnificent peaks have a wonderful creation story. This aboriginal Dreamtime story tells of three beautiful daughters named Been, Wimlah and Gunnedoo, who lived in the Jamieson Valley with the Katoorma tribe. The daughters fell in love with three brothers from a neighboring tribe but were forbidden to marry because of tribal laws. The three brothers decided to take the maidens by force and declared war between the two tribes. When the battle broke out, and the women were seized, the witch doctor of the Katoomba tribe tried to save the girls by turning them into stone, hoping to return them to their natural form after the war. During the battle, the witch doctor was killed and no else knew how to break his magic spell. To this day the three beautiful maidens wait encased in stone until someone can free them.

Just like those sisters, I too felt, in a way, that I had fallen under a magic spell. The land and the people of Australia had bewitched me. I had only one more day here in this land of Oz and part of me wanted to stay on forever.

The last night I had a performance at the Resistance Club which was a real political hangout for The Green Party. When I entered the building, I was met by a huge painting of the Statue of Liberty with her eye poked out and blood running down her face. Despite the horrendous first impression, the club's clientele were friendly and I met some very interesting folk.

Leann's parents drove down to see me perform, as did a few other friends, so it was kind of my farewell concert. We did not get in 'til very late and with a bit of melancholy we had another round of drinks and toasted our friendship.

The next morning Leann drove me to the airport and helped me check my instruments into the plane. Then after a few cups of coffee, a few hugs and a sad so long and good bye, I climbed aboard that big plane bound for home.

FUN AT THE BOSTON INTERNATIONAL FESTIVAL

A few years ago, I was asked to perform at the huge Boston International Festival held at the Bayside Expo Center. A nice woman, I had met at another show decided to sponsor my performance in memory of her Polish mother. Arriving in Boston, I found myself walking into the gargantuan convention center to entertain about 8000 high school students. At one show I had to follow a fashion show with my Polish bag pipes and I found it almost an impossible task, when the models turned up with see-through blouses and no underwear.

Now, I have had to follow a lot of crazy acts in my time, but trying to go on and play music by squeezing a dead goat to a mob of teenagers, who were just exposed to a bunch of young risque models, proved to be quite a task, not to mention the screaming of the outraged teachers and parents. If this was not enough, later the organizers scheduled me to appear live on the NBC's WBZ evening news with a few other artists including a 40 piece Indonesian Gamelan. It all started well enough, the first group, Inca Son, did their performance without a hitch. Then, when the host came over to interview me and had the camera man filming my hands as I played the bag pipes. That's when it turned into a musical noisy display.

In the middle of the shot, one Indonesian man must have been a bit nervous and dropped his mallet onto his gamelan. All at once his band mates looked at him as if he had given the signal to begin. In a flash, the whole gamelan took off in a cacophony of bells, pings and pongs. Dancers in full regalia started prancing out and fanned across the stage while singers darted out and began singing at full volume. All of this occurred, of course, while the cameraman was still filming me. Hearing the mix of Polish bagpipes and Indonesian gamelan was just too weird and everyone just started laughing. The TV host just lost it and broke out laughing too, saying to her viewers, "Well, it's live TV!"

"HEY EVERYBODY, IT'S POLKA TIME!"

One of the strangest gigs I ever did had to be the weekend I was booked at Donald Trump's Taj Mahal in Atlantic City for a Polish Polka weekend. It drew, no fooling, over 40,000 people and had nonstop polka music from 9 A.M. 'til 11 P.M.

The big star was Jan Lewan and his band, but there were about ten other bands during the day. I was hired to play my Polish pipes and try to give polka fans a more folk roots presentation in this gala of polka music and Polish cultural appreciation. Every day I played a few hours in between a gaggle of loud polka bands in a non stop show starting at nine in the morning and ending at eleven at night. On the last day's final performance, for the grand finale, all the performers, polka bands, me and my Polish sheep dog, Koza, were called up to do a tribute to our armed forces.

Surrounded by a wall of trumpets, saxophones, accordions and clarinets, we blasted out "The Marine's Hymn," "The Caisson Song," "Off We Go Into the Wild Blue Yonder," "Anchors Aweigh," "America," and "God Bless America." Just when I thought I was lost in a patriotic frenzy, with flags waving and red white and blue streamers raining down from the ceiling, a familiar tune came blasting out of the lead trumpeter horn. It was Woody Guthrie's song, "This Land Is Your Land." Like an old friend paying you a surprise visit, this old melody roared out from the polka bands coming like a prayer from the heavens, and filled the room. with the true spirit of what America means to me.

As I stood on the stage, blinded by the bright spotlights, I could almost see the images in Woody's song; the wheatfields of Kansas, the mighty Pacific Ocean, the rolling Oklahoma hills and the Statue of Liberty standing in New York harbor. As the song intensified, with ten polka bands joining in, on the stage, Koza's skin quivered and shook from the sheer energy and raw power as Woody's spirit came shining through.

LOT AIRLINES. POLAND AND BEYOND

While I was on my school tour, I kept telling the schools to send their thank you cards, letters and drawings to the main office of LOT Polish Airlines, as they had sponsored my last tour. Little did I realize that kids from all over America were writing to LOT and thanking them with pictures and letters, until they filled an entire filing cabinet! While I was still out on the road, the LOT sales department head tracked me down. Mr.

Ziebinski, who was my main supporter with the company, was overwhelmed with the response I was getting from the children. He said, "Ryki, I don't know what you are doing out there, but, it is working to get people interested in Poland and we could use your kind of enthusiasm in building our next year's tour."

Mr. Ziebinski set up another appointment for us to get together, at LOT's main head quarters, in New York, during my winter break. Mr. Ziebinski was happy to see me again and even showed me some of the letters that the children were sending. " Now," he said, "We have talked it over and have decided it would be a good thing for you to help us plan out an ultimate tour of Poland. You have contacts that no one else has, plus a vast knowledge of the folk culture. Of course we understand that it will take time for you to organize this tour, but we are willing to help you and give you anything that you may need." Mr. Ziebinski then handed me a plane ticket and said, "See if you can go to Poland during your vacation, and make a few contacts." He smiled and said, "This will be the first of many such trips, so you will be seeing a lot of Poland."

It did not take long to get everything in order and get on the big Polish jumbo jet and head back to the old country. Once, I was back in Poland I went right to work. I knew that this was an important tour not only to teach Americans about the wealth of Polish folklore that still exists, but also to help out my friends. After the Berlin Wall came down it brought rapid changes to the entire Soviet Bloc countries. When they gained their freedom and autonomy they lost any kind of support that was provided for the arts. When the Soviets were in power, they provided a healthy atmosphere for the folk arts. They sponsored festivals, concerts, dance groups and even raw materials needed to create folk crafts. Now, with their support gone, many of the artists were just starting to feel the pain. One of my hopes for my tour was that it would create a new market for their work while putting a few dollars into their pockets. My idea of an arts tour that supported the artists had a certain appeal to it. Most of my friends were intrigued and agreed to participate. After traveling around Poland for a few weeks I had all the contacts I needed to make Ryki's Polish Folk Arts Tour come to life.

MERRILY KISS THE QUAKER

As my flight returned to Montreal, Marianna was on her way to pick me up at the airport. Once I landed it was a quick drive to the US-Canadian border.
When we went through custom's, the American customs agent was asking a few questions about who we were, our nationality and reasons for coming to Canada. As he looked me over he asked if we were related. Immediately Marianna piped up with a smile, "He is my fiance." The official smiled and waved us on. We both laughed as we drove into Vermont realizing that this was the first mention of our getting married. On the way home I asked

Marianna, "Do you really want to marry me?" She laughed and said, "Well, I told it to the customs guard, so I guess it's official."

After I completed my year's school tour, Marianna and I began to plan out our wedding. We decided to keep it simple, by holding it at a local Quaker meetinghouse, but also decided it would be fun to give it an ethnic flair. In our invitations we explained how music, dance and traditions were essential to our lives and in keeping with that spirit invited our guests to dress in clothing that in some way reflected their own cultural background. The wedding was simply beautiful, with friends and family coming from near and far to celebrate our marriage. The night before the wedding both Marianna's family, and mine, gathered for a pre-nuptial party. Besides our relatives, a small group of my Polish friends came all the way from Chicago to join in the festivities. My mother at first was not in the ethnic mood, but once she heard my friends playing the sweet melodious melodies from the land of her ancestors, she broke into tears and danced around the room. That night I went to sleep at a friend's apartment and would not see Marianna 'til she arrived at the old Quaker meetinghouse.

While Marianna prepared herself, my family also was getting ready for the big event. I wanted to have many of the old Polish wedding rituals in our wedding, so I not only dressed in my Polish outfit from Istebna but had enough Polish costumes to fit both my dad and two sisters. My mother had told me that she was not going to wear any old Polish folk costume and that she had already bought a nice dress for the occasion, so I was surprised to see that she had procured Tina's dress on the morning of the wedding. When I asked her about it, she said "When I heard that music from Poland, I knew that I just had to wear this outfit!" Tina understood and luckily brought along another dress.

Even though my father is half Polish, he really did not know much about the culture. He was surprised when I handed him the heavy wool pants and overcoat of the Gorali and told him to put it on. Later, when we all entered the churchyard we made quite a scene with our colorful outfits of embroidered wool, satin and beadwork. When some of my friends saw my father they said, "You look great. Do you wear this often?" Of course my dad said, "Oh yes, we wear them all the time!"

While we were busy greeting the guests, Marianna and her family showed up. Marianna was dressed in a blue Swiss styled dress made by one of the Von Trapp family, Her long hair reached almost to her knees and was topped off with a crown of flowers with long silk ribbons hanging down her back. She was a beautiful bride!

Our whole wedding party looked like something out of an old movie with Marianna's sister dressed in an eastern European dance outfit. Our friends Tom and Monica, and our friends from Chicago, were dressed in Polish outfits plus many others dressed in colorful vests, shirts and hats, all linking them back to their own ancestors.

We also tried to incorporate a few very Old World traditions by carrying a ring of rue, a Polish wedding herb, and having our wedding party arrive in a horse-drawn wagon.

After the Quaker wedding, we all headed back home to ride in the wagon to the reception that was held in a friend's barn just a few miles from our house. It rained a bit while we rode over to the reception but by the time we pulled into Jean's barn, to the sound of our Polish band, the rain stopped and a little rainbow appeared over the farm. While the fiddlers sawed away, Marianna and I stood in the wagon while our friends and family toasted to our future.

The reception was almost like a mini festival, with Tom playing his Polish bagpipes, Sean Folsom, playing hurdy-gurdy, and almost every kind of bagpipe that you could think of. Besides the piping there was storytelling, harp playing and an evening contra dance that had almost a different caller for each dance and more than ten fiddlers.

The whole day was amazing! We were so happy and knew that we were just at the beginning of a long life together. A few weeks after our wedding, we were off to our honeymoon. Well, it was not just the two of us, it was more like eighteen people, as we went off to lead my very first tour of Polish Folk Arts.

RYKI'S POLISH FOLK ARTS TOUR

We had been working on my tour for months, getting out ads, and even doing a little TV commercial to help create interest in the tour. By midsummer we were able to attract eighteen people, just the number we needed to make it happen.

In planning out my tour, I wanted it to be the ultimate tour of Polish folklore, the kind of tour where everything that you wanted to see and learn, would all take place in the span of a two week period. Even though I had set up the tour, with my limited language skills I needed help to carry out my vision. LOT provided a very knowledgeable tour guide named Kasia, to help me coordinate all the activities. Kasia was young and vivacious. She loved to have a good time and had an interest in Polish music and dance. She also knew more about the history of the country than I would ever learn in a life time. In short, she was a perfect fit to complete our objective.

When our first trip came to life in 1992, we were met at the airport by our tour guide and a folk group dressed in full regional regalia. The band welcomed us with song, dance and the traditional greeting of bread and salt. As our group of Americans all danced to the sound of the big accordion in the busy airport terminal, they realized that this was not going to be just another tour of Poland, it was something completely unique.

It did not take our tour participants very long to start relaxing and sort of slip into the shoes and souls of the Polish people. In my plan, each stop on our tour was in some way connected with Polish folk arts. Sometimes it would be in the interest of music, art or dance. In some cases, the place itself was part of the folklore tradition. In these stops our tour guide would often read us the old folk tale connected with the city we were visiting.

My tours continued from 1992-1996, each of them having their own special memorable moments. Rather than give you a detailed tourist's itinerary, I thought it would better to give you a few of my personal highlights and share with you why I think that these areas are so important to Polish folklore and culture.

WARSAW

As my Folk Arts tour both began and ended in Warsaw, I will give you a little taste of the capital city of Poland. But before I get into the city itself, I thought I would share with you one of the stories that tells of how the city found its name;

THE LEGEND OF THE WARSAW MERMAID
(BASED ON AN OLD FOLK TALE)

Long ago, there lived a beautiful mermaid named Zawa. She had deep green eyes, long blond hair, green scales, a leathery tail, fins and the voice of an angel. She was said to live in a palace made of amber deep in the Baltic Sea. One day, she swam down the mighty Wisla River, sat on a large rock, and sang as she combed her silky hair. Two poor peasants saw this lovely creature and thought they should try to capture her and bring her to the king, for there would surely be a large purse of gold for a gift as wondrous as a mermaid. Knowing that the mermaid's voice might entrance them they stuffed beeswax into their ears so that they could not hear her, then threw a large net over the rock and caught their prize. As they had a long way to travel to reach the king's castle they looked for a place where they might be able to rest for the night. They came across a little house with a barn right alongside the river.
The house was owned by a young fisherman named Wars.
The fisherman had just finished docking his boat, when the two peasants approached him about lodging for the night.
When he spotted the unusual fish they were carrying in their net. Wars asked with wonder, "Now, what kind of fish is that?"
The two peasants told Wars about their prized mermaid and asked him if he wanted to see her. As one of the peasants pulled the netting away from the mermaid's face, tiny iridescent

tears flowed down from her emerald green eyes. As Wars looked
upon the helpless mermaid his heart broke and he immediately
fell in love with her.

As the two scoundrels boasted that they were going to take her to
the king and collect and handsome reward, Wars was already thinking
of how he could outwit them and help out the young girl. As
everyone made plans for a good night's sleep, Wars offered to stand
guard over the barn. The two peasants plugged up their ears and gave
the fisherman a lump of wax to fill his ears, for they knew that without
stuffing their ears, they would be enchanted by her seductive singing.
While the two peasants slept, the mermaid sang to the young fisherman
who was watching her from outside the barn. In her song, Zawa begged
him for her freedom. Wars could not resist her haunting melody and
released her from the net and carried her to the river. As Zawa swam
away she cried out to Wars, "I have tried to live with the people of the
land, but they have disappointed me, but you, Wars, have saved me and
returned me to my home in the sea. Though I must leave now, I will
return whenever your home is threatened and if need be, will defend
it with my own sword and shield."

She pointed to a bank of land up the river. Using her powers to see
into the future, she said "I can see that someday they will build a great
city, here on the banks of the river that will remember your courage and
bravery, and my love for Poland by giving this town our name," and then
she swam away. Years later just as the mermaid had predicted a great city
was built and it did bear their names, Wars-zawa.

This is just one version of the old tale, there are many more, with some telling that
Wars and Zawa later married and their children became the original inhabitants of Warsaw.
Just like the tale of the mermaid, the city of Warsaw has its own history of tragedy, love
and hope. Through the centuries the city has had both a colorful and turbulent history. As
it would, literally, take me writing another book just to tell you about Warsaw's place in history, I will instead concentrate on its place on our Folk Arts Tour.

Though there is a lot to see, learn and experience in Warsaw, we spent most of our
time seeking out the places that most exemplified its rich folk arts history. One of the
best ways to start our education was to spend a morning at the ethnographic museum. The
museum has a vast collection of folk crafts, costumes and musical instruments.

I wanted us to get a good background of the Polish Folk Culture and this huge
collection was a great way to educate our tourists to the wealth of Polish folk arts. As I

listened to the group "ooh and ah" over the exhibits, I knew the very things that they were excited about in the museum would soon be a part of their special folk encounter. But instead of seeing them behind glass they would be experiencing them as part of a living tradition.

LOWICZ

The city of Lowicz is only a few hours ride from Warsaw, but it is a world away from the bustling city streets of Poland's capital city.

In the center of town is the regional museum. The museum complex consists of a large museum combined with a few historic houses filled with regional folk arts. In the main building there are many examples of the traditional style of architecture, woodcarvings and a huge collection of Lowicz weaving and costumes.

Up until the 19th century, woven fabrics only came in one color and were made on hand looms. The weavers of Lowicz soon developed new techniques to add a rainbow of colors to their woolens and linens. Their regional folk clothing is a fine example of combining fabric and decorative embroidery, to create one of the most striking costumes in all of Poland. Like many other regions, the citizens of this area only wore their outfits primarily on Sundays, holidays, weddings or other special occasions. While the notion of wearing folk costumes is dying out in most of Poland, in Lowicz it is still quite common to see both women and men wearing their colorful outfits early Sunday morning walking their way to church. Besides the colorful regional costumes this area is also noted for another very unique folk art called wycinanki. This art form is constructed by folding brightly colored glazed paper into symmetrical designs, cut out with large sheep shears.

The craft came in the 1850's, when the peasants would decorate their homes for the coming of spring. During the long winters, the women would often spend hours cutting out delicate images of roosters, flowers and scenes of everyday life. In preparation for Easter, they would whitewash the walls and then paste their cutouts onto the walls, ceilings and chimney covers. During spring the houses of Lowicz were often a blaze of color. They would leave their wycinanki up all year long and then next spring whitewash over them and put up new designs.

In between the time of the first and Second World War, wallpaper became available and the need for wallcovering declined. After the Second World War the Soviets encouraged the people to continue their folk traditions. Wycinanki took on a new life with contest, competitions and schools to teach the skill and increase the appreciation for the art form. In many towns regional folk arts stores were built so that they could sell their wares. Soon tourists from all over the globe were decorating their homes with Polish paper cutouts and the work of skilled artists was highly sought after.

Our mission on my Folk Arts Tour was not only to view and appreciate folk arts, but to really get a hands-on experience by creating our own folk arts. We were lucky over the years to have a few of America's finest paper cutters; Carolyn Guest from Vermont and Judith Myers from Colorado, on our tour. Both Carolyn and Judy were fascinated by the Polish papercutters and not only participated in the papercutting workshops but also gave away samples of their own work. As I watched the interaction between the Polish and American artists, I could see that all my work was well worth the efforts for we were all experiencing the true gift of multi-cultural exchange.

POZNAN, THE LAND OF GOATS AND BAGPIPES

Even though the modern city of Poznan is the home base for a huge International trade show it also is an area filled with historic buildings and folklore and contains one of the oldest and most picturesque squares in all of Poland. It is on this square in the old town hall that another old folk tale grew.

Legends say that many years ago, two goats had a battle, locking horns on these very steps. The goats caused such excitement that a huge crowd had gathered to watch their antics. As the goats fought, someone had noticed that the building had caught fire. With the large crowd already assembled it was easy to put out the blaze and save the town from destruction. To commemorate that event the town's people later erected a large animated clock, at the top of its tower. Even today, when the clock rings in the hour, two doors swing open and reveal two wooden goats that butt their heads together. The mechanical goats are a reminder of the two heroic goats that helped save the city, so many years ago.

Just a short walk from the town hall is the Museum of Musical Instruments. The museum contains one of the finest collections of musical instruments in Europe. The collection is full of instruments from around the world, priceless old violins, brass instruments and a special room of instruments and memorabilia once owned by Fredric Chopin. While we were taking our tour, we were surprised to hear our guide tell us that the violin has its roots deep in Polish soil. He went on to say that around the same time of the celebrated violin craftsmen of Italy, there were also some very noted Polish violinmakers in the city of Krakow. Even some scholars suggest that perhaps the present day violin may be more of a Polish innovation then we realize.

The collection that was of special interest to our tour was the room filled with Polish folk instruments. We able to get a personal tour by the museum's curator, followed by an evening of Polish bagpipe pipe music from a local group. Of all the bagpipes in Poland, this region's instrument is probably the most popular. Every few years the city hosts a bagpipe festival that can attract up to a hundred pipers. As I had already met a few of the local pipers, I was able to arrange a little concert for my tour. My group was amazed as four pipers entered the room dressed in the regional costume. There were three men dressed in bright red coats with black hats, boots and pants, and a lovely young girl dressed in a colorful dress and a large lace-like headdress. The pipers entertained us for about an hour and then I was asked to join them. I quickly left my seat and strapped on the bellows and, to the amazement of my group, played along with these pipers as if I had known them all my life.

ISTEBNA

It was a long bumpy ride through the mountain roads to reach my friends in Istebna. When we arrived, my teacher, Jozef Broda, was there to greet us with his group of young children. As I stepped off the bus Jozef's voice rang out with my favorite song "Groniczki." It was in Istebna that we really got away from all the typical trappings of a group tour by staying not in a hotel, but in tiny little wooden huts.

The next day, we spent at the cottage of Jan Kawoulok's, listening to his daughter Suzanna play all the instruments that her late father had made. Our tour marveled as Suzanna demonstrated a wide variety of flutes, whistles, bagpipes and the long wooden trumpet. I was filled with personal pride for being able to bring my tour group to meet the very best of the traditional artists.

ISTEBNA WEDDING

Later that evening we had something very special in store for our tour group. They were going to attend a mock wedding, complete with traditional music dance and food. Two members of our group would play the role of bride and groom, and go through all of the old wedding traditions.

As ours was just a mock wedding, I thought it would be more interesting to describe a real Polish Highlander wedding that I was once invited to. It was back during one of my planning trips that I was invited by one of the young boys, Stash, from Jozef's dance group, to his wedding and I just could not resist.

The day started early with all of the groom's friends and relatives gathering at his parent's house. While the groom was getting ready, his family passed around food and drink, then all circled 'round him as his parents laid down a large tablecloth on the floor. Stash kneeled on the cloth as his mother and father brushed a twig of an evergreen tree across his forehead to remind him of the mountains and forests where he was raised. Then they kissed him on the cheek three times, as is the custom, then wished him well as he went on his new life.

After the little ceremony, the groom's family, accompanied by a little brass band, headed in the direction of the bride's home. As the cars honked their horns along the narrow back dirt roads, they were often met by a very strange sight. The family of the bride would barricade the road with a crazy assortment of baby carriages and dolls. The bride's family, who were all dressed in masks, would demand a kind of tariff before they would let the groom's family through. In order for the wedding party to pass they would have to give their new relatives a bottle of special vodka that has a label that has been prepared just for this occasion, marked with the wedding couple's names and date. After getting passed by the bride's relatives, the groom's family made their way to the house of the bride.

The home of the bride was easy to spot as it was decorated with a pretty floral arrangement arched around the doorway. When we reached the front door, the groom asked the band to play until the father of the bride appeared. When the door opened the bride's father appeared to be not interested in letting him in.

Bride's Father: "So what do you want?"
Groom's father: "Why, can't you see that we are all in our best clothes and have brought this wonderful band of musicians because we have come to marry your daughter?"
The bride's father (laughing): "Your clothes look shabby and the band sounds out of tune." Then he slams the door!
The groom's father knocks harder on the door 'til the bride's father opens it again.
The father of the groom tells the bride's father that his family and friends have traveled far to come to his house and celebrate this happy day, why we even have a guest from America. (At that moment I step forward and tip my big Stetson.)
Bride's father says (smiling): "Oh you have important guests" as he invites us into the house.

Once inside, we experienced another old time tradition - the "buying of the bride." In this old ritual, the groom's father had to pay the father of the bride a sum of money before she will enter the room. After the money was collected, the father went into the back room and brought out a little girl who was dressed in white holding a bouquet of flowers. As the bewildered guests laughed, the bride's father called out, "You see, if you give me only a small amount of money then you only will get a little bride!" Laughter filled the room then quickly hushed as the young girl recited poetry. In her beautiful poem she tells that she is not the bride, but someday she hopes to grow up to be as lovely as the bride is today. After the young girl was finished with her poem, the father passed around the big plate to gather even more wedding money. This time when the door opened, it was still not the bride, it was the bridesmaid. As the laughter continued, the bride's father snatched the young girl off her feet and held her in the air proclaiming, "This one is for me, but she is not the bride." Yet again, the plate collected even more money until everyone's pockets were empty. Now, that the bride's father was satisfied, he opened the kitchen door revealing the blushing, beautiful young bride.

When the bride entered the room she was dressed in white with her hair hanging loose and decorated with tiny little flowers. This goes back to old days when, on the night before the wedding, the bride's girlfriends would unbraid the bride's long locks (braids were considered a symbol of maidenhood) and tied her hair with long ribbons making the transition to married life.

As she reached the center of the room her parents spread out a large blanket on the floor, thus repeating the old mountain custom and giving their blessing to the marriage. Then the entire wedding party was led to the nearby the church by the beat of the little brass band.

After the religious church ceremony, the whole wedding party went over to hall in the firehouse, where the reception was being held. In the old days, a Polish wedding would last three days, have at least a hundred guests and they would consume at least five hundred bottles of vodka. While this wedding didn't last quite that long, we did consume an awful lot of vodka. As this was a traditional wedding, the bride and the groom were not dressed in modern day wedding clothes, while many of the guests and the band all dressed in the traditional clothes of Istebna. After many hours of songs and dances, the bride gathers around her old girlfriends and her new female relatives for another old custom.

In the old days, near the end of the wedding party, the bride's girlfriends would sing her the last songs of maidenhood, while, her new relatives would shear off her long hair. Once her hair was shorn, they would fit her with the customary lace cap and headscarf of a married woman. Today this ritual is performed in the spirit of good-natured fun, with the bride fighting her way from her friends, refusing to put on the cap and leaving her hair alone.

During our mock wedding, we went through many of the same old rituals including a traditional style wedding feast. we hoisted our newlyweds up to the ceiling in two wooden chairs and sang the song all Poles love to sing "Sto Lat." (One Hundred Years)

UNDER THE DEVIL'S HOOF

One trip, we decided to eat at a very unusual hunter's cabin. Almost from the minute we got there, calamity was in the air. Many of my group were losing their balance and falling to the ground, while others had headaches and even were arguing with each other. As I was just about to tell our bus driver to move on to another restaurant, the owner caught me just before we pulled away. The owner apologized, but then explained what were really experiencing; "When I first bought this house, I heard many stories from the local people about the house and its first owner. You see, this cottage is very old. It once belonged to a hunter who was said to have been possessed by the devil. He actually hung himself from that very roof. From that day on, everyone who bought this house has had problems."

There are even stories that the devil himself would often appear on the roof and bang his hooves while he engaged in his mischief. There are also tales of priests who came here to remove the devil's power only to have him return his vengeance by sending a bolt of lighting from the sky. Of course, at first I did not believe these stories and thought they were just old folk tales. Then as my little restaurant became a tourist attraction, I too saw that perhaps these stories were true after all. It was when the restaurant was doing very well that, from out of nowhere, a bolt of lighting hit the roof and the cottage caught fire. We had to work hard and fast to save the building from total destruction, and we did manage to save most of the old cottage. After the fire, I began to seriously look into and research some of the old stories.

While I was doing my research I came across a book of regional folklore that contained some information about my old hunter's cottage. At the very end of the story it said, "There is only one true way to rid the cottage of the devil's power. You must put a rooster or cock at the top of the roof. As everyone knows, the devil fears the rooster, and at once, upon seeing it, he will stamp his hooves on the roof." He continued the part of the story that really interested me. "The legend says that as the devil stamps his hooves, silver coins will pour out onto the roof and then he will be gone."

"So you see my friends, if you look at the top of my roof you will see the symbol of a large rooster. Since the day that I put up the rooster this restaurant has been very successful. And, if you are wondering about the silver coins, you might say those coins keep rolling in!"

After the owner concluded his fantastic story, he said, "Now, my friends, come and please join us for a wonderful meal of fresh trout broiled over a hot fire." Our whole troop bounced out of the bus. They each grabbed a stick and a freshly caught trout and roasted it over a small grill. After we had finished our meal, I heard many of the tourists say "It is not that often that you get a chance to eat at a haunted house."

DANCING AROUND THE CAMPFIRE

I had invited all of the town musicians to visit and, much to my delight, everyone was able to come. All day long the women of Istebna kept busy, making the special foods for our party like fresh kielbasa, hand made pirogue, potato pancakes, glumpki and a batch of Highlander tea spiked with strong vodka. By nightfall, the fire was lit and from all corners of the woods came my musician friends, playing their fiddles, bagpipes and accordions. Even Jozef brought along his long trumpeta and blasted out a signal that rang through out the hillsides.

For me it was like a dream come true to be back with my friends and listening to the music that I love. As my friends heard of Marianna's and my wedding, they gave her a traditional village costume as a wedding present and asked her if she would honor them by wearing it tonight. Marianna disappeared with some of the young girls and in a few minutes returned looking as if she had lived here all her life. She looked radiant dressed as a Goralka and showed my friends that I had made an excellent choice as she effortlessly danced with them round the campfire.

The party lasted 'til the wee hours of the morning and by the time it was over, every drop of vodka was gone and many of celebrants just fell asleep right where they stood. By the next morning, yours truly woke up with one of the worst hangovers that I had ever experienced. To top things off we left Istebna in the early hours to visit, of all things, a brewery! Needless to say it was a long hard day.

ZAKOPANE

I have been fascinated with this town since my very first trip to Poland back in 1980. I love everything about this colorful town, the hand-hewn log houses, the panoramic Tatra Mountains and the fantastic music.

As I have made friends with many musicians in this area, they agreed to give my group a personal tour. Ironically, it was not in Poland that I met my friends, but right in my own living room. Back when I lived in Poland in 1984, I kept hearing about a master piper named Tomek Skupien. Though I never had the chance to meet him, I did have a Polish friend write to me an introduction to Tomek just in case our paths ever crossed. A few years later a group from this region came to play at a festival in Vermont and stayed at my house. As these fine musicians were from the same town as Tomek I thought it would be worth a try to ask if they knew this legendary Polish piper. After a few minutes of showing them around my house, I hunted up that old piece of paper and handed one of them my note. The musician, whose name was Mietek, laughed as he passed the note on to another fellow, who was more or less the leader of the ensemble. To my surprise he stepped forward and tipped his hat and said, "I am Tomek Skupien."

That was the beginning of my friendship with Tomek and all of the members of the Bartusia Obrochty. After our initial meeting I was later invited to visit them back in their homeland. Through the years, Tomek and his friends taught me about their style of music, instruments and folklore, and even made me a beautiful set of Polish bagpipes. When my friends heard that now I was putting on this folk tour they said, "No problem Ryki, we will take care of everything," and they did.

On the day of our arrival, Mietek met us at the hotel and arranged to travel on our bus to our first destination, the popular tourist area known by the Poles as Morskie Oko or the Eye of the Sea. Mietek was very knowledgeable about the region's folklore and history. He gave us his own personal tour, as we rode along up the tall mountainside. "Since the late 1870's, travelers from all over Europe have come to the Tatras to get a taste of its gray-bluish, jagged mountain cliffs and colorful and exuberant folklore. He told us, "At one time, only shepherds lived in the area. They would bring their flocks to graze in the high mountain meadows, producing wool and make a special type of cheese called Oszczypek, prized by us mountaineers. Eventually this area became an artist colony, then a tourist town that attracted people from all over the world, to hike and ski in our magnificent Tatra Mountains."

As our bus stopped, we were directed by Kasia to follow her to the long wagons that were waiting on the side of the road, for this is as far as the paved road would take us. There is something very relaxing about riding in a wagon. Perhaps it is just the clip-clop of the horse's hooves or just the slow pace, but what ever it is, it is a fine way to travel. The wagon trip lasted about an hour 'til it we arrived at an absolutely gorgeous blue mountain lake surrounded by the magnificent stony needle-like peaks of the high Tatras.

The mountaineers call it the Eye of the Sea referring to an ancient legend of a long tunnel that once connected it to the Adriatic Sea. We spent a few hours admiring the beautiful panoramic view of the rugged Tatra Mountains then started on the long way back. Much to our surprise the wagon only went one way, so we would have to hike the trails to get back down. It was a beautiful hike. As we walked along the trail, we saw bursts of sunshine flooding through the tall trees, deer, wild mountain flowers and even edelweiss, a flower that one only expects to find in the Alps. By sundown, we had made the long trek down the tall mountain and boarded our bus for our evening dinner and a concert hosted by my friends from the dance group.

We were met at the restaurant by a group of Gorali fiddlers, who were playing a greeting song, as we made our way inside the thick wooden walled building. After we sat down, we were treated to a whole evening of culture and fun from our mountaineer friends. The dancers and musicians were all decked out for the occasion; the men were dressed in a heavy white wool cape called a cucha, wool pants with colorful embroidery running down the front pockets, (These designs are called Parzenica. They are somewhat like the Scottish tartan plaids, for many regions and even families have distinct patterns), and leather moccasins called kierpce, a broad rimmed hat decorated with sea shells and an eagle's feather sticking out from the red leather hat band. The women, not to be outdone by the men, wore sparkly vests made of colorful beads and sequins, bright flowered dresses, coral beads around their neck, white lacy blouses and leather moccasins tied around their feet.

Bartusia Obrochty began their program with a variety of regional songs and dance. The music was so lively that just about everyone in our group released their inhibitions and headed straight for the dance floor. The party went on for hours 'til everyone was practically floating in vodka and beer. Near the end of the evening, my friend Mietek summoned me to come forward and to my delight placed a bagpipe in my hand. As this pipe was a mouth blown pipe that I had not had much experience with, I struggled to get out a tune. My friends, noticing my difficulty, struck up the band and, with their support, I was able to regain my confidence and made them proud by playing one of the fast bagpipe tunes of the region. I think we could have stayed there all night but as everything must come to an end, so did this wonderful day.

RAFTING DOWN THE DUNAJEC

Not too far from Zackopane is the Dunajec River, in the valley of the Pieniny Mountains. For centuries, river men have used wooden rafts to pole their way up and down the shallow riverbed. The rafts are long log-like boats that are lashed together with heavy rope.

On each long raft is a river man who guides and poles you down the narrow riverbanks. Like the Gorali of Zakopane, these river men are also dressed in their distinctive attire. The mountaineers of this region often wear a bright blue vest covered in highlander embroidery and also sport the same bowl-like cap of the Gorali. They sometimes even suggest that the seashells often worn around the crown of their hat come from the old stories of river men who traveled all the way to the sea and picked up the shells as a memento of their long journey.

While we were riding along, our guide was spinning out the tale of a famous highwayman named Janosik. Even though he is originally from Slovakia, many of his exploits are said to have taken place right in this area. It is with great pride that this region boasts of his heroic exploits. It was back centuries ago when this one-time shepherd came from Slovakia and crossed the Tatra. He was said to be extremely handsome with long dark hair and a large moustache. Legend has it that he became a highwayman after he experienced the cruelty of the noblemen to their peasants. In his quest to right the wrongs of the petty gentry, he would rob them in a Robin Hood-like manner, giving the money back to the poor. As his legend grew he became a mythical figure.

One story tells of how the witches endowed him with magical powers by giving him a red shirt that would make him invisible, and a belt that would enable him to leap across the high gorges. With his magical tricks he was always able to outwit his adversaries. At one point of the raft ride, the rivermen often refer to a huge gorge that Janosik was said to have been able to leap across and gain entry from Poland to Slovakia. Sad to say, like many of the old Polish tales, this one too does not have a happy ending. Janosik was finally captured and hung from a meathook when his girlfriend betrayed him. But his sprit lives in these mountains and you feel his soul every time you see and hear the Gorali's (Polish mountaineers') music.

KRAKOW, THE CITY OF THE DRAGON

Legends say that when Poland was a very old nation, it was besieged by all kinds of mythical creatures; mermaids, gargoyles and even fire-breathing dragons. Such is the tale I am about to spin. It was long ago, where the city of Krakow now stands, that there was once a terrible dragon. All of the people who settled nearby were frightened by its power. The dragon was said to be a huge green monster with thick scales, able to breathe fire, and to have a taste for the flesh of young maidens. The men of the village tried to kill the beast, but their spears and swords were no match against its thick leathery skin.

One day a shoemaker's apprentice named "Krak," who also had the knowledge of a chemist, arrived at the village and said that he had a plan to destroy the dragon. At first, no one believed that he would be able to defeat such a mighty dragon, but they decided to give him a chance.

Krak asked for a sheep, and a bag of sulfur. At once, he went to work smearing the sheep with sulfur and magic potions. Later that night he placed it just outside of the dragon's lair. When the dragon saw the sheep he pounced on it and gobbled it up in one big bite. It did not take long for the sulfur to react with the fire in its belly, sending it straight to the river to get a drink. When the dragon drank the water, it reacted with the sulfur and he began to swell and swell until the dragon exploded! Once the dragon was killed the townspeople were so impressed with his courage, valor and intelligence that they invited him to be their new ruler. Eventually, they built a fortress above the old dragon's den and named the city Krakow after their brave ruler. Today, at the very bottom of the castle, you can still see what is thought to be the dragon's lair complete with a true fire-breathing monument that pays tribute to the old legend.

The Wawel castle has stood for over 500 years and has been one of the centers of Polish cultural life. Inside the walls of the castle are tombs of many Polish kings, queens, poets and national heroes. Kosciuzko, Poiniatowki, Pilsudski, the poet Michkiewich and many more are all laid to rest behind its massive walls. Not far from the Wawel is a large city square that reminds one of the plazas in Italy, with its flagstone market place, flower carts and pigeons. It was known as one of the largest squares in medieval Europe.

One of the biggest attractions is the old medieval cloth hall. This huge complex is a shopper's Mecca, lined with booths filled with amber, dolls, costumes and folk arts. It is also just a great place to sit and relax over a hot cup of coffee and watch the world go by.

Another famous building in the square is the Mariacki church. The church is one of the finest examples of Gothic architecture in the country. Every day a trumpet sounds from the top of one of its two towers. This haunting melody known as the "Hajnal" is a reminder of a Tartar invasion and it honors the brave watchman who was killed while sounding the alarm. The melody stops abruptly in remembrance of the exact moment that the Tartar's arrow took the trumpeter's life.

KAZIMIERZ

For centuries, Poles and Jews had shared the same land, ever since King Kazimierz the Great chartered this area in 1335 and put out the welcome mat. The old Jewish area of Kazimierz is just on the outskirts of the town of Krakow. It is interesting to think that for many years Poles and Jews were able to live side by side and live in peace. Not always were times as peaceful as we would like, but for hundreds of years they did co-exist. But peace ended abruptly for just about everyone who lived in Poland at the beginning of the Second World War. Jews. gypsies, union organizers, communists, scholars, homosexuals, and Poles were all terrorized at the hands of the Nazis. But there is no doubt that the Jewish community was hit the hardest. In Poland, there are many grisly reminders of the atrocities that took place at the concentration camps. I have been in some of the smaller ones and even in those you can feel the horror and still imagine the stench of death in the air. To think that so many innocent people were sent to death in these camps is almost incomprehensible. But it did happen and these camps are here to remind us so that it never happens again.

After the war, the Jewish population almost disappeared and those who did survive left Poland to start a new life in Israel and the Americas. Now that Poland has once again changed its politics, some Jews are coming back to Poland. In the old Jewish town of Kazimierz there are now two little Jewish restaurants serving not only Jewish cuisine but also presenting Jewish Klezmer music. Our tour group dined on Jewish-style cuisine and danced to the marvelous melodies of this vibrant culture.

In the center of this little town, there is an old synagogue. Behind it there is a massive stone wall. The wall is made from the remnants of the old Jewish gravestones that were found after the war. Today it stands like a patchwork quilt of names, dates and symbols, honoring the people who lived in this once spirited and strong community.

POLISH EASTER EGGS

In Poland, eggs have always symbolized life and resurrection. Some Poles believe that they hold magical powers. Believers say that the first Easter eggs originated with the Virgin Mary when she begged for her son's life with a basket of colored eggs. Others say it was Mary's own tears that colored the eggs when she cried at her son's crucifixion.

In Poland there are many ways to decorate eggs. In some regions they just boil the eggs in onionskins, while in others they dye them blue and then use a sharp knife to carve away the dye leaving behind a sketchy design. In Lowicz, they use wycinanki cutouts and paste them on to the eggs, and in Zakopane they carve wooden eggs. But of all the styles, there is none so demanding as the technique they called pisanki, a word meaning "to write." I discovered a little museum in the center of the old town of Rzeszow, and was able to find a few women from the area who were quite skilled in this old folk art that dates all the way back to the tenth century.

The women explained they used wax and colored dyes to make the eggs. They demonstrated with a large egg, and a tool stylus (a stick with a tiny funnel tied on the end), filling the funnel with melted wax, and making the fine designs on the egg with its fine tip. After the first designs are drawn, the artist would submerge the eggs into a pail filled with a light colored dye. This process is repeated over and over using darker colors until the egg is covered with thick wax and is dyed a dark black, red or blue. Once the design process is finished the artist slowly passes the wax-covered egg over a hot candle flame. Finally, the hot wax is gently rubbed off the egg with a towel revealing the beautiful design.

After our demonstration, we all had a chance to try our own hand at making these eggs. We found out very quickly with our eggs cracking and rolling off the tables that this was a skill that was best left to the masters. We left Rzeszow and slept the night away in an old Polish castle, then made tracks for our final destination.

After two weeks of experiencing the sights and sounds of Polish folk music it was time to head our LOT Tour bus back to Warsaw for a Polish folk arts banquet. My tourists were now well educated about Polish folk arts, so they were quite surprised by the bland tourist show which was presented. Perhaps this is when they realized how much they had learned and how different it was to really experience the folk arts rather then just see a staged commercial facsimile. On our flight home, the airplane was buzzing about their favorite moments and places. Even long after the trip was over we would be getting mail from our new friends.

I did these tours for LOT for about four years. Each tour had its own special moments and frustrations. The tour eventually included stops in Gdansk, Czetochowa, Nowy Sacz, Torun, Lancut, and the wonderful salt mine in Wieliczka. Without a doubt, the strangest trip was the year that our bus broke a fan belt and the driver fixed it by using our tour guide's pantyhose. Unable to find a replacement belt, he continued asking our tourists for pantyhose donations until we made it back to Warsaw. We ended up going thorough a half-dozen pairs. I guess you could say that trip ran on pantyhose!

By the fourth year of our tour, things were changing both at LOT and in Poland. My dear friend and supporter, Mr. Zebinski, was promoted and all of the people that I knew at the office in New York were slowly being replaced. With my supporters gone, it was getting difficult to convince the new people about the need for preserving the folk arts. By 1996, it was almost a lost cause. The new director in charge of the tours wanted me to change my tour, adding in more castles and the general tourist destinations. Poland was also in flux. The people were being force-fed a diet of free market economy, and when our tour arrived in Warsaw in 1966, I realized that I was in for a whole different trip than the one I had envisioned.

TOUR 1996

When western philosophy and culture first exploded into eastern Europe, many of us expected change, but I never thought it would come as fast as it did! Only five years before I had put together my first folk art tour to expose Americans to Poland's rich traditional folk arts. In that short time, the old culture had been almost eaten away by our heavy western influence.

Very few musicians are still playing the traditional music or making the beautiful folk handicrafts. The young people associate folk music with being connected to the old Soviet times and want to get as far away from it as possible. One of the traditional musicians told me, "The only way we can get the young people interested, is if we play the old songs with a modern beat and electric instruments!" We witnessed some of this multi-cultural schizophrenia in a festival in the Baltic Sea port of Gdansk. During the festival some performers were still dressed in the old traditional costumes, with the old folk instruments but they also had an electric band.

What we saw was almost unbelievable! The women and men sang the old songs while the band wailed away in a cacophony of sound without even an attempt to play the same melody. It was not folk, it wasn't jazz nor rock, it was just an explosion of strange sounds. In visual terms it would be like Grant Wood trying to paint like Jackson Pollock!

During that show, one of these new mixtures did blend into a pleasant new music - a blend of Polish highlander & Jamaican reggae. In one of the songs the vocalist sang "Grandpa is crying because they don't sing the old songs any more!" It is not hard to see why. Our ways are taking over. In every city you see a McDonalds, Pizza Hut and Burger King. The stores are filled with western products, billboards advertising American cigarettes and coffee are painted on old buildings and the voice of MTV pours out of hotels, and train stations, and can be heard in the poor ramshackle houses of the countryside.

After two weeks in Poland we took a train to Berlin, Germany to do an hour interview with Michael Kleff on his radio Brandenburg Show. While in Berlin we once again felt the pressure of western expansionism. Old buildings torn down, old factories bought out and closed by western competitors, anything remotely connected with the Soviets was being removed. We drove out to see the few concrete slabs of what was once the Wall, and there on the top of the soviet control tower of Check Point Charley now stands a huge golden Statue of Liberty. Yes! The wall is gone, freedom reigns and now everyone is free as long as they have money.

I experienced this personally during my return to Poland to catch my flight home. As the tour host I was given a free ticket, by LOT Polish Airlines, but when I tried to get on the flight we found it was over-booked. Marianna had bought her ticket so she could fly back. But I was told only people who paid full price could get a seat. I watched as Marianna hugging my banjo case walked on board the LOT aircraft then flew away. I had to stay behind on standby. The attendants treated me like all the rest of the poor souls who only had a standby ticket as we were pushed away from the gate.

I spent another night in Warsaw and gazed out my hotel room to the bright neon lights advertising casinos and American company logos. As I fell asleep the words to an old calypso folk song filled my head;

MONEY IS KING by the Tiger

Now if a man has money today,
people run to shake his hand right away.
Yes, if a man has money to spree
people don]t care if he has leprosy.
He can commit murder and get off free.
And live in the governor's company;
but if you're poor why god help you
even a dog is better than you.

I waited in line again the next day and at last boarded the plane and said goodbye and farewell to the old traditions that I loved.

Rubber Tramp

RUBBER TRAMPING ACROSS AMERICA

Some performers like to follow the example of the professional businessman or woman, using airplanes, rented cars and staying at fine hotels. There are others who have a less expensive and simpler method of travel, using their vehicles for not only transportation, but also as a hotel on wheels. Some of my friends take it to extremes by welding racks onto their exhaust manifold so they can cook meals while they drive along. No fooling, there is even a cookbook out so you can follow simple directions to cook savory meals on the top of your engine. Now that's what I call road food. I also know of a couple who like to do their laundry as they drive. They put a big tub in the trunk, fill it with soapy water, throw in their dirty clothes, seal up the tub with a tight lid then go off to their show. After the gig, they dump the bucket, wring out the clothes and tie them on to a roof rack and when they get to their next gig, they have clean clothes.

As for myself, I have found that the best way to survive on the road is to "follow the trucks." I do most of my traveling in my truck camper named "Apache "which is a slide-in pop-up camper that fits onto my Toyota pick- up. Inside the camper are two beds. There is a large bed that you have to pop the camper to reach, and a tiny bed, so that even when the camper is not popped up, I can still squeeze inside to sleep at night. When Apache pops up, she is like a full hotel on wheels, with the two beds, a four-burner stove, an icebox, storage cabinets, heater and a sink. As you can't drive around with her popped up, I have to wait until I can park at a festival, campground or friend's house before I can really open her up.

On my trips, I plan each day of travel with the idea of sleeping at a truck stop at the end of the day. I find out where the next truck stop on my route is by looking over a truck stop guide sold at most truck stops. They will tell you exit by exit which truck stops have food and overnight parking. Truck stops can be like an oasis, with hot showers, laundromats, phone booths and even free movies for truckers. The best thing about truck stops is that they are usually safe. You can park in the parking lot, grab some coffee, use the bathrooms, get a good cheap meal, and get a good night's sleep in the back of your vehicle, unlike staying in rest stops which can be very dangerous. Many truckers will avoid rest areas at night because as they say, "You can get yourself killed at a rest area."

If you've never been on this type of tour, it's hard to imagine just how many days of driving you have to sit through to really get anywhere. To give you an idea of what my life on the road is really like, I'll take you on a little cross country jaunt across America.

Don't worry, I have ridden these roads many a time, so buckle up your seat belt, partner, and hold on. We are off to one hell of an adventure.

My tours usually last from one to two months and can cover almost the whole country. I leave mid-February just around the time of one of the biggest folk events of the year at the International Folk Alliance.

HOBOS ON ICE
THE CLEVELAND FOLK ALLIANCE

It was just a short drive from Vermont to this year's Folk Alliance held in Cleveland. The Folk Alliance is an organization that promotes folk music and dance in many forms. Each year, thousands of performers and people from the music world, gather together to celebrate the world of folk music. This year's event was held in that city by the lake, Cleveland, Ohio.

My participation was being sponsored along with a group from the hobo community, and the National Hobo Association (NHA). We travelers, from the school of hard knocks, were there to have another round of fun songs and stories and put on a few workshops and panels. Last year Buzz Potter, the NHA President, and Clark Z. Branson Productions brought a group of hobos together in Albuquerque, New Mexico. This was one of the first times that the folk community had the pleasure of experiencing the hobos. This year the NHA brought in a true master of hobo song and lore, U. Utah Phillips, "The Golden Voice of the Great Southwest." Utah is a master orator, knows more about trains and hobos than most folklorists, and through his countless concerts and radio programs has become, as his mentor Hood River Blackie would say, "One of the Golden Ones" or one of the keeper's of records for the hobo family.

Now, you might be asking yourself what do hobos and a couple thousand singer/songwriters have in common and why should a bunch of hobos be hanging around with a horde of young musicians?

Traveling songs, history and lore have always been a strong component of the hobo lifestyle. For dozens of years now the old hobo songs have been passed on, first by cowboy singers and country and western bands, then later by folk singers such as Burl Ives, Woody Guthrie, and Pete Seeger, and most recently rock bands like The Grateful Dead. These old songs capture a spirit of wanderlust that we all can relate to and perhaps are one of the hobo's greatest legacies. Standing at the threshold of a new century, many of us are concerned about the next generation and how to pass the torch, so that even when it becomes impossible to ride trains, that the old songs, stories and train lore survive, and that those people who lived by the code of the road are remembered with pride and dignity.

Cleveland, Ohio in February does not seem like the ideal place to get together for a hobo gathering and then to think of it, a hobo jungle on the tenth floor of a Sheraton Hotel seems almost absurd yet, that is exactly what took place. It's hard to imagine a swanky mid-town hotel holding such a folksy event. Slowly the stately hotel let it's hair down as multitudes of performers from all over the world flew in like a swarm of bees, opened their instrument cases and let the music take over. Even the dourest sourpuss had to smile when the musicians hit town. In just a few hours, the upscale hotel got a facelift as performers plastered their flyers on any space they could find. First posters started appearing on the tables, then on walls, in elevators and even in the bathrooms. Truth be told, you could not escape from the endless barrage of colorful images, calling out like a siren's song, to come to their showcase.

This is a far cry from the jungle camp where hobos gathered to pass the time while waiting to catch out. This is business, show business, where everyone wants to be a star. At the Folk Alliance, Utah joined in with some of the usual suspects who, with music and stories, brought our presence to the forefront of the event. There were two nights of Mulligan Stew gatherings. These were casual evenings, where we dreamt up a campfire and sang songs until the wee hours of the morning. Just like in a real jungle everyone was invited and the room overflowed in song and spirit. One of the highlights came the night when Woody Guthrie's daughter, Nora, came up to join in the fun and sang along with one of Woody's personal favorites, "Hobo's Lullaby."

Early Saturday morning Banjo Fred hosted a panel called, "Why We Ride." This was a formal panel where our distinguished speakers had the opportunity to tell of the hobo's desire to roam and lead a nomadic existence. Banjo Fred put together a crackerjack group of musicians including Larry "Cream City Slim" Penn on guitar, U. Utah Phillips, and Luther the Jet, Clark Branson on dulcimer and Banjo Fred & yours truly on the old five string.

Our music, together with New York Maggie's and Connecticut Shorty's poetry, turned out to be just the right mix to give a real taste of the old campfire jungle. During the panel, New York Maggie and Connecticut Shorty told the young audience about their father's hobo life and showed them the bandanna he left behind from his forty years on the rails. Then Connecticut Shorty explained in detail how she prepares for a train trip, what she wears and carries along with her every time she hops freight. It seems Connecticut Shorty can fit more stuff into her small traveling pack then I can fit in my camper. When she mentioned taking a bedpan, Utah glanced at my banjo and said with a grin, "Rik takes along his own style of bedpan." All jokes aside, both of these well-traveled women had a big effect on the younger women in the audience in saying that you, too, can take control of your life and live by your own rules. As I looked into the young audience, I could see many youthful eyes beaming out, "Yes!"

A special showcase of Utah Phillips and the Rose Tattoo took place later that afternoon. The room began to feel like a can of sardines as people sat on beds, on the floor and stood down the hallway of the hotel just trying to get a glimpse of this mythical outfit. The Rose Tattoo is a group of singers and storytellers, just the kind of folks that Utah likes to hang out with. Few people really know how many are in the group or where they all come from but one thing is certain, each of them bears the mark of the Rose Tattoo on their left arm and they are all a bunch of real characters. This event brought together a group of four Tattoos: Utah, Larry Penn, Al Grierson, and Rik Palieri, plus two special guests, Saul Brody and Hobo King Luther the Jet. You could almost smell the coal and feel the train roll as these veteran performers took the stage. One fan came up after the show and said, "Wow! My skin was quivering when you guys sang. I've been looking for real music all this weekend and when I heard the Rose Tattoo, I knew that I had found it. You are the music!"

All too soon, it was time to leave the hotel and hit the icy highway to the last show over at Oberlin College. Banjo Fred once again had organized the event and really outdid himself by putting together a very memorable show for the young students. After the concert, we went over to a student's hangout for pizza and beer. We asked them to turn down the canned music, took out our instruments and transformed the joint into a 1960's style hootenanny. Soon the young students pulled their chairs close to our table and joined in the singing until we made the rafters ring. A storm of rain and ice came in, and after a careful drive back to Cleveland, we went our separate ways.

After four days of non-stop partying in the hotel, it was time to jump back into old Apache and continue my tour.

It was another day of hard traveling until I hit Nashville, Tennessee. It was late already so I started looking for a place to park my rig for the night. I was so tired that I missed the truck stop I was heading for and had to keep driving as I looked for somewhere, anywhere, to park. Now it was way past midnight, and I was still looking when a fog started coming through. My eyes were so tired that I just knew I had to get off the road before they started to close. I knew there was a rest stop ahead but, just my luck, it was closed and under repair so I kept driving. Now it was two A.M, I had been on the road since five A.M the previous morning, and I ws starting to drift. Just then a sign told me that there was a truck stop just twenty miles ahead. I pushed myself to make the next exit then bedded down for the night. It was my second day of travel and I went out like a light. It takes me a few days until I get back to the rhythm of the road but once I get the swing of it, I can drive forever.

NASHVILLE, THE CITY OF BROKEN HEARTS

I woke up in the big 76 Truck Stop about twenty miles from downtown Nashville. I had been coming to Nashville for a number of years to play at the legendary Blue Bird Cafe which gained it's notoriety from the film "A Thing Called Love," telling the stories of the singer/songwriters who flock to Nashville hoping to hit it big.

The cafe itself is not downtown, but on the edge of the city across from a little mall. The Blue Bird runs shows every day, but it is the Open Mke and the Songwriters Nights that really bring out the mobs. On Open Mike nights, long before the doors open, a line of guitar-toting hopefuls stretches out into the parking lot. Once inside, you find yourself in a comfortable room lined with photos of all the stars who have graced this stage.

Over the stage is the club trademark, a glowing neon light depicting a blue bird in flight. The seats fill up fast and everyone has to share a table but this really works out well as you can meet other songwriters and cheer them on during their performance. The night really begins when the stage host has everyone sign in. You write your name on a card that gets tossed into a basket, after which the stage manger draws out the names and assigns them a slot to sing one or two songs. As there are more people than time slots, the spots fill up fast and there are always a few that never get on stage.

When the show starts, the room fills right to the brim. You never know who is going to be in the audience, as many of the talent scouts from Music Row often come here to check out new acts. There is an almost legendary story about a very well known singer playing the Blue Bird when he was just starting out. He was the last person to perform that night and there was only one person left in the room when he sang. Even though he had an audience of one, he still sang with all his heart and gave a stunning performance. That one person turned out to be a record A&R man, and that night he signed him to a recording contract. I guess it is stories like this that keep people coming from all over the world to give it their best shot at the Blue Bird. The club is also like a training ground that works on all levels.

After you go a few rounds at the open mikes you can get a spot on Songwriters Night. Here a few songwriters are selected to do a fifteen-minute set. After that, if you do a good job, you might be selected for the best of the songwriter's picks. By having songwriters working through all these levels, it gives them a real chance to hone their writing skills. I always have fun at the Blue Bird whether it is the songwriter's night or just the open mike.

As I was just passing through, I took my chances at getting a spot. When my time came, I strolled up to the stage, standing underneath the neon bluebird light and gave it my all. After my show, I hung my hat in Nashville for a few days and exchanged songwriting ideas with some Nashville songwriters. One veteran writer told me, "It's not like it used to be, you know. A few years ago when a top artist was cutting a new disk, there were about 10 cuts that went out to the 2500-plus in the Nashville song writing community. Today, the producers are co-writing with the artist and now we only get a crack at two cuts per CD, with the artist and the producer taking the rest. Another problem here is airplay. If you're not in your twenties anymore, it's hard to get airplay! You would not believe how many popular artists, who had some major hits, are on their way out." As they went on and on about the hardships of Nashville, I drifted, back to the hopeful faces of the young singers I saw at the Blue Bird still believing in Nashville dreams.

JIMMY DRIFTWOOD AND PICKING ON THE COURTHOUSE SQUARE

Traveling west on I-40, I thought it was a good time to take a little detour and pay a visit with Ozark balladeer, Jimmy Driftwood. As I traveled the backroads to see my old pal, I thought back to our first meeting.

I first met Jimmy when I was doing my long school tours. I was aware of this legendary figure back from the days when I was just a kid listening to my grandmother Kay's Hi Fi and hearing his song "The Battle Of New Orleans." I also remember reading about him helping to organize the Ozark Folk Heritage Center in a place called Mountain View. As I was performing near Little Rock, I thought that it might be worth it to head up to the Ozarks and have a look around.

It took over an hour to reach Mountain View from the main highway. There is no easy way to get to Mountain View. The roads out there have more twists, turns and bumps than an Australian camel. My road was so snaky that you could get seasick riding up and down the long curves before reaching the town. It looks like many other small towns with a main street lined with old brick buildings, a post office and a few stores surrounding a courthouse square. On closer inspection, you will notice that right on the square is a music store with a large open lot next door.

I saw a group of guitar pickers, playing away, sitting in folding chairs next to a large wood stove. These men looked as old as the vintage guitars they were playing and made a joyful sound as they passed the time away. I decided to have a look around at the music store and found to my surprise a large number of high quality instruments for such a little town. I also noticed, on the wall, hundreds of photographs of people playing music around the courthouse. The salesman told me that there would be a big jam around the wood stove later tonight and reminded me to see the Ozark Heritage Center. I could not help but notice the many snapshots of an old fellow dressed in a bright red shirt, and black Stetson hat, holding the strangest guitar I have ever seen - something that looked like it might have been made from a cigar box. As I walked out of the store, his image was glued in my head. Who was this strange character?

When I reached the Ozark Center, I was totally amazed. The Center was filled with little log buildings used as exhibit houses. Inside the cabins, guides explained the history and culture of the area. There were also demonstrations of Ozark crafts, dulcimer making, quilting, wood carving, herb gardening and log cabin building.

They also had a large auditorium where there were even more exhibits and a large stage for musical events. That afternoon they had a band called the Arkansas Mountain Band that featured a few guitar players, mandolin, bass and banjo. The banjo player was a real poker-faced fellow who was thin as a beanpole. He played bluegrass-style on an old Gibson Mastertone. After the show, I went back stage to meet the band.

At first, the banjo player was a little reserved. He was tired, wanted to get home, and did not want to hang around talking to a Yankee. When I told him that I played a bit of banjo, he was unimpressed and only reluctantly handed me his prized possession. When he saw my hand frail the strings of his banjo, his jaw dropped and he fell back in his chair. "Not many people can pick like that around here," he said, with a big warm smile. He continued, "The only one that I know of is old Grandpa Jones, most of the others died years ago." We sat around and traded licks until he said, "Are you going over to the courthouse tonight? There will be a great big jam near the wood stove and I hope you can make it." We shook hands. He packed up his instrument and left.

Later that night, when I drove back into town, I noticed the whole area near the courthouse packed with cars. Around the square, it almost looked like a picture from an old postcard: there was a huge circle of pickers sitting around a smoking wood stove with women busy knitting and old men whittling away with their Barlow knives. As I was a stranger, I sat away from the circle, just plunking away, until a friendly man called me to join in the circle. As my banjo frailed along to the old fiddle tunes everyone clapped along to the bouncy beat. The friendly face, who invited me to join in, wore an old farmer's cap and was strumming on an autoharp. His name was James Yancey, but everyone just called him by the name of the town he grew up in, Snowball.

Snowball and I fired up a couple of hot tunes and were soon joined by a big strapping man known as Big John. Dressed in bib overalls and feathered cowboy hat, Big John was always the center of attention and, despite his massive presence, he had a gentle voice. During each song, he would call out the name of the instrument that he wanted to take a lead, while thumping away on his old Gibson Hummingbird flattop guitar. After one guy struck up a hot fiddle tune, a few gals jumped up out of their seats and danced and clogged their feet to the beat of the old "Soldier's Joy."

It was almost midnight, the fire was burning low and a cold wind was blowing through the square. As everyone packed up, Snowball came up to me and said, "Well you sure kept up with everyone tonight and you fit in real well. You know I think that Jimmy would enjoy meeting you." "Jimmy?" I said, "Jimmy, who?" Snowball smiled, "Why, old Jimmy Driftwood. He's a good friend of mine and I just know he would like your kind of picking. By the way, where are you staying tonight?" I said, "I'm just sleeping in my camper." Well, Snowball said, "You better not camp here in town. Follow me and I'll show you a good place to camp, don't worry, it's not far. Just follow me." I followed Snowball's pick-up a few miles down the winding back roads to a town called Timbo. He told me to park right next to the schoolyard and then said, "You sleep here. No one will bother you, but come morning (he pointed to a small stone cabin) you go over there and have breakfast with Jimmy." Snowball smiled and drove off into the darkness and as I wrapped myself in my sleeping bag, I started thinking, "I'm going to have breakfast with Jimmy. Is he joking?"

The next morning I was greeted by an old, gray haired man, wearing a bright red shirt. He knocked on my window and said, "Howdy, breakfast is on the table, come on in." It was Jimmy Driftwood.

When I walked into Jimmy's stone cabin, I found my self surrounded by his mementos. Jimmy asked me to sit down while, his wife, Cleda, fixed us both a cup of coffee. He told me that Snowball had called early that morning and told him that I was in front of his house, sleeping in my van. He then walked over to a large table piled high with old instruments and said, "Old Snowball told me that you pick a fine banjo." Jimmy handed me an old 5-string and I took to it like a duck to water. Jimmy said, "All the old-timers who played that style are not living anymore. How did you learn it?" After a short run down on my life, Jimmy started telling his own story:

Jimmy was born James Morris, in a saddleback log cabin, in the Ozark Mountains, on June 20, 1907 in Mountain View, Arkansas.

He grew up in a musical community and his family, who moved to Arkansas from Tennessee after the Civil War, were all music makers. His father, Neil Morris, and grandfather Elijah, played the guitar. Jimmy's grandmother sang old ballads and his neighbors played fiddle and banjo at country-dances. It was no surprise that Jimmy, too, took an interest in music.

As a young boy, Jimmy taught himself to play the guitar, fiddle, and banjo. He also learned to read and write music and practiced the art of shape note singing with his father. Jimmy soon joined his family singing at parties and dances, collecting ballads and old folk songs wherever he went.

Although music was his first love, he realized, at a young age, that it was not going to put bread on the table. He began thinking of how to combine his interest in music with his enthusiasm for learning. Becoming a schoolteacher seemed like the right choice. Jimmy started teaching in a one-room country schoolhouse at age sixteen, right after he graduated high school. He earned his college credit, between terms, at John Brown

University, Arkansas College and the Arkansas State Teacher's College in Conway, where he ultimately received a Bachelor of Science in Education.

He married Cleda Azalea Johnson, a pretty lady of Cherokee ancestry, in 1936. Cleda was one of Jimmy's former students. She shared Jimmy's interest in music and loved working with , so it was only natural that she also became a schoolteacher. Together they continued teaching and collecting old songs and ballads, while farming and raising four sons.

Jimmy began to put his musical skills into the classroom. He wrote songs based on American history and used these songs to teach his students. Jimmy's reputation as "The Singing Ozark School Teacher" spread throughout Arkansas. He became a favorite at folk festivals and was invited to lecture in schools and universities to demonstrate his unique teaching method.

As the news of Jimmy's singing and songwriting traveled, friends like Hugh Ashley and folklorist Dr. John Quincy Wolf urged him to take his songs to Nashville. His songs had already reached the ears of some of the well-known Opry stars, and they were eager to hear more of his music. In 1958, at age fifty-one, Jimmy packed up his rusty truck with his old guitar, a few boxes of cheese and crackers, and over one hundred original songs, and drove with Cleda, over the Tennessee state line.

In Nashville Jimmy sang his songs to song publisher Don Warden, who later introduced Jimmy to Chet Atkins of RCA records. They both became interested in Jimmy after hearing a little song that he wrote as a history lesson for his high school students called "The Battle Of New Orleans."

In 1958, Jimmy was signed to RCA and began recording an album entitled Newly Discovered Early American Folk Songs." At first, he got little airplay. Then late one night, fate stepped in. Country singer Johnny Horton was on his way to the Louisiana Hayride show at 2 A.M, when he turned on WSM radio and heard Jimmy sing "The Battle Of New Orleans."

Horton fell in love with the song and recorded it for Columbia Records. Horton's version, with a drum introduction, was released on April 26, 1959. The song was an instant hit and became a million-copy seller. It flew up the charts for twenty-one weeks staying six weeks as the number one song.

Soon other country artists like Eddy Arnold, Hawkshaw Hawkins and Homer and Jethro followed Horton's lead by recording Driftwood's songs. On September 19, 1959, there were no less than six Jimmy Driftwood songs on the top 10 and later that year, he won three Grammy's including Top Country/Western Recording and Song of the Year.

With Jimmy's songs on the tip of everyone's tongue, the offers came pouring in and everyone from the Grand Old Opry to New York's Carnegie Hall wanted to hear Jimmy's music. He performed at colleges, folk festivals and, later, for President Kennedy.

After meeting the President, Jimmy was asked to tour the world for the United States Information Service as the first Goodwill Ambassador of Arkansas. He later did tours throughout Europe, Asia and the Pacific Islands.

As Jimmy traveled, he noticed that, while college students were playing his Ozark music, it was almost dying out back home. Jimmy and Cleda started a campaign to re-vitalize the old music. They beat the bushes for all the old musicians they could find and formed a club for the preservation of Ozark heritage called The Rackensack Society.

The Rackensackers first gathered in homes, storefronts and the Mountain View Stone County Courthouse. As the numbers of Rackensackers continued to grow, Jimmy thought about getting a better place to showcase his Ozark roots.

In 1963, some of the town merchants in Mountain View wanted Jimmy to help run a local craft fair. Jimmy had the idea of expanding the craft fair into a folk festival, and called on local performers. Soon Jimmy was promoting the show during his college lectures, inviting everyone to come to Mountain View. That spring over twenty thousand people took Jimmy up on his offer and came to the first Arkansas Folk Festival.

With the success of the folk festival, Jimmy's dream of getting a proper building for his Ozark folk music and culture came into focus. The idea of creating an Ozark Heritage Center was born and Jimmy became so involved, with this project that he realized he would have to stop touring if he was going to get the job done right. He retired from touring with the Grand Old Opry, and then rolled up his sleeves and went to work.

Jimmy contacted Arkansas Congressman, Wilbur Mills and set up an appointment with the Ways and Means Committee. He flew to Washington and brought along his merry band of Rackensackers to serenade the US Congress. They sang to the tune of 2.1 million dollars for the proposed center plus another 1.9 million dollars for town water and sewage improvements. Jimmy's efforts paid off. He got the center and was soon appointed as the unpaid musical director.

Soon the small town of Mountain View, with its courthouse square, post office, school and one filling station was turning into the home of The Ozark Heritage Center, the Folk Capital of the World. It was a huge complex containing a large amphitheater and a little village of log cabins which featured crafts, herbs, regional, and folk arts, gift shops and a restaurant. Not far from the huge Heritage Center, Jimmy and Cleda built a more intimate setting to showcase the Rackensack Society in the Jimmy Driftwood Barn. Jimmy and his friends welcome everyone to free concerts of down home music. The shows feature old folk songs in a beautiful setting where you can sit in the far corner of the room and still see the whites of the singer's eyes.

Jimmy, who is now eighty-four, had a bad car wreck last year in which he and his wife slid off the road and crashed into a ditch, leaving both of them in bad shape. Cleda recovered fully but Jimmy was having problems. His memory was foggy and his guitar playing was nothing like it used to be. Luckily Cleda's memory is as sharp as a tack and she fills in any missing information.

Jimmy looked at me as he strummed his old weathered guitar. "You know," Jimmy started, "This guitar has quite a story. My grandpa Morris came from Tennessee. His family traveled by horse and wagon and settled here near Mountain View. Back then guitars were hard to come by, so when my grandpa saw some of the other boys playing, he wanted to play, too. He didn't have any money to buy a guitar but what he did was take the old headboard from my great grandmothers bed and used it to make the top and back of his guitar. Oh, he got a bad whipping when his father saw that big hole in the headboard. Then he found an oxen yoke to make up the sides and used a fence post to carve the neck."

As Jimmy handed me the old guitar a knock came at the front door. It was a group of friends who had played in last night's show at Jimmy's barn. Soon the house was filled with people. All the pickers reached for their instruments and filled Jimmy and Cleda's kitchen with the sounds of fiddle and banjo. Jimmy sat in his chair singing along and swapping tales as he slapped his leg along with the beat. Jimmy also slapped his leg when he laughed and if you don't watch out he will be slapping your leg as he let out his big bellowing laughs. After a few hours of picking, Jimmy brought out his old mouth bow, an instrument he learned from the Cherokee Indians who lived near by. Jimmy said, "The Indians used to play songs on their hunting bows while they sat around the campfire." He picked up the bow and placed it near the edge of his mouth and as he plucked the string he changed his mouth opening to produce a series of different notes, almost like a Jews harp. After his demonstration, Jimmy handed me his bow to give it a try and coached me as his friends looked on. After a few minutes, he said, "Hey, I think he's got it!"

That first meeting was the beginning of our friendship and from then on, I always went out of my way to visit with Jimmy and Cleda. We'd sit at the kitchen table, passing his guitar back and forth, as he tried to remember some of the six thousand songs he wrote.

Jimmy had aged considerably since my last visit and now, at the age of almost ninety, he was only a shadow of his former self, yet he still held the magic spark that made him a national folk icon. As Cleda poured more coffee into Jimmy's cup, she looked at me and asked smiling, "Coming to play at the barn tonight? Jimmy likes it when you play." "Sure," I replied, as I unpacked my banjo and handed Cleda a bottle of our homegrown honey. We sat at the kitchen table, with Jimmy's old guitar in my hand, swapping tunes together. We sang "The Worried Man Blues" and "Going Down the Road." Then I sang one of my new songs, "Plant A Tree" and Jimmy fumbled through one of his old song books and said, "Now, Rik, did you ever hear this one?" He picked up his old guitar and sang the old Civil war song, "When We Meet at the Golden River." Jimmy told me it was a song that was sung by both armies the night before battle. Often they would sing it together, both Rebels and Yanks, with their voices mingling over the riverbanks. As he sang the last chorus, Jimmy faded away and drifted off to some other land.

After the song, Jimmy bounced back and we talked a bit about folk music. I told him all about Folk DJ and our cyber-space community. Old Jimmy was happy to hear about it and was in favor of anything that kept folk music alive. Then we talked about folk music, and the new singer/songwriters, and Jimmy said, "You know, some songs are over five hundred years old and people don't sing 'em any more, because they've had their run. Then someone writes a new song about the same idea, and people start singing the new one and before you know it, it becomes like a folk song too. Why a new folk song might be written tomorrow!"

Later that night we played together at the barn. His fans cheered him on as he took the stage and once more created the magic that endeared him to all those who have met him.

As I was about to leave, Jimmy and Cleda, came out to say goodbye. Jimmy played a last little tune on my mouth bow and said, "You come back now, and hopefully I'll still be Driftwood and not deadwood." Jimmy laughed as he and Cleda climbed into their car and drove off, with Jimmy still waving from the window with his big happy smile.

WOODY'S HOME TOWN

I got up the next morning and made a pilgrimage to the town of Woody Guthrie's child-hood home, in Okemah, Oklahoma. It is hard to comprehend what an impact Woody has had on the world. He started out as a young curly-headed kid playing the harmonica, shining shoes, and playing music for the poor county farmers and oil derrick roustabouts. Later he took up the guitar, and hoboed around the country by freight train, thumbing rides and often just walking down the road with a guitar slung over his back. His songs, "This Land Is Your Land," "So Long, It's Been Good To Know You," "Hard Traveling," and "Pastures Of Plenty," have become classics and are now part of our American culture. Woody was also one of a few songwriters who combined music with social action. On his guitar he had a slogan that read "This Machine Kills Fascists," and he meant it. Often Woody would play for union rallies, jungle camps, progressive parties and wherever people needed a bit of music. His music came from the heart of our soil and he spoke and sang with a voice that was of the people. No other singer in American folk music has had more of an influence than Woody. He was and still is a true original.

As famous as Woody is around the world, it is sometimes strange to hear that in his own hometown the citizens have mixed feelings. Some people just don't like him while others have a hard time with some of his more radical views. Up until recently, he was hardly thought of at all except for having his name on the town's water tower. Now, local peoples' views are changing and they are inviting songwriters from all over to gather in Okemah to sing his praises, and are honoring Woody with a huge summer festival.

I first stumbled into Okemah a few years back when I did perform there at the schoolhouse and I found this town, even though it is a bit run down, to have a bit of magic to it. Perhaps it's old Woody's spirit still lingering around but, whatever it is, it makes me want to make a stop, whenever I am passing through.

Walking through the downtown, the main street looks almost like the days back in the dirty 30's of the Great Depression. The main street is lined with ramshackle buildings, with "Going Out of Business" signs hanging in the windows and crumbling concrete falling from the buildings into the alleyways. I walked up the main street looking up and down the street. Next to the fire station, stood the old police station, now just a store-front. Peeking into the doorway, in the corner of the concrete sidewalk was scrawled "WOODY 1927." I knew, from a previous trip, that Woody himself had put that there years ago and it was only found, recently, when the town was repairing the building. For years, it was hidden underneath an old piece of molding.

When I asked for directions to the old Guthrie homesite I was told that it was torn down years ago and now is just a wooded lot next to the library. I drove my truck up the hill, parked next to the library and saw a nice wooded lot filled with big trees. I sat there for a few minutes and thought of this little fellow who made such a huge impact on the world, then drove off with Woody on my mind.

I left Woody's Oklahoma hills and headed north to my next gig, up in the wheat fields of Kansas. There is a certain kind of peace that comes from these graceful flat lands of grain elevators and windmills that is hard to explain to folks who do not know Kansas.

Kansas. There's nothing to see in Kansas. Well, perhaps it's the nothingness of the wide open spaces that I enjoy so much. I had great shows in Kansas and made a whole crop of new friends up in Lindsborg, then blew out of Dodge just in time to be clobbered by a whale of a snowstorm.

I spent the night in a truck stop right on the Kansas-Oklahoma border then woke up to one of the most beautiful drives on the whole tour, the route over the canyons of Cimarron, NM. What an earthly delight, a new postcard picture at every turn of the road. The huge canyon walls glowed with blood red rock as I twisted my way up the high canyon walls and I did have to use my four-wheel drive a few times, but it was worth it!

I had a show in Taos the next evening, so I had a little free time to relax, and as it was St. Patrick's Day, what better way to spend the night than at an Irish party complete with bagpipes. I found out that a friend of mine, Charlie Raferty, was playing at the local bar. When I got there, the house was packed and the aromas of Irish corned beef and cabbage filled the air, while Charlie's band cranked out the old Irish melodies. Charlie invited me to play; I begged off but did take him up on his offer to spend the night at his place. I should have known that I was in for an adventure, when he said. "What are you driving? Oh, you've got a four-wheel drive. Good, you'll need it."

ADVENTURES ON THE MUDDY MESA

I followed Charlie's friend, Paul, out of town and turned onto a dirt road. The dirt soon turned to mud, then ruts, holes and finally to no road at all. My truck bounced up and down, like popcorn popping, throwing my pickup and myself in every direction. At last, my leader's taillights disappeared as he sank down, into a very deep hole. I jammed on my brakes and shouted out, "Oh, no. No way," only to be waved on by my mud-covered friend now standing at the top of the huge ditch. Slowly, I clenched my teeth, threw my truck into low four-wheel drive and, like an old pro, we flew down into the muck and up again in a flash.

It was now only a few more miles until I reached Charlie's underground log hogan. It was a house unlike anything I had experienced, with a short tunnel leading to a huge circular log room supported by a huge log decorated with eagle feathers. Inside, there were only a few slim windows, a dirt floor, a table, a small library and sleeping area. We played a bit of music that night, then all crashed. In the morning, our jam continued with the wildest assortments of sounds coming from any one room you could imagine from a small tuba, violins and Polish bagpipes. Even though it sounds like a strange trio, the music we made flowed like melted butter.

After our jam, Charlie mentioned casually about how he could sure use a hand in picking up a junk truck, ending his plea with "It should only take an hour." Being the nice guy, I said, "No problem, I'll be glad to help." In a few minutes, we climbed into his truck and slid through the mud on the way to the local junkyard. As we were riding along, I noticed that the shacks that I had seen at night were really houses made from trash. They call them earth ships. They look pretty good when they are finished and covered over with cement, but left uncovered they are just a mess of tires, garbage, windows and doors thrown together, looking like a set from a bad science fiction movie.

We got a long chain to pull the truck from the junkyard and then raced through the mud to find his new pick up. We pulled up to a field stacked with an army of broken refrigerators standing guard around a fortress of garbage. "You mean this is it?" I asked. "Someone lives here?" Before Charlie could answer, an old fellow with gray Rastafarian braids, popped up from a wall of garbage with a line of dogs yelping behind him. The old fellow said, "Well, there she is," pointing to a real wreck of truck. As we looked closer, we noticed it was up on blocks. Needless to say, it took hours and hours to pull wheels off other wrecks, before we were ready to roll.

After our long ordeal with the truck, we drove into town to wash the mud off before my show. To my surprise all of the hippies that I met during the day, out on the muddy mesa, made a pilgrimage out to my show. That night we had a real blow out, kids dancing, people joining in with drums, harmonicas and finger cymbals while our voices raised the roof. Everyone smiled as they sang their way out the door, and drove back to their muddy mesa homes.

DEEP IN THE HEART OF TEXAS

It took most of the day to drive and reach Texas. The route that I drove took me all the way down to the very southern tip near Brownsville, right on the Texas-Mexican border. In the town of Donna, I met up with a few friends from the hobo community. Hobo Queens Connecticut Shorty and New York Maggie were my hosts. We had a grand time together doing a little show at a campground. The next morning we drove the Hobo Queen's RV, Patches, and crossed over the Mexican Border.

The town of Progresso is, like most border towns, a maze of tacky stores lined up on a street filled with cars and trucks waiting to get over the bridge. The "Winter Texans" spend a lot of time here trying to get the cheapest meal or health care that they can find while poor Mexicans sit on the sidewalk and panhandle or walk up and down the streets trying to hawk their goods. We walked around the shops, had a bite to eat and just took in the scenery. As we walked back across the bridge, over the Rio Grande River, you could hear the shouts of the little children wading in the river, carrying long poles attached to a small plastic funnel and begging for money. We drove back to the campground caught up with all the news and said our goodbyes.

It was another day and a half of driving to get back north to Dallas for the next show with the Dallas Folklore Club, set up by my friend Charles Loubert. This was a fun evening. Everyone sat in a huge living room, with their instruments in hand, picking away until the evening show began. I did the feature spot and had a really great show, and then we moved into the kitchen for some snacks and there grouped again for an old-fashioned song circle. Around the circle, everyone was encouraged to join in. There were folks of all different ages and abilities. Almost everyone had a guitar, some had banjos and one fellow even played a hammered dulcimer. Sometimes they would sing an original song or a cover tune but most often, it was just an old song that everyone could join in on. Evenings like this can be pure magic. It's so nice to see that this kind of house concert is catching on and perhaps it's one way that our love for community music will continue. After a nice country-style breakfast, including grits and bacon and eggs, it was time to pack up my truck, so I waved goodbye to my friends Charles and his wife and hit the road again.

A VISIT WITH AL

Looking over the map, I realized that it was only a couple of hundred miles out of my way to make a stop over in Luckenbach to see fellow-worker, Al Grierson. I first met Al at the Kerrville Folk Festival and then started corresponding with him through the cyber folk community on Folk DJ. Over the years, we have become like brothers, sharing a passion for songwriting, unions and the Rose Tattoos that we wear. Even though we have known eachother for years and talk almost everyday, this would be the first time that I was going to visit him in his school bus parked at the Armadillo campground.

After a long ride across Texas, I saw the tiny sign "Lukenbach" and followed the country road over to a seed store, to look for a phone. The seed store was surrounded by tall grain silos and was the only place around that had a telephone. Within minutes after my call, here came old Al, driving a rattrap of a car. I followed Al a few miles to the center of town where, the main building of town (I think there were only two buildings in town) was a combination Post Office, grocery and bar, and the other, a community dance hall. Al told me that this town was almost a ghost town, until a fellow named Hondo, fell in love with it and bought it.

Hondo was a well-known storyteller and picker who began to attract all of his Hollywood friends here and, in a short time, Luckenbach became famous as the "biggest small town in Texas." Al has been channeling old Hondo's spirit and has a whole basket load of new songs in his honor. I first heard these new gems, as we traded songs in his untouring bus in the Armadillo Campgrounds. Al's bus did not run when he bought it, so he had to tow it over to the campground where it is now settling into the Texas dirt while he attempts to make it into an affordable, livable abode. I liked to tease Al that he was living in an abandoned school bus and Al would jump back and say, "It's not abandoned. I'm living in it." The bus is outfitted with a kitchen area, (where Al brews up gallons of tea) and a bed with just enough room left to hold his records, books, tapes and CD's. Al and I spent the evening sharing songs in his bus. It was fun for me to pick along with him on my banjo and yodel together on tunes like his "Wild Dogs of Kitawonga." I spent the night in the back of my pick-up and surprised Al in the morning by walking around his bus playing the Polish bagpipes, it sounded great to hear sounds of Poland echoing through the vast Texas wind. In the morning I was off again heading north, deep in the heart of Texas.

THE GUITAR-PICKING, PISTOL-PACKING PREACHER

West Texas is just a big tumble-weedy kind of place where oil derricks sprout like wild flowers along the highway. There are miles and miles of sand, dirt, snakes, lizards, scorpions, a few blue bonnets and not much else in between. It's the kind of place where you keep checking your gas gauge and pray that you don't break down.

After a long day like this it is always nice to check in on old friends, so I pulled off the highway to visit to the home of Walter Lee, the guitar-picking, pistol-packing preacher of Coahoma, Texas. Walt is a fine picker and songwriter. He is an avid hunter (he keeps his freezer stocked with venison, some of which goes to feed the hungry) He is a man of the cloth, and has occasionally been drafted by the sheriff's office as part of an armed posse! With a combination of skills like that, you know that it is worth driving a few hours through Texas to visit with him and his family.

I first met Walt at Kerrville and ever since have been coming out to play at his community coffeehouse and a few schools. I could not survive doing music full time if I did not do some schools on each tour. I also have been a big believer that as a performer you should try to reach the whole community and not just those at the folk clubs or coffeehouses. I book my tours with this in mind and always include shows in schools, libraries, senior centers and sometimes nursing homes, together with the usual coffeehouses and folk clubs and radio interviews.

It did not take long to get Walter to take out his old Martin guitar and show me some of his new songs. As is my custom, I spent way too much time singing and telling stories so I hardly had any time to sleep

My tours seem to have a hidden theme that helps drive them along. I did not know it yet, but the theme for this tour was to be around songwriting. This soon became apparent when I started telling Walter about the fun I have been having with a songwriting group we started back in Burlington, Vermont at the Burlington Coffeehouse. I told him that every month, we get together and talk about songwriting, exchange ideas and even do a monthly challenge. Walter was excited about this concept and asked if we could write a few songs together. He came up with a few ideas and in a few hours, we were hard at work writing songs.

In between running to schools, Walter and I were passing song ideas back and forth like friends sharing a soda and by the end of my stay, we had written four new songs in five days.

During the visit, the conversation turned to the political mood in various parts of the country. Walt showed me a video which a friend had loaned to him. It was on the Branch Davidian siege outside of Waco. lots of people in West Texas were still concerned about what happened, particularly after a jury had acquitted the surviving Davidians of all the more serious charges. As a preacher, a Texan, former deputy, and gun enthusiast, he was very concerned about what took place at Waco. The video was alarming with infrared film showing the compound being fired upon from troops and tanks on the ground, and helicopters with mounted machine guns firing from above. It showed bodies being run over by tanks and it pointed out that they targeted the room where the woman and children were, at which to throw the tear gas. This film was very disheartening and reminded me of the worst side of America. One of the weirdest moments of the film was when our government troops played Nancy Sinatra's "These Boots Are Made for Walking" endlessly over huge speakers aimed at the compound. While the music played, the elite soldiers dropped their pants and mooned the women and young girls whenever they approached an open window. "Our Government troops in action." Even though I'm not a hunter or a gun owner, I found this video both tragic and fascinating.

On these tours, I often stay with people from every race, creed, color and socioeconomic background. On my first visit I say, "You know, we won't agree on every issue, but we can both learn from each other." This usually opens up some very though-provoking conversations.

One night, Walter and his wife Mary, took me out to see a movie. As luck would have it, as we walked out the door, Walter noticed a famous Texas Radio personality, Tumbleweed Smith. Tumbleweed specializes in unusual people and stories and has his own syndicated radio show heard on 240 radio stations throughout Texas.

When Walter introduced me, Tumbleweed's wife recognized me from a story in the local paper. I asked them if they wanted to see some of the instruments and led them over to my pickup. Within seconds, I had my Polish pipes out and was piping away while stopping traffic in the parking lot. Tumbleweed became very interested in my story and wanted to tape it and share it with his listeners. The next day Tumbleweed came early with his mikes and tape recorder and did a long interview, then taped my whole show. It was a fun show with lots of stories mixed into my usual folk bag of tricks of banjo-picking, mouth bow playing, original songs, and sing-a-longs. At the show's end Tumbleweed said this show was going to be a winner and thanked me repeatedly for letting him tape it.

THE MARFA CAT ROUNDUP, THE MYSTERIOUS BLINKING LIGHTS AND NUCLEAR WASTE

From the tall oil derricks of Coahoma I streaked along the interstate and drove most of the day down to the next show in the west Texas desert town of Marfa.

Last year I'd had some great shows here, so I was excited to come back. It also gave me a chance to hang out with my pal, Gary Oliver. Now, Gary is an interesting fellow. He is a blind cartoonist by trade but also one of the nicest and politically on-target people, you could ever meet. Gary and I had first met on a peace walk up in Vermont when he was part of the Texas contingent that came up to join us. Well, they really didn't come to join us; they came to alert us that Vermont was planning to dump nuclear waste near their home in Texas. You might say that they were not exactly happy about Vermont, or even us Vermonters, but it did not take long for us all to realize that we were all victims of the politicians and that most Vermonters did not even know much about the issue. It did not take long for the Texas Radiation Rangers to educate us and, in a short time, we were all marching together, not only to end nuclear weapons but also to stop nuclear waste.

Gary and his group worked hard to stop the dump and turned over every stone to help the cause. Through their research, they found that a dangerous faultline ran through the proposed dumpsite. Because of all the protesting and community awareness that they created, they won their case and stopped the proposed dump in Sera Blanca. However, the story does not end there. It seems that our politicos had found a new dumpsite near Pecos, Texas and so the battle continues with a new community at risk.

As I was driving to Marfa, Gary asked me to visit one of the new town organizers to see if we could pull together a little concert to help get things moving. I drove down another dusty road, found myself in front of a nice stone house, and parked my rig. Laura Burnet and her mother were not your typical activists. They were just regular townsfolk who got involved because their home and future were being threatened. They were very enthusiastic about putting on a concert to drum up more support. We ate some chili and beans together and planned out some ideas at the kitchen table, then waved goodbye 'til the show,which was set for the next week.

This part of Texas, known as the Big Bend, is like a completely different world, with huge mountains of red and brown rock leaping up to the sky wherever you look. It is not hard to see why these honest Texans fought so hard to keep the nuclear dumpsite out of this area as it is, as they say, "God's Country."

The town of Marfa is a true Texas desert town with houses and stores made of adobe brick. The town became famous because many films were made here including James Dean's last film Giant. Marfa was also the home of a well-known artist named Donald Judd and is now a Mecca for new emerging artists. The Judd foundation hosts workshops and conferences in Marfa. It looks like this tiny town is getting ready to sprout wings and fly and some residents fear it will become Texas's answer to Santa Fe.

Another well-known attraction in the area is the famous Marfa lights. Just a short drive from town there is a spot where tourists pull over and scan the sky for these mysterious lights. No one really knows where the lights come from. Some say they are flying saucers. Some say it's a strange magnetic field. No matter what is out there, it sure draws folks into Marfa.

While I was there, the Budweiser Beer Company wanted to do a goofy TV commercial about buying the rights to the Marfa lights to go with the Michelob light campaign. When they walked in with the idea to the mayor's office, he agreed to the little spoof, but when the cameras were rolling, and he was asked about buying the rights he looked at them with a gruff face and said, "Buying the Marfa lights? I'm not too sure about that."

Gary lives in an old adobe home that is still in the reconstruction mode. That means there is nothing much inside but a few chairs, a little table, records, books, a shelf for food and about twenty-five cats. Gary could not stand to let any stray cat not have a home so he decided to invite every cat in Marfa to come to live in his house. There are cats in the living room, cats in the bathroom, cats on the roof, cats everywhere.

My first show in the area was at a reform school, which I played at last year, called High Frontier. This place is, as they say, the last stop before jail. It's really a huge complex of buildings. I could not see any barbed wire fence or any locked rooms, though the site is pretty far from the road. The kids inside range from twelve to eighteen years of age and both boys and girls all live together in small groups on the site with each group lodged in small bunkhouses. The whole idea is based on working in peer groups so the group bears the consequences of each member. For my show, the kids walked in, group by group, and during the show a whole group might have to leave at once if just one member got out of line. Despite all the regimentation, we had a fun time. In fact, I had proposed an idea the kids really took off on. I told them about the Poetry Slams that are going on around the country and a few kids came up and read a few poems of their own. This sparked the idea of a weekly Poetry Slam being staged by the kids. We later talked about producing a video of their work on my TV show. As the kids were still minors, their faces would be hidden behind masks, when they read their poems. It is hard to imagine that these young kids are in fact in some way a risk to the community. I guess if we can turn a few kids around by this program at High Frontier, than it's worth the struggle.

The next morning at Gary's was a big day, as it was the day that the veterinarian was driving in from Fort Davis for his annual visit to vaccinate all the cats. Gary and I spent most of the early morning collecting cats and putting them into cages for the vet and, as you can imagine, this was not an easy job as the cats had their own ideas about this and wanted no part of it. Gary caught all the easy ones first while I tried my best to keep them from getting back out of the house. Then he went after the real wild cats and with his never-ending patience managed to get most of them. When the vet came, there were twenty-three cats in the house ready for their shots. The vet smiled as he carefully gave each one an injection then opened the door to let them have their freedom. As we got to the last few, Gary realized that two were missing. After a brief search, the vet had to go as this was his first stop before setting up at the town for a day long clinic. As soon as his truck sped away, the two missing cats popped up from under the bathtub!

After the great Marfa Cat Roundup, we headed over to the library for a kid's show, only to find out there were no kids at all. It was spring break so most of the kids were out of town. To my surprise a group of adult tourists, who really looked way too old to be kids, turned up. I switched gears quickly and did a show that I knew they would like and I guess they did, as many of them showed up later that night for my evening show.

That night the library moved all the tables and chairs to get ready for the show. Soon the room was filled with all kinds of people, kids, ranchers, activists, seniors, local musicians, artists, writers, and a few Mexican-Americans. It was a great night, as I was able to play some old favorites on the banjo to get them singing, and then did a lot of my own songs like "Ghost On The Highway," "My Father and Me" and "You're Just A Car." Then I told a story about Jimmy Driftwood and played a tune on the Ozark mouth bow. Later, I played a nice Native American melody on the courting flute, and sang a few songs with my Polish bagpipes. I followed this with a brand new song, about my friend hobo King Frog, called "Riding On The Westbound." I ended the evening with my yodel-along "Freezing in North Dakota." No one wanted to leave or for the music to stop, but soon we were putting the tables back in order and saying goodnight.

The next day was to be my last show of the area, a concert for the people fighting the nuclear dumpsite near Monahan. Gary and I drove up the long winding roads until we reached the community center. Only a few cars were there. "I guess they could not get that many people out," I said, as we walked into the brick building, stumbling along with all my instrument cases. I could tell from the look on the few faces that greeted us that perhaps they could not get the word out in time and it might be a small turnout.

I said, "It doesn't matter. I'll sing for whoever shows up." We started placing the chairs in a half circle, getting out the cookies and getting my instruments in tune. Then as the concert time was near, people started slowly walking in and soon we had the room almost filled. I did the first half of the show myself, and got everyone singing, then Gary joined me and we did the second half together. We sang old chestnuts like, "Down By The Riverside," "We Shall Not Be Moved," and my song about nuclear waste. Then Gary sang a bunch of songs that he wrote both in English and in Spanish about the dumping issue. Later, we joined forces and did Woody Guthrie's "This Land is your Land" and included a new verse that I just wrote.

As we were walking along the march line,
we sang together while waving peace signs.
One rainbow nation, for liberation,
this land is made for you and me.

Then Gary sang a few more verses until the room was ready to bust apart from all the positive energy. After a few encores, we ended the performance with moving rendition of "Amazing Grace." By the time, we were finished, everyone was singing with all their heart and the applause almost brought the roof down. The organizers passed around my big Stetson hat and it came back filled to the brim with their appreciation.

IN THE TOWN OF EL PASO

It was hard to leave but I knew my job was done, so I jumped into my truck and drove west to El Paso. I always get excited coming into El Paso at night, as it is another boarder town from which you can see Mexico just over the Rio Grande. As the city is enclosed by huge mountains, you can see the low watt blue lights of Mexico, face-to-face with our American bright white lights. It is like a mini festival of lights as the blue and white lights dance together on the border.

The El Paso Polish Community had worked with me before with very successful results, so for this year's tour they got together and decided to sponsor a show at the poorest elementary school in the city. Since this school has a very low operating budget, and no funding for the arts, this sponsorship enabled them to have their very first School Assembly.

I spent a full day with these mostly Mexican and African-American students and taught them the art of Polish paper cutting and later did a full-blown concert for the students, faculty and sponsors. Dressed in traditional Polish mountaineer regalia, I did my multi-cultural school program of Polish folk arts and introduced them to an exotic world of bagpipes, flutes, folk tales and folk dancing.

The students roared with delight as I brought their teachers up to join me in the dance circle, then howled with laughter as I taught them an old Polish courting dance and knelt and kissed their teachers over a woolen handkerchief. During one part of the show, I asked three students to join me on stage and try to blow a note on my long wooden trumpets. Their classmates went wild as they tried to blow signals to warn the community of a make-believe attack on the big ten-foot long trumpeta. At the show's end, I asked the students to clap out a rhythm and the whole room reverberated with energy as I led a long line of kids and teachers around the stage in an old traditional dance of the highwaymen known as The Robber's Dance.

If you ever wonder if your work has made an impact, you only had to read some of the three hundred and fifty hand-written notes the kids wrote about my show. Their letters were a wonderful affirmation of the importance of artists in the schools, though I sometimes wonder what parents may think when they find a crumpled up piece a paper with my autograph, stuffed into their kids' jeans. Rik Palieri? Who is Rik Palieri?

After the show, my sponsors drove me around the streets of El Paso. We went to see, Rosa's Cantina, the old log and stucco building near the border where the famous ballad by Marty Robbins was inspired, then we drove along the narrow Mexican border. As we were staring at the shacks across the border, we tried to take a few photos from behind the tall barbed wire fence. My driver took a dirt road that went right through the fence to get a better view. Within seconds, the big green and white jeep of the border patrol greeted us with, "Where do you think you're going?" Lucky for me, my driver, Bernie, was a retired Army man who knew the right lingo to avoid any problems and even convinced the border patrol to let us drive down the tiny strip of no-man's land.

Over in Mexico, the ramshackle dwellings are so dilapidated that it is hard to imagine there's just a stream of water and a tall fence dividing these shacks from the wealthy houses on the other side. It is so sad, that it made me think that, for years, we in America clamored about Russia's Iron Curtain, and now, we went and built our own!

DUST STORMS AND TOMBSTONES

With Texas in my rearview mirror, I jumped into my truck and drove off to New Mexico, the Land of Enchantment. By afternoon, it was windy and cool and my truck, Apache, was having a hard time just getting up the hills of New Mexico, with the wind so strong it blew the side-view mirror off my truck. Then, right on the Arizona state line it happened. I ran into a huge dust storm.

I had heard about these kinds of dust storms but never experienced one until now. A huge black cloud raced across the prairie. The dust was so black and thick that I had to turn on my headlights and, yet, could still not see anything ahead of me. The police, fire department and rescue units were soon on the scene and they stopped all the traffic. Slowly we kept inching along the highway as the black clouds stormed across the road. We were told to get off the highway so I ended up pulling into a truck stop and spent the rest of the day and night there as the wind shook my truck in the parking lot. Later that night it snowed.

Waking up to the Arizona desert covered with a fresh blanket of snow is a truly wonderful site to see. The cactus and reddish mountains of sand and rock take on a completely new dimension when snow-covered. The snow did not last long in the morning sun and I wiped the remaining snow off my windshield and headed down to the old town of Tombstone. Even though it is only about a half-hour drive from the interstate going to Tombstone, that short drive is like taking a trip back in time. When I passed the huge gravestone marker welcoming me into town, I looked for a side street to park Apache. I spent the day watching the stage coaches pulling tourists up and down the main street, visited the court house museum and passed the famous OK Corral. Even though it is often portrayed as a gunslinger's town, it was really a miner's town, springing up from the silver mines of the early 1880's. Though the town today is mostly a tourist trap, it is still rich in both history and lore, if you are willing to seek it out.

One of my favorite spots is the original Bird House Theater. This is one of the few buildings in town that is left in its original state. They say that even the dust in the basement has not been cleared off the poker table since the days when Wyatt Erupt walked the streets. The building was known as a theater, but it also served as a brothel. Back in the 1880's the red light district of Tombstone was a thriving business with theaters, parlors and cribs through out the town. The houses were run by madams and were stocked with women from America, Mexico, Africa, France and China. Some of the young girls were bought as slaves and sold as property, while others, like the young French girls, were imported from European prostitution rings.

Many of these "Soiled Doves" were just poor farm girls enticed by the glamour and adventures of a boomtown and with hopes of finding a rich husband. When they arrived, they found that there was little work and that there was more gold in a woman's body than in a miner's pocket. Some of the women, who worked in tiny one-room cribs, made only a pittance while others plied their trade in fancy parlors and theaters like the Bird House. Back in the heyday, a painted lady, working in a parlor, could make as much as one hundred and fifty dollars a week, at a time when the miners only made $3 a day.

The gals who worked at the Bird House were of the more refined class like Josephine, who was the lover of Wyatt Earp, Madam Moustache, Crazy Horse Lil, Blond Marie, Lizette, China Mary and Big Nose Kate. These "Hells Belles," and many more like them, worked in the theater, serving drinks and selling their wares to miners and wealthy gentleman from two rows of balcony boxes that were suspended from ropes hanging from the ceiling. These boxes will always be remembered by that classic song "She's Only a Bird in a Gilded Cage." Walking inside of this old building you can almost feel the presence of these beautiful young women, with their lost souls, still swinging in their elaborate cages

Not far from town lies the original Boot Hill Cemetery. Today, it is run by a tourist shop, complete with postcards, popcorn and T-shirts. You have to walk through the gift shop to get to the cemetery and this is just another grisly reminder of how we treat the history of the American West. Once inside the actual grounds, the tourist trappings fade while you are looking over the sandy soil and the graves of the men and women who lived and died on the streets of Tombstone.

"Here lies Les More,
Shot down with a 44,
No Les, No More! "

THE PHOENIX HERITAGE FOLK FESTIVAL

It was a long ride past columns of prickly cactus up to Phoenix for the annual Phoenix Heritage Folk Festival which is one of my all time favorite festivals. It is the kind of festival where everyone is a star and there is no separation between the audience and performer. In short it is a true folk festival. The day before the festival I performed at a small coffeehouse called the Back Door. This show was a great introduction to the very active Phoenix folk community. The Back Door Coffeehouse is a large room behind a church that, for some time, has been featuring nights of folk music. They started this evening off with a song circle, where everyone had a chance to pick and join in, then a showcase of some of the out-of-state performers who would be playing at the next day's festival.

The person who runs this big shebang is a tall lanky fellow named Lon Austin. It is safe to say that there would not be any festival at all if Lon, and his wife Sandra, were not at the helm. Don't let Lon's white Stetson with the Montana peak fool you, he's no ordinary cowboy. Not only does he have reins on just about every folk venue in town but he is also a fine storyteller and singer in his own right, sounding like a cross between Woody and John Prine. Besides the normal cowboy-poet act, he's in a songwriting group that is into science fiction as a basis for their work. They call their songs Filk Songs. Lon comes out with some of the strangest songs on this planet, telling stories about rusted space ships and ghost towns that are inhibited by toothless vampires. Sometimes, Lon shares the stage with his song writing buddy Dean, and together they sing humorous songs like "Bras Across the Canyon," a song written about an artist who wanted to fly bras across the Grand Canyon as environmental art. Part of the chorus goes, "Send us your bras, we artists need your support." Yep, Phoenix would sure be dull with out Lon Austin.

When I arrived, Lon and Sandra were both a little under the weather from fighting the flu, but it did not take long to get out Lon's old Mossman guitar and make a bit of social noise. The day just flew by at Lon's house, playing songs, swapping stories and learning more about Native American culture and crafts. Soon the festival was just hours away as the house filled up with guests making festival food while passing around the guitars.

Early the next morning the festival got under way, with five stage areas and pickers just about everywhere. I noticed that only the main stage had a P.A., with most stages being nothing more than a sign and a circle of chairs. This was folk music the way that I remembered it, with people singing together and exchanging tunes and tips. No one was left out. Everyone was a STAR. They had workshops for banjo, kid's songs, hobos, song writing, blues, chorus songs, cowboy songs and many more. I ran myself ragged going to as many as I could, plus trying to have some time to just pick with the folks.

The next day it all started again, only this time I had more work to do as I had to become the Polish piper and had to put on the heavy wool pants, and vest in the hot Phoenix sun. They had never seen anything like this, so once I got going about half the festival came to see this funny fellow, dressed in wool, squeezing a dead goat. After my show, I found a room to shed all that wool and rejoined the festival as just another picker. It seems like almost everyone at this festival played a bit of banjo though some wouldn't admit it. By the festival's end, the last few picking circles were trying to get in their last licks. Two fine banjo players invited me into a jam, which lasted so long that by the time we stopped to look up, everyone else was gone and the festival was over. Lon had organized a few more shows for after the festival, to help fill my gas tank.

THE POOR MAN'S SHANTY

I had a truly magical experience playing at a club called The Poor Man's Shanty. The Poor Man's Shanty is a small but interesting club, run by a fiddler named Sol. Just looking from the outside you can tell it is not going to be an ordinary gig. One of the first things you notice about this shack is this narrow staircase, with quotations and poems taped to the railing. Near the top sits a huge plastic owl next to a box that hides a plastic spider. Inside the shanty, the walls are festooned with photographs, pictures, paintings and old memorabilia, filling every corner, nook and cranny of the building.

The room held about thirty chairs stacked on top of furniture and tables and was definitely one of the most outrageous places I've ever played. I was told, before I went on, that many people have written songs about Sol's Shanty and perhaps I should give it a try before I left and I kept this thought in mind as I did my show.

The show was a blast with people sitting almost on top of each other, singing their hearts out. After the show, I had a talk with Sol, about his shanty and a little bit about his life. He told me when he first moved in, he was so broke that he didn't have a thing in his rundown shack. Soon friends came by and started giving him things, and now there is hardly any space left. "So now," he said, "I have to give away stuff to keep from having too much." I asked Sol, "What is your philosophy on life?" He replied with a smile, "If you only have one lemon, you can stir up lemonade." After talking to Sol, I worked out some verses to a traditional tune and by morning, I called Sol with the finished song.

Little Poor Man's Shanty in the Lane

There's a little yellow shanty, just outside of town,
In Phoenix Arizona, USA
Though the outside, needs repair, there's love and friendship there,
With songs to help, chase the blues away.

There's an owl on the staircase, and spiders everywhere,
With pictures on every wall and frame.
Sol, can fiddle up a tune, as we howl up to the moon,
In his little poor man's shanty in the lane.

You'll never feel Despair as you walk around and stare,
At the poems and the writings on the wall.
Hot Coffee's on the boil, with treats for one and all,
with home-spun advice from Uncle Sol.

"If you only have one lemon, you can stir up lemonade,
If you have too much already, give the other half away.
If you only have a Shanty, you can fill it up with love,
give as you receive, you'll always have enough."
If you're feeling down and blue there's one thing you can do,
to forget about your trouble and your pain.
Go knock on Sol's back door, you'll be welcome that's for sure,
in his little poor man's shanty in the lane.

There's an owl on the staircase, and spiders everywhere,
with pictures on every wall and frame.
Sol, can fiddle up a tune, as we howl up to the moon,
in his little poor man's shanty in the lane.

I had such a great time in Phoenix, it was hard to leave, but I knew I still had a few more jobs to complete.

I was staying with my old high school buddy, Jim, his wife Rita, and their wonderful little son, Nicholas. We were celebrating Nicholas's fourth birthday. To mark the occasion, Nicholas and I collaborated on a song. Nicholas had this great line, "I like breakfast with a brownie on the side" that I hooked together with a few more of his clever words and then sewed it all together with an up beat rendition of "John Brown's Body." Before I left, it was time to get it all down on tape. Nicholas sat on the floor holding a little wooden train whistle and played along on every chorus with a short "toot, toot" while Jim ran the recorder, and was almost in tears, as he watched his young son make his first musical recording. For me, one of the best parts of my work is sharing my music and life with my friends. Of course, "I Like Breakfast With a Brownie On the Side" will never make the pop charts, but I'm sure it will be on Jim and Rita's hit parade, for years to come.

Finally, everything was coming to an end. We did one more fun concert together at the Peoria Library. Lon filled up my Stetson (it pays to have a big hat!) with gas money and I blew down the highway the next morning.

I drove north through the beautiful Arizona mountains, past cliffs of green cactus with their spiny arms like bandits reaching for the sky. I had a little time to kill before heading to my next show so I took a little detour and drove out to Gallup, NM. I went into one of the oldest trading posts, in the region, Richardson's Trading Post, right in the heart of downtown Gallup. This was the kind of place you dream about, with old silver concho belts laying out like rows of wild flowers. Lon Austin had taught me a great deal about what to look for when looking at Indian crafts, so I knew that this was a treasure trove of silver and turquoise. Of course, everything was way out of my price range, so I just enjoyed the experience. Later that night, I pulled my truck into a truckstop for the night and as I was sitting eating some fast food, a young Indian fellow looked at me pointing to the bracelet and ring that I wear. "Nice work," he said, "You don't see that kind of work anymore. My family makes jewelry so I know." We got into a fantastic conversation about his family and growing up in the region.

Ricky went on, "Well, I'm a builder, and build houses, but my family, for as long as I can remember, have been carrying on the old ways by making silver jewelry, Navaho rugs, and raising sheep. We live up at the top of the world in a place called Crown Point up along the Great Divide, an elevation 8,000 feet. My grandmother is almost one hundred years old now and she still lives in a hogan even though I built her a modern house on our land. She doesn't want to live in a modern house. She likes her hogan, and she likes to wear clothes that she made herself. All my family makes crafts for the stores in Gallup. I tried to do the same, but found I like building houses more. I do still make my own arrowheads. I find the old rocks and then carve them into arrowheads. Yeah, I make bows too, and go hunting. Last season, I got a big elk with my bow. I was alone so I had to tie the elk up into a tree, lift it high into the air then pull my pick-up under it just to get it into my truck and back home. Boy, it was hard to do it by myself." I then told him about my life as a musician and the places that I have been. We talked for a few hours and then I said, "Hey, I've got something for you," and gave him my CD. We talked a little more then he said, "Let's walk over to my truck." We went outside to his pickup and he pulled out a little sack, then he reached inside and lifted out an arrowhead. "It took me a month to make this," he said, "I worked on it whenever I had some free time." Then he placed it into my hands. The arrowhead was a fine piece of work, a real piece of art. "It's really nicely made," I said. "Yeah," he looked at me and said, "I want you to have it." I said, "Oh no, don't you want to keep it or sell it?" "Nah, I want you to have it. String it on a piece of rope and wear it around your neck," he smiled. We walked over to my camper and I showed him what I travel in. "You know," I said, "I think I have something for your grandmother," and reached in my camper for a jar of our honey. I said, "It's from our bees on our land in Vermont." Ricky smiled, taking the jar of clear amber colored honey, "We like it on fry bread." "Good," I said, "Then take it and enjoy it." "Well, it's getting late, better hit the sack," he said as he walked away with the honey and disappeared into the night.

PANNING FOR GOLD IN CALIFORNIA

My next stop was Mariposa, in the old gold mining area where I was to play a concert for Bob and Doi Dewitt. Bob and Doi are very interesting people. Bob was once known as the Barefoot Realtor of Topanga Canyon and together they ran a theater that attracted famous folk and jazz acts from around the country. For years I have been hearing stories about this loving couple, so I was thrilled to get to meet them in person.

When I first walked into their round clay-roofed house, Bob and Doi greeted me with a fresh salad and cup of herb tea. Bob pulled out an old photo album and showed me some pictures of a young looking Utah Phillips dressed in a bright purple shirt and rainbow-colored beret, looking through a telescope with a much younger Bob pointing the way. There were also photos of Bob, Doi and Kate Wolf, plus a few family photos. "Utah and Kate used to come here often, as did lots of other good singers," Bob said, "but Kate was always our favorite. We still listen to her music every day." We sat in the only heated room in the house, with all of us very close to the wood stove, as Bob fed the fire and reminisced about the old days.

"We were living up in Topanga the first time we met Woody Guthrie. He was walking by our place with a guitar strapped around his back, just walking up and down the street. We kept asking him to come in, but he just kept on walking. Later that night he was over at Will Geer's house. Will introduced us to Woody and he eventually moved in with us. He later bought himself a little piece of land that he called Pretty Polly Canyon. He was a strange bird back then. Even though he carried that guitar everywhere, he never would sing a note. He'd just keep playing the same old Spanish fandango over and over. Once word was out that Woody was here, all kinds of folksingers showed up at our door. The first time Ramblin' Jack came, he was so cold that when he came inside, he hugged the stove. Those were fun times. Then, later, when we left Topanga and moved up here, we started bringing all our friends to do shows here in Mariposa. Soon a whole bunch of new singers like Kate Wolf and Utah started doing our shows. Now we still try and bring in a concert when we can, but at my age (87) it's getting to be a lot of work, so we don't do as many as we used to."

We spent hours talking about the old days, and then Bob, walking barefoot, showed me the whole ranch. He pointed to a little clearing near a stream and said, "That's where we had Kate Wolf do her show. Right there, near the water. The kids just ran up and down the riverbank as Kate sang. We never had a P.A. - didn't need one. Look, here's an area I built for Utah. I made it for him to recite his poetry. He did, but never with an audience." As I looked over at the large circle of rocks, and the funny face painted on an old gas tank, I could almost see Utah reading his poems out to the river and sky.

My show was held at a room at the nearby hotel, and it attracted a delightful crowd of people. Throughout my whole show, you could hear Bob's zany vocals singing along. I could tell that this couple knew their music well and hung on your every word. After my show, we headed back to the ranch to relax and eat.

I soon learned how much Bob cared about his performers. "Rik, I really liked your show," Bob said, "But I've got some advice," he grabbed my red cowboy shirt, "Get your-self one made of all cotton, not this cheap stuff, and your song, "Ghost On The Highway," don't whisper the words, scream it out like you mean it. Don't be afraid to let the people see your anger, it's not a gentle song!" Then Bob went back and fed the fire.

I walked through the darkness and somehow managed to find my way to my pick-up where I bedded down for the night. In the morning, I was woken by a sudden jar, then another big bump. When I opened my eyes, I was face to face with a huge cow trying to eat the latch off my back window. As I got a better view, I realized I was surrounded by a whole herd of cattle and they were treating my pick up as the new toy in the pasture, crashing into it from every side. I banged on the window and the leader of the pack jumped back. Then I opened the window started yodeling, and cleared the pasture in min-utes, with the herd running for their lives.

This was my last time with Bob and Doi, as I had to move further south for the next gig and I thought it would be fun to sing a few songs over breakfast. I slung my banjo over my shoulder and walked into the house playing "It takes A Worried Man." Bob jumped up from the table and started dancing while Doi sang along from the kitchen. Our songfest lasted for about an hour, singing many of their favorite old folk songs. As we sang our last song, "Hobos Lullaby," Bob looked me straight in the eye and said, "This was the best concert, and you did it just for us." I thanked them again for all their hard work, talked about coming back next year, slipped my banjo over my back and walked out the wooden gate.

FOLK DJ AND A VISIT TO MR. WAGMAN'S NEIGHBORHOOD

Radio has always played an important part in my life. I listened to both AM and FM stations as a kid, filling my head with all of the day's pop tunes. Later, as I pursued my own musical career, I found that radio was one of the best ways to both build an audience and connect with the community. My first radio shows were with Gareth on little college stations in New Jersey. We would be crammed in a tiny studio, which was sometimes barely large enough to accommodate the two of us, and sing into one big microphone. The young DJ's would ask us to play a few numbers then ask about our music. Many times, we would get a copy of the show to take home. It was always exciting to be on the radio as you knew that you were reaching a large audience. I always tried to fit in a few radio shows when I was out on the road, but the discovery of Folk DJ's on the internet opened up a whole new world.

I was never enthusiastic about computers until I saw a tiny story in Sing Out Magazine mentioning some thing called Folk DJ. My wife Marianna helped me to sign on to a thing they called a list server, showed me how to work the computer (a skill I'm still working on) and hooked me up to this new cyber world.

A woman named Tina Hay, at Penn State University, started Folk DJ. Tina had gathered a number of DJ's around the world to write post about their shows. Eventually, as more and more people signed on, the list grew to include not only DJ's but also performers, agents, managers and fans. The accessibility of radio stations made it possible for anyone who had a CD to get airplay. With the help of DJ's posting their play list, it also made it easy for the artist to track airplay and set up interviews. This new cyber-community lets you have a daily dialogue with DJ's around the globe, and as you were reading their posts on Folk DJ, it made everyone on the list feel like old pals. On this tour, I had visited a few radio stations already, so when I contacted Bill Wagman to appear on his show, Mr. Wagman's Neighborhood, he didn't hesitate to give me an early morning spot.

I had to be there by 6:30 AM. Now, anyone who knows me will tell you that I'm not a morning person, and at 6:00 A.M. I'm hardly a person at all, so I must have looked like quite a sorry sight as I dragged into Bill's studio with all kinds of cases strapped to my body.

We soon got everything set up for the interview and turned his orderly room into something looking like a stall at a flea market, with all my instruments scattered about the room. I started off with "Coffee on My Mind" because the coffee shop was still closed and if I couldn't drink some coffee, I could at least sing about it! The song must have done it's magic, as no sooner had I finished the song, than one of his staff produced a steamy hot cup of java and placed it in my hands.

I have often read Bill's comments on Folk DJ, so it was a real treat to see him in action. Bill got me on a roll. I got to play a bit on the banjo, tell a Jimmy Driftwood tale, played the mouth bow, did a song on the Native American flute, did a few originals, and even tried to play the pipes, but as they were still asleep, we ended up playing a cut off my CD. Before I knew it, two hours had rolled by and it was time for one last song. As I was heading up to spend the day with Utah, I knew I just had to sing his classic "The Telling Takes Me Home." I said goodbye to Bill then pointed my truck towards Nevada City.

A VISIT WITH UTAH PHILLIPS

Utah now lives, with his wife Joanna, out west in the old gold mining town of Nevada City, California, where he continues his legacy of performing people's songs, and is host to his own radio show called Loafer's Glory. I first met Utah when I was only 15 years old at the Philadelphia Folk Festival. He had a magic about him that made me an instant fan. As Utah has lived a very unusual life and is one of my mentors, I thought it was worth a few minutes to tell his story.

Bruce was born into a family of radicals in Cleveland, Ohio, in 1935. As a boy, he learned how to play the ukulele, inspired by the Hawaiian music he heard on the Arthur Godfrey radio show. His family moved from the mid-west to Utah, when he was still in his teens. Frustrated with home life, he ran away and learned to hop freight trains. At a young age, he fell in love with the notion of roving around the country riding in boxcars, while working at odd jobs. Away from home, he continued his family's tradition of radical politics by joining the militant workers union, *The Industrial Workers of The World.*

The Wobblies, as they are sometimes called, have a romantic history of initiating strikes, raising hell on picket lines, and organizing workers from every trade and nationality. Their motto, "An Injury To One, Is An Injury To All," fit in well with young Bruce's personal philosophy and gave Bruce a feeling of commitment, motivating him towards living a principled life.

He took on the nickname of U. Utah Phillips as a tribute one of his favorite country singers, T. Texas Tyler, when he was working at a camp in Yellowstone National Park. As he rambled about the woods of Wyoming, he met up with a crew of road builders, who taught him some basic guitar chords and introduced him to his first taste of railroad and work songs.

Utah kept traveling, collecting songs, and learning to play the guitar. He began to tell his own tales in verse and song, while singing around jungle campfires. In the freight yards, Utah encountered old hobos with names like Hood River Blackie, and Frying Pan Jack. They taught him their parlance, poems and stories and they influenced his song writing.

He served in the Army and was sent to Korea in 1956 to 1959. As he says, "I wanted to learn a trade, but all they taught me was how to shoot. What I really learned in the Army was how to be a pacifist."

After his stint in the Army, he continued his nomadic existence and roamed the country trying to make sense of his life. "I hopped the trains," he said, "because I was mad as hell! I hated what I did in the Army and I wasn't sure if I could live in this country anymore or if I could even live with myself."

He stumbled into Salt Lake City and ran into Ammon Hennacy a Catholic pacifist and anarchist. Ammon ran a house for transients called the Joe Hill House. As Utah puts it, "Ammon sobered me up and became my mentor. He taught me about anarchy, got me away from the bottle and gave me the tools to civilize myself."

Once Utah cleaned up his act, he decided to run for a seat in the Utah State Senate on the Peace and Freedom ticket. He garnered over 6000 votes in a very conservative state. Utah made an honorable showing but lost the election and found himself unemployed.

Now with the election over and no job on the horizon, he intended to go to New York City. He planned to sell off all of the songs he had written over the years, for a flat fee of $5000 to refinance his next campaign.

While in Saratoga Springs, New York he fell in with the folk community who gathered at Cafe Lena's Coffeehouse. Utah had never thought of making a living with his music, but being exposed to performers, who traveled the country sleeping in old cars, appealed to his wanderlust nature and made him reexamine his life. At the age of 35, he committed himself to honing his craft and soon became a full time songwriter and coffeehouse entertainer.

He started playing the small coffeehouses and later moved on to major folk venues and festivals. Working together with Folk Cooperative's like Wildflowers, Wooden Shoe and, later, the infamous Rose Tattoo, Utah started building up his audience. He teamed up with his long time friend, Rosalie Sorrels, who was already on the circuit, and began to pop up at well known folk festivals all over the USA and Canada. Even though Utah was moving up, he never moved away from the small coffeehouses. Instead, he dug in deeper, building a firm foundation with his fans and the folk community. "I always remember the ones who helped me out on the way up and thought of these small coffeehouses as part of my extended family," he said.

He recorded his first album in 1960 back in Utah. As Utah relates, "My first recording was on a label called Prestige and that's about all I ever got out of it. That record really stinks, but later I found some friends up in Vermont who were interested in recording an album of train lore and songs of the railroad, and that's how I hooked up with Philo."

The stories of the Philo barn-studio up in the hills of Ferrisburg, Vermont are now almost legendary. At that time, many of the artists lived at the studio while recording, and Utah purchased a railroad caboose and set up camp right next to the barn on fifty feet of railroad track. Utah's Caboose caused a big concern with the local zoning board. They had considered it a trailer, and the area was not zoned for trailers, so they wanted him to move it out of the township or face a heavy property tax. At one meeting, a turbulent argument took place with the zoning board and, in a frenzy of rage, Utah threatened to get a helicopter, pick up the caboose and toss it into Lake Champlain. While the zoning controversy went on, he started singing at the local Grange Halls and soon found out that his music was the key to smoothing things out. The locals soon realized they liked Utah the man, his music and his outrageous sense of humor. They lobbied the zoning board to rezone Utah's caboose as a hunting camp as long as it was used only six months out of the year.

While living in the caboose, Utah recorded one of his personal favorite albums entitled Good Though. This album captures all of Utah's love for trains and hobos complete with the sounds of steam locomotives, train bells and whistles as introductions to his songs. Many of the songs from this record are now folk standards. "Daddy, What's A Train," "Rock Salt and Nails," "Going Away," and his hilarious epic story of "Moose Turd Pie." As Utah's songs were parceled out to the masses, they were picked up and covered by Joan Baez, Emmylou Harris, John Denver, Flatt and Scruggs and most recently hip-hop artist Ani Defranco.

Utah has been a friend of mine for a number of years, so when he invited me to spend the day with him and his wife at their home in Nevada City, I jumped at the chance.

This was my first time at Utah's place. And to mark the occasion, I brought along a small bouquet of red and yellow roses. As I pulled up to the little green house, with a vintage red pickup parked in the driveway, Utah came to the door and said, "Rik, what is this?" I told him it's for Joanna. "Well, the red roses are for her, and the yellow ones are for Marianna. It's to honor these women who believe in us and have worked hard to enable us to do our work." Utah smiled and said, "That means more to us than you'll ever know." He then gave me a quick tour, leading me around their neat cheerful little home. The house is very comfortable, with a music room, filled with tapes, records, his old guitar, Joanna's cello, and all kinds of recording equipment for his radio show. There is a bright little kitchen, a bedroom and a spacious living room lined with books. On the side of the house is a little sunroom where Joanna and Utah are already working on this year's garden.

Utah brought out his old Guild guitar and started telling me the history of the instrument. "You see this crack? I got this one on a picket line. This one was so bad, it got clubbed in a rally, but I fixed it myself!" Utah's hands gently walked over the entire face of his old friend, explaining every battle. He handed me his big old guitar and then I said, "On Bill Wagman's radio show I sang your song "The Telling Takes Me Home." It's one of my all time favorites." I started picking out the melody and we sang a few verses together, then I asked Utah, "How did you write this song?" Utah sat down and thought for a minute, and then he said, "I wrote it while I was living in Saratoga Springs. I was feeling a little homesick and I started writing about the west that I knew, way out in Utah. Sometimes you can get clearer images when you are far away. Like the verse about the rusted Cadillacs, that came from thinking about an Indian tribe who sold away some land and then bought Cadillacs for everyone. In a short time the cars fell apart and now there's a long caravan of Cadillacs just rusting away in the red dirt."

"Rik, when you sing it, be sure to always end with the verse about 'I'll sing to you an emptiness the east has never known, Where coyotes don't pay taxes and a man can live alone, where you have to walk forever just to find a telephone,' because that's the most important image and the one I want to leave with the audience."

Joanna soon came in and rushed about the kitchen putting some soup on the stove. We all sat down together to eat and discuss their new adventure, a weekly radio show called Loafer's Glory. Utah and Joanna have been spending all their time trying to get it syndicated. This week's show was to feature baseball. Utah has been researching and getting a hold of old recordings of "Casey at the Bat," newsreels of Babe Ruth and even an off-beat poem about Fidel Castro as a pitcher for the New York Yankees.

After brunch, Joanna flew out the door and Utah and I spent the next few hours exchanging stories and songs. Utah then went looking for a song he wanted me to help him with. He handed me a song called "Pass It On Again," a tribute to Pete Seeger. The first two verses and the chorus were from Utah, but the last verse was from Pete. Utah wanted me to put some music to it. I was honored and stuck the sheets into my pocket. Before I knew it, the sun was going down and it was time to leave. I gave Utah a big hug and told him that I would visit again. He called out, "And keep calling from the road, it's always good to hear from you." As I drove away from his big smiling face, I said to myself, "I love that old fellow!"

I rode out to I-80 east and reached Donner's Pass by noon. At the top of the pass, snow was blowing and visibility was a struggle, but it was a light spring snow so it did not last that long. Leaving California I followed the trail out to Idaho.

My next show was up in Idaho Falls at a place called Lost Arts. Near the end of the show, I asked them to move the tables and had them dancing to an old Polish folk-song, played on the bagpipes. They had a great time, but later the owner told me, "We were lucky that no one looked through the windows and saw us dancing." I said "But, why?" He said, "It's Sunday and there's a law here, No Dancing on Sunday; we could have all been arrested."

One of the nice things about being on the road, is that you sometimes get a day off and have the chance to visit old friends. A few years back I spent a few weeks touring Idaho, so now I had many friends to check in on. One was the rancher, logger and buckskinner named, Nielus Cook, who lived way out in Prairie, at the top of a huge Canyon. When I reached his wooden cabin, Nielus was busy making primitive bows and arrows out of native wood. He stopped his work, and made some coffee. We talked a bit, and then spent the rest of the night singing and picking. After picking with Nielus, I realized just how important these visits are. People need music and art in their lives and they really look forward to taking a break and sharing a few songs together.

My day's drive ended in Wells, Nevada and before I hit the sack, I gave my pal, cowboy entertainer Ernie Sites, a ring. Ernie invited me to come for a visit on my way to my gig.

A VISIT WITH ERNIE SITES

I first met Ernie at an airport in NYC a few years ago. I was sitting, waiting for a plane, when this big-hatted, mustachioed cowboy came by and said, "Hey partner, looks like you and me have a few things in common." Ernie was laughing at my agglomeration of instruments and pointed to his chair that looked almost the same. We both laughed and exchanged tapes before we had to catch our flights. A year later, I met up with Ernie again at the Portland Folk Alliance, where we really had a chance to get to know each other and even do some picking together.

Ernie is a good singer and picker, but he can also spin a good tale and even does some fancy rope tricks. Spending time with Ernie is like standing next to a wild bronco. He is so filled with energy that sometimes you think he might explode. Ernie lives with his folks out on a small ranch just outside of Wendell, Idaho. I met up with Ernie in Wendell and followed his big yellow Eldorado, to his family's log house.

Inside Ernie's room is a cornucopia of hats, boots and chaps, plus a corner devoted to guitars, mandolins, banjo and an old Martin uke. After talking for a spell, Ernie handed me a banjo, picked up his Martin and suggested that we pick a few tunes.

We dreamed up a campfire, then rode along the Colorado trail, saddled up Old Paint, rode along with the little doggies, danced with Buffalo Gals, married Sally Ann, tied a knot in the devils tail and got buried on the Lone Prairie. After the campfire burned out, we walked outside into a small pasture.

Ernie had just bought this piece of land from his dad and is planning to build his own little homestead. We walked around the grassy land that led to a big white trailer. The trailer was stacked to the roof with cowboy hats. "Well, I love hats," he laughed. "I've over a hundred of 'em but someday I'll use this trailer to hold the tools to help build my house. Right now, I still have to pack for tomorrow's flight to New York." I asked Ernie how it feels to spend so much time in New York City and he replied, "Well, I do get a lot of work there and made lots of pals too, but when I'm away, I do miss the mountains. Sometimes, when I'm in the city, I look up at the skyscrapers, squint my eyes I can almost see the Saw Tooth Mountains!"

I followed Ernie's big Cadillac out of town and we went for some homemade soup at a local diner. As we were eating, people started, coming up to Ernie, "Haven't seen you around, Ernie," said one old man. "Still playing your music?" "I saw your show, Ernie," said the nice young waitress, "You're great!" Ernie's red face smiled and he waved to other old friends in the shop as we walked out the door.

BIG WOOD BREAD

My last show was at a bakery run by two ex-Peace Corps workers. It was called Big Wood Bread, named after the river that runs through town. Big Wood Bread bakes up some of the best bread on earth and attracts a real nice crowd of people from all walks of life. Now that their name is spreading, they are booking folks like Brain Bowers, Walking Jim Stolz and Rosalie Sorrels.

"The Bread" is one of my favorite all-time gigs, so it was nice to end my tour there. Rob and Al were happy to see me and insisted that I go over to the house that Rob is care-taking to relax in the hot tub.

I drove through the fancy neighborhood, past the big houses of Clint Eastwood and Arnold Schwarzenegger, then pulled into a circular driveway and entered a living room that was bigger than most houses. The place where I stayed was a "modest" mansion worth over two million dollars. It was decorated in a western motif including an original Andy Warhol of AIM leader, Russell Means, and a wooden canoe suspended from the ceiling over the stairs, with carved wooden fish swimming through the staircase. I made my way to the back of the house, slid into the outdoor hot tub, and slipped away into dreamland. As I closed my eyes, I thought of all the new friends I met on this trip and all the adventures I went through. When I opened my eyes, I was stunned by the breathtaking beauty of the foothills of the Saw Tooth Mountain range, as they reached into the indigo twilight sky.

At last, the show was ready to take place and I drove past Arnold's house back to the bakery. The people started coming in and there was enough time to greet and meet with my audience. Many were repeat customers from two years back who brought along their friends.

Soon the lights went dim and the show began. It was a fun show, with almost one hundred people in the audience. Two hours rolled by like a wink of an eye and it was already time for the last song. I looked around at the space and said, "Well, we're going to do something different, after this next song. I want you to push the tables into the corner and join me in the center of the room." We did my yodel along "Freezing in North Dakota," and then with laughter still ringing in the room joined hands to form a big circle. I told them we were going to do some Polish folk dancing, explained the steps and walked them through it. I pumped up my bagpipes and made the old tradition come alive. Everyone joined in and danced around the room with the big old goat droning away. As the crowd left, their eyes glowed with happiness and I once again knew that I had done my job.

I left the ski town of Ketchum and headed across to see The Craters Of The Moon. This godforsaken place once made the early settlers think that they had reached the bowels of hell. It's not surprising why. The land is made of hard volcanic rock with strange and wondrous of sculpture like formations and it has to be one of the weirdest sites on earth.

From Idaho, I traveled northwest through West Yellowstone. The center of the park is closed until April, because of the snow, but I had arrived just in time. As I entered the park, the road was blocked with snow-covered buffalo. Buffalo don't like humans and even the scent of our body can turn them into deadly menace. I waited as these big lumbering beast cleared the road and then I proceeded up to Old Faithful. This old geyser is one of the parks most visited attractions. As it was still pretty cold outside, geyser's base was covered in a thick sheet of ice. Just like clockwork Old Faithful started rumbling below the ground right on time. Then it shot straight up into the clear blue sky wetting every one who was with in reach. After getting soaked, I thought it was best to move on. As I threaded through the park, I saw herds of elk and deer and even caught a glimpse of a bull moose while heading out the park. After Yellowstone, I wanted to make a short detour to visit another one of my hangouts in Cody, Wyoming. The road to Cody was closed, so I had to go up through Montana and then down to Cody. I know it seems a bit out of the way, but it just wouldn't be a tour without a stop at Buffalo Bill's Irma Hotel, for beer batter pancakes. From Cody I went through a route that took me to Ten Sleeps, WY. This was the most fantastic ride of the whole trip. Twisting through huge canyons of rock, then up snowy mountaintops, it was one of the most scenic roads that I have ever seen.

KEVIN'S SWEAT LODGE

While I was on the road in South Dakota, I thought I would drop in at Mobridge, to meet with my friend, hoop dancer and flute player, Kevin Locke. Kevin is known as a national treasure and keeps alive the old traditions of his Lakota people traveling the globe introducing people to his culture through music and dance.

I first met Kevin when I was performing at a school in his town a few years back. On our first meeting, I told him that I was interested in learning about the Native American flute and a little about the Native American culture. Kevin invited me to a sweat lodge and later shared some tips on playing the flute. Kevin had spent many years collecting the old songs from the elders.

He told me that the flute was a gift from the Great Spirit, passed on to his people through the woodpecker. There is an old story that tells of a young boy's vision of a woodpecker that had perched on an old cedar tree. The woodpecker reached down and pecked five holes into a hollow branch. When the woodpecker flew away, the branch broke off and as it sailed through the sky, it played music as a gust of wind rushed through it.

The flute became associated with romance and was used in courting rituals. If a young man fell in love with a woman, he would often compose a song for her to win her heart. If she accepted his song, it was a symbol that they would be together. If the man or boy were not musical, he would contact a shaman to compose a song for him. These shaman were often called the Elk Dreamers and had a gift for composing wondrous melodies and often a boy would bring a horse in exchange for their gifts.

Kevin encouraged me not to try to learn the traditional songs of his people, as some of these songs are sacred, but to use the flute to compose my own melodies. We spent a whole evening sharing stories and music and ever since have enjoyed spending time together whenever our paths crossed.

On my recent visit, he asked if I would like to join him and do a performance for the kids on the Reservation. I had played at Little Eagle school on a past trip, so it was fun to come back to perform again with Kevin. The kids were all excited as Kevin played the "Flag Song" on the flute, while the local men joined in singing and drumming. He played a few more songs then brought me up to play on my Polish bagpipes and flutes. He played a few more songs, and then called on his friends for some dance music. Kevin whirled in circles as the hoops spun around his body. Near the end of the show he was able to get all these hoops of red, white, black and yellow (the colors of the human race) to form a ball. He held it up in the air and said, "If we all were able to come together like these hoops, what a beautiful world this could be. But if we take out any one hoop, the whole world (or ball) would fall apart."

Later, Kevin asked me to stay and join him at his sweat lodge. Kevin is Baha'i and proudly spreads this message around the world. When he is at home, he tries to have a "sweat" at least a few times a month. To prepare for the sweat, we gathered some big logs of driftwood, lit them and covered them with rocks. We let the wood burn until it was just hot ash and the rocks were glowing red. Using a long pitchfork, we scooped them up and laid them into a small pit, located in the center of a cloth-covered dome of twisted branches and then Kevin and I crawled inside. He closed the door tightly, and began to pour water over the hot rocks. The lodge was pitch black, and was filling up quickly with moist steam as Kevin began singing songs in his native Lakota tongue, while he shook his gourd rattle. We sang and prayed as the air became scorching hot and, after a while, we went out to breathe the fresh air. This was to be a healing sweat for one of Kevin's friends and one of mine. As it would take three more cycles, we crawled back in the lodge to continue the ceremony. Once again, Kevin poured on the water and in an instant, the air was filled with steam. My body was dripping with water, and my hair felt like a river, as we prayed and sang through the hot mist. I asked Kevin to teach me some words so I could join in. He did and we sang together, then we prayed for our friends' health. During the last cycle, Kevin prayed in Lakota and finished by linking an old familiar prayer with a song of his people.

Kevin handed me the water pot and I slowly prayed and kept pouring out the water. It was getting hotter and hotter as I poured the rest of the pot on the rocks. Then Kevin and I crawled out of the lodge and felt the cool breeze from the river. It was done!

The next morning I set off for home. The route that I like best takes me through Minnesota, the farmlands of Wisconsin and up over the Upper Peninsula of Michigan. I discovered this route when Marianna and I took our first trip west. It is a beautiful ride right along the coast of Lake Michigan and I often plan to camp overnight in one of the many pull-offs near the lake. The next morning was a short ride to the Canadian Border where I shot over the Sault Ste. Marie canals into the Canadian wilderness, into New York, over the friendship bridge at Cornwall, and then back to the hill's of old Vermont. As I drove the last few miles, I thought of all the roads that I had traveled and how nice it was to see Vermont's rolling hills once more.

When I pulled into our long dirt driveway, our big white sheep dog cocked her head as she saw the old pickup and ran down the hill barking wildly to greet me. As I walked in the door, Marianna who was sitting on the floor reading, jumped to her feet and said, "Rik, you're home." The next day was Easter and we packed a little knapsack and climbed the big hill behind our house. After twenty minutes of walking through the woods, we came to our favorite spot, a rocky clearing that looks out across the mountains. There, with Marianna and Koza sitting close by my side, we exchanged our journals, and soaked up the warm spring sun, while the birds flew across the beautiful Vermont hills. It's good to be home!

Hobos and Heros

THE NATIONAL HOBO CONVENTION IN BRITT, IOWA

For years now, Utah Phillips has been telling me about the National Hobo Convention in Britt, Iowa. This weekend I made my way through the open fields of grain to check it out. What I found was quite amazing. Since 1900, the small town of Britt has opened it's arms to hobos, honoring them with parades, a hobo museum, the Hobo Cafe, a hobo jungle complete with showers and cooking facilities and even a hobo graveyard for hobos when they catch that last train.

When I arrived on Saturday, this tiny town was packed with over a thousand tourists. There was a carnival atmosphere about, with a flea market, rides and games blocking Main Street. I parked my rig near the hobo jungle and meandered down Main Street and there, in front of the Hobo Museum, sat my pal Danville Dan, the Singing Hobo playing his old resonator guitar. Danville asked me to play a few tunes as he introduced me all around. It was nice to see such a friendly bunch of folks exchanging stories and songs on the street and, as we jammed, a crowd of onlookers started filling up Danville's guitar case with dollar bills. He said, "Rik, this is great. You do the work, and they put the money in my case."

After a few more tunes, I headed out to see the parade. There was a long line of chairs around the parade route and I got there just in time to hear the first fire truck send out it's signal, welcoming every one to the 98th Hobo Convention. The parade followed, with a few marching bands and politicians in antique cars ending with the Hobo Float crammed with hobos of all ages. After the parade, there was a line up for free Mulligan Stew made by the Boy Scouts. This is a tasty soup filled with meat, rice and lots of fresh veggies. The soup line circled around the town green and park gazebo where all the day-time activities were held. After we chowed down, it was time for the crowning of the Hobo King and Queen. Since the beginning of this Convention, this event has been one of the highlights. Every year a new King and Queen are selected, by a show of applause, by the hobos and audience. It was a moving event when the reigning King "Frog" and Queen "Minneapolis Jewel" said their farewell speeches and announced the nominees for this year's election. Four men and four women were announced and stepped up to the microphones. Each delivered a speech about their philosophy and what they could do if they were elected. The audience applauded, then a hush fell on the crowd as the votes were tabulated. The MC called out the winners and pandemonium broke out as this year's Royalty greeted their kingdom. The new king, New York Slim, a huge 6 foot 7 inch

African-American, and Cinders a small tubbish woman from a railroad family, were given the crown (a straw hat with a cut up coffee can on top) red and blue robes and royal walking sticks.

The news media gathered around the new royal couple, like sharks around bloody fish bait as the hobo musicians entertained the crowd. I was honored by the hoboes by being allowed to help with the festivities and pitched in with some of the singing hobos, Liberty Justice, Bojangles, Windy City Tom, Fishbones, Frisco Jack, Wisconsin Del and Danville Dan, just to name a few.

Later that night there was a big feed and concert down at the hobo jungle. The jungle is a field on the outskirts of town with a large open air kitchen and an open box car, to sleep in, which is available, year round, for traveling hobos. As this was the "Big Convention," the fields were covered with tents and sleeping bags. The town paid for the free meal and the hobos provided the entertainment.

Today there seems to be two groups of traveling communities: the older hobos and a group of young "Punk-Thrashers" who call themselves "Flintstones." These young riders, dressed in black shirts, combat fatigues, big black biker boots and skinheads, are into body tattoos and seem to avoid soap and water. They use freight trains as a way of travel while the older hobos carry on the old tradition of working odd jobs, story telling, playing music and traveling.

These two groups are at odds as the older hobos are a very friendly group who are carrying on the old hobo ways, while the Flintstones are of a more violent nature, almost a Lord of The Flies riding freight trains.

The evening's concert started off with the older hobos singing old songs and reciting hobo poetry. It was family entertainment. Later, after most of the townspeople went home, the New Kids took the stage. At first they sang a few songs to a borrowed guitar, and then sang old folk songs, unaccompanied. They asked everyone to sit into a circle with hands joined and then, together created a "Sound Wave." Everyone added some sort of note, wail, yell, bellow, or scream, producing a sort of New Age Harry Parch kind of music. Then they picked up bits and pieces of scrap wood and started beating them into tribal rhythms. One of the group sprang up with two lit sticks and did a fire dance, walking into the camp fire, bare-footed, swishing the flames around his body. He then held up his head and spit a ball of fire into the air. The group then found the kitchen pots and plastic tubs and pails and continued drumming. Two men jumped up and started dancing around the campfire and peeled off their clothes. Soon a young woman joined them, stripping off her dress as they all danced to the throbbing rhythm of the drums. The drumming continued as the police cars pulled into the jungle. The young naked woman disappeared into the darkness as the police surrounded the campfire. The police did not seem to know what to do, as now it was about 2:00 A.M. and there were fifty or more young kids still beating on their drums. The old-timers stood shocked as they watched this new generation perform their tribal rituals around the old jungle campfire. I sat there thinking, "Next time I'll bring my didgeridoo!"

SIS CUNNINGHAM

I first met Sis Cunningham, back in the mid-70's. A friend of mine was visiting her and asked me to come along. Sis, and her husband Gordon Frisen, lived in NYC in an old brownstone apartment and, even though I came as a guest, I still dragged along my old 5-string banjo. Sis was one of the founders of Broadside, a political songs magazine that first published songs by Bob Dylan, Tom Paxton, Janis Ian, Phil Ochs, Len Chandler, and many more. She was also a member of the old Almanac Singers and a wonderful song-writer, in her own right. The idea of meeting Sis was very exciting and that wonderful evening later developed in to a nice friendship.

When we walked into Sis's apartment, the first thing I noticed was the large red flag of the United Farm Workers Union. As I had marched in support of the Farm Workers I could already feel the presence of kindred spirits in the room.

It did not take long for Sis and Gordon to find out that I was a young folkie, and when Gordon asked if I could play them a song on my banjo, the stories really began to fly. There were tales about Woody Guthrie, Leadbelly, The Almanacs, Bob Dylan, Phil Ochs and one of her personal favorites, Native American songwriter, Peter Lafarge. She went on about the Greenwich Village folk scene, the blacklist and about the creation of Broadside Magazine.

After a short while, Sis pulled out her worn old guitar and started illustrating her stories with songs. I sat there in awe, listening to Sis sing old Almanac classics like "Union Maid," "I Don't Want Your Millions, Mister" and Aunt Molly Jackson's stunning "I Am a Union Woman," with the unforgettable chorus "Join the CIO. Join the CIO." Then Sis talked about her group The Red Dust Players, and how she would play her big squeeze-box on the picket lines or even calling square dances to "Everyone Here Is Union Made."

Sis, put down her guitar and brought out her accordion. She had not played in quite some time, so when she began to pump up the bellows dust squirted everywhere. We all laughed. She said it was Oklahoma dustbowl dust! Then she sang one of my all time favorites. "How Can You Keep On Moving?"

"Oh how can you keep on moving?
Unless you migrate too, they tell
You to keep on moving
But migrate you must not do.

The dusty old accordion, Sis, singing along, Gordon smiling, me in my youth plunking away. Oh what memories. Sis was so excited, she wanted me to come with her to meet Sammy Walker and Phil Ochs, who were doing a radio show that night. It was a little too much for this young folkie, and I declined (one of my many regrets) but I did keep visiting Sis and Gordon.

When Sis's husband Gordon became ill and was confined to his bed, my visits became shorter and when I moved up to Vermont we kept on communicating through the mail.

The last time I saw Sis was at a Carnegie Hall concert. Pete had asked a bunch of the Clearwater Sloop Singers to help on stage. So we all sat up there at Carnegie with mikes all around and helped Pete sing on the choruses. Pete sang a few tunes, then he said, "Hey, there are lots of old friends here tonight... Let's bring up the chief editor of Broadside and old Almanac Singer, SIS CUNNINGHAM!" There came Sis, with her long gray braids, filling that big hall with some of her Oklahoma dust.

Years after I wrote this little story, we had big tribute to Sis to thank her for her many contributions to the folk music world.

Many of her long-time friends were invited to sing a few songs in her honor. The house was packed with so many of her friends and fans that we singers only had enough time to sing one or two songs each. The MC was old Izzy Young who once ran the New York Folklore Center. Izzy's charm and wit was just the right touch to turn this huge theater into an intimate love bath for Sis.

All of her long time friends were there including Pete Seeger, Sammy Walker, Julius Lester, Matt Jones, Oscar Brand, Sonny Ochs, Pat Humphries, yours truly and many more. One of the special guests was songwriter Len Chandler. Len flew out from California just to honor Sis. Even though Len penned a great kid's song, "Beans In My Ears" not to mention the classics "To Be A Man" and "Keep On Keeping On," he chose to not sing his own song but instead premiered a song from a young Californian songwriter, a touching piece about the tragedy of Tiananmen Square.

At the very end of the show, Sis, who was sitting in the center of the stage, picked up her walking cane and made her way to the microphone. The room fell silent as Sis began to sing. At first she seemed a little frail but as she sang she grew in her strength and even let go of her cane as she stood proudly in song. The music empowered her being, singing with a power that lifted the whole house and left not a dry eye in the building.

For the last song, Matt Jones, a black activist, had us all lock hands together and sing "We Shall Overcome." The room rocked in rhythm as we sang, and if for just one minute the rest of the world could have seen us, black and white, young and old, gay and straight singing together maybe, just maybe, the words of this song could come true!

RAMBLIN' JACK ELLIOTT

Ramblin' Jack Elliott has always been a hero in my mind. He has been a role model for many people who want to recreate, reshape and take charge of their life. Jack was born a doctor's son in Brooklyn, New York. At an early age, he found a love for cowboys by reading western novels by Will James. He saw his first rodeo in Madison Square Garden and seeing the cowboys in real life ignited a spark in the young boy. He knew that he too, would follow the cattle trail and learn how to rope and ride and become a real "cowboy." He ran away from home in his early teens, hitch?hiking a ride with a trucker down to Washington, DC where he found work at a rodeo, cleaning out stalls and grooming horses. He was beginning to lay down his future when the rodeo boss discovered that his young hired hand was really a runaway. When Jack was confronted with the news, he admitted that he was from New York and still only a teenager. His boss told him that he had to get back home and finish his schooling. When the old cowpoke saw the sadness in the young boy's face he said that once he finished his schooling he could be and do anything he wanted, including being a cowboy. When Jack said, "Even though I'm from New York?" the cowboy replied, "We don't care where you came from. It's where you're going that matters."

Jack went back home, but his heart was still living in the west. When Jack was at the rodeo he met up with a cowboy clown who showed him a few chords and songs on the guitar. Now, back in the streets of Brooklyn, Jack decided that even though he couldn't be in the west he could at least sing about it and learned how to accompany himself on the guitar. Jack took to the old flat top like a duck takes to water, spending hours on end perfecting his flat picking technique. He supplemented his growing list of songs with the tunes that he heard on The Grand Old Opry. As Jack was discovering old cowboy singers, he came across one that really called out to his soul, an Oklahoma dust bowl balladeer named Woody Guthrie. Jack learned that Woody was now living in New York City and one day called him up. Woody was in the middle of an appendix operation but told Jack to come by the next day. Right from the get-go, Jack and Woody hit it off. Woody invited Jack to hang out with the Guthrie household and he didn't have to ask twice.

By this time, Woody was already experiencing the first signs of the disease called Huntington's Chorea. Woody inherited this condition from his mother and, now in his late thirties, was experiencing its early signs. As Woody's condition worsened, Jack became not only his musical protege but also his care-giver. Jack would make sure that Woody would get to where he was going and picked him up when he fell. All the while, Jack was soaking up not only Woody's songs but also his whole lifestyle. Woody once said, "Why, Jack sounds more like me than I do."

As Woody started hitting the road again, Jack was right there beside him traveling out west. He then followed Woody down to the swamp lands of Florida until Woody's condition deteriorated to the point that he could no longer continue his rambling and admitted himself into the hospital.

With Woody no longer able to sing, Jack took on the job of keeper of the flame. He traveled the country by thumb spreading Woody's songs and spirit wherever the four winds blew. After Woody checked into the hospital, Jack married a young folklorist and shipped out with his bride to England to collect songs. While in Britain, he gained a whole new group of admirers, exposing them to a wealth of American folk music. As Jack's reputation grew he was soon recording and became a fixture at many of the English folk clubs. His shows were getting so popular that he asked his lean, goateed banjo-picking pal, Derroll Adams to join him. Together Jack and Derroll made quite a pair dressed in their big Stetson hats and pointed cowboy boots. They traveled all over Europe hauling their instruments on two Vespa motor scooters, creating a scene wherever they went.

Back in America, the folk boom was taking off and the news of Rambling Jack's European success was creating quite a stir. Jack headed back to the States and started playing the Greenwich Village coffeehouses. As the folk boom went into full swing, Jack was more popular then ever. He was a favorite at the Newport Folk Festival, had a major recording contract and was playing at every folk club on the map. As the years went by, Jack became a living legend, playing the top folk festivals, appearing with Johnny Cash on his TV show, performing with Bob Dylan's Rolling Thunder Review, winning a Grammy and even receiving an award from President Clinton.

My introduction to Jack came from a chance meeting with a singer and guitar picker named Rick Robbins. I had met Rick in Memphis at the Folk Alliance and knew from the first minute we met, that he was the kind of guy that I could be friends with. Rick is a fine musician with a rich baritone voice and he has the kind of warmth and love for his music that makes you feel real comfortable. He has that kind of easy sound that brings your mind to sitting on a back porch, relaxing with friends on a hot summer's day.

Rick grew up in the Hudson Valley and met a kid named Arlo Guthrie while attending the Stockbridge School in Interlaken, Massachusetts. Arlo was already into playing the guitar when the two met and soon introduced Rick to a host of his family's folk singing icons. Hanging out with Arlo, Rick was able to meet Rambling Jack. Rick says that when Arlo and I were kids, "Jack was our hero. We studied and learned everything we could from Jack." Rick and Arlo went traveling the country looking for the footprints of Arlo's dad and his pal Cisco Houston. Together they crisscrossed America, driving in an old sports car that was forever breaking down along their rambling folk club odyssey. As the years passed Jack and Rick became close pals. When Rick was recording his first CD, he asked his pals, Jack and Arlo to join him. After recording together, Jack asked Rick if he wouldn't mind helping out with his annual Mud Season Tour as part tour manager, part guest singer.

I met with them in a small hotel just out side of town. The show was in a Community Hall in Rhode Island and it was packed with people. Rick Robbins introduced me to Jack and I could tell that Jack was everything that I imagined and more. He seemed like a long lost brother, and we hit it off right away. Jack started the show with the 'San Francisco Bay Blues" and did a lot of my favorites like "South Coast," "Buffalo Skinners," "If I Were a Carpenter" and "Don't Think Twice," just to name a few. After his first set, we all went backstage where the only place to sit down was in a tiny broom closet. Crammed inside the closet Jack asked me if I had brought along my banjo and if I did, to go get it. A few minutes later, I walked back in and squeezed back in the closet with Rick and Jack, fighting for a few inches in between the brooms and pails. Jack was sitting, holding a big old Guild (a real cowboy guitar), Rick had his old Martin and I was holding my banjo and, without thinking, we just started playing. The song we kicked off with was "Going Down The Road Feeling Bad" and moved right into Woody's "Hard Traveling." It was so natural that I felt like I was jamming with old pals. The minutes flew as we pounded out, Woody's dust bowl ballads, 'til we heard a knock telling us that it was time to go back on. Jack smiled at me and said, "Do you want to do a song, next set?" I said, "You bet!"

Jack did a few songs and then brought up Rick Robbins. Rick did a wonderful guest set, singing "East Texas Red," "Beautiful Brown Eyes," and "Handsome Molly." After Jack took back the stage, he did a few more numbers and then brought me out saying something about Rik "Salierie" (Mozart's nemesis) I cracked up after Jack's introduction and then swung into my yodel-along, "Freezing In North Dakota."

Needless to say, the room turned into almost an Alpine Convention, with yodeling screaming through the wooden walls. After I got through, Jack told a funny story about how the yodel was born in the west and blamed it on the horn of a western saddle. It was Jack's night and they would not let him off the stage. Each time he tried to leave, they stood clapping so loud that he could not let them down. After the show, Rick and I went back to the hotel, where we played more music until we both went to sleep. In the morning we all had breakfast together, with Jack spinning out endless tales about him and Woody Guthrie, his love for boats, trucks, cars, his old horse Young Brigham, riding freight trains, and he just kept on rambling 'til his ride came to bring him to his next show.

A VISIT WITH PETE

On my trip out to the International Festival in North Carolina, I stopped over to see Pete Seeger. I drove down along the Hudson River and found Pete's driveway. His driveway is a gravel road filled with bumps and humps, confirming my belief that anyone worth visiting has a difficult driveway! At the top of the hill is a circular drive that leads right to Pete's place. His 50-year old log cabin is to one side of the yard and a red barn, with a new addition, looking out towards the Hudson River, is on the other. Pete was in a great mood as we sat around and talked a bit, in between the many phone calls.

Then Pete brought out the work gloves and asked if I wanted to help him transplant a large rose bush. I feel it's really not a proper visit at Pete's unless you do a bit of work together so I was more than happy to pitch in and help, and besides Pete can turn the most mundane chore into a fun adventure. There is another reason that I always enjoy helping Pete. He has given so much to me that I want to give something back. One of the things that I know I can contribute is my strength and energy.

As we walked outside, we first went to dig the new hole. The ground was hard and rocky so, Pete had to get out the pickaxe. That led to a conversation about Leadbelly, with Pete singing a few work songs while swinging the pickaxe. "Wack...wack...wack," he said, "Rik, I just love to chop! I think it's the fun of just going WACK." Pete swung the pick high over his head and threw it down with another big "WACK" and starts to sing, "Take this hammer ... Wack!... Carry it to your captain ... Wack!.... Take this hammer ... WACK!... and carry it to your captain ... WACK!... Take this hammer ... Wack!... and carry it to your captain ... WACK! ... Tell 'em I'm going ... Wack!... tell em I'm gone."

As the pick broke up the earth, we started shoveling out the dirt. Once the hole was dug, Pete went off to get out the wheelbarrow. He filled it up with compost, and then started to wheel the heavy load up the hill. Pete gets a little out of breath and calls out for help. Yep, it was pretty heavy, so we rolled it over to the hole. Hours go by, (hooray, with no phone calls!) so we could really talk while we worked and did a little singing, too. Now the hole was dug out and we start digging out the rose bush.

Pete gets the idea that once we get the rose bush started by digging around the roots, we can use a come-a-long to finish the job.

Rik; "Hey Pete, did you ever do this before?"

PETE; "Nope, but I think we can figure it out."

We kept digging, working up a real sweat. Now the afternoon was gone and Pete dragged out the come-a-long and a big heavy chain.

PETE: "OK, Rik, we'll latch it on to the tree, but first we have to protect the tree."

Then he dragged out an old mattress and we wrapped it around the tree, and then wrapped the chain around it. I had dug all around the rose bush and we were ready to try and yank it out.

PETE: "Rik, Toshi is going to be so happy. We have been planning to do this job before the winter sets in so it's good thing you came over."

RIK: "Glad to help out."

OK, back to the work. Pete tied a knot in the cable but it failed. We tried again. Pete tied a bowline knot, and then we played tug of war to get the knot good and tight. Then we slipped the cable around the roots of the bush, attached the chain and started cranking her up. The bush slowly crept up from the ground, while Pete kept taking up the slack.

By God, it was working. A few more minutes and we had pulled the bush out of the ground. We picked it up and moved it to the new hole. Then it was time to fetch the buckets and throw some water in the hole. We started up a whale of a conversation about how Pete built his log cabin, while filling up the buckets;

Rik; "Pete, can you tell me about your log Cabin?"

Pete; "Well, I built it back in 1949 and 50. Cut all the trees with my ax. Then I had work parties with my friends, but soon found that many of them were not strong enough to lift the logs. So I found a neighbor who had a draft horse and he used that horse to skid the logs. When I built this place, I didn't know that much about building with logs and I used some bad wood. The cabin roof leaks now, so we moved over to the barn but I lived in that house most of my life."

Then I start talking about drilling my well and how I used the help of some old dowsers to find where to dig.

RIK; "Did you use any dowsers to find your well?"

Pete; "We did find someone to come by and dowse. He used a long forked stick."

Rik;" Yeah, we had a real problem with finding water on our ridge. Most wells in our area are about 500 feet or more, and drilling down that far can get mighty expensive so we called up two dowsers. The first guy was a local fellow who walked the land with a forked stick, and then sure enough, that old stick shot straight down. I marked that place and, just to be sure, called a dowser from the Danville Dowser Society. He came over and brought these metal rods. He walked the land and came almost to the same spot." He said, "Dig here and at 150 feet you'll hit potable water. I called up the well drillers and asked the if they could drill on the spot and told them what the dowser said. The driller said, "OK, but you'll never hit water at 150 feet on this ridge." He started drilling and in a half-hour he yelled, "Rik come over here. We hit something." He was amazed that at 120 feet he hit a stream of water, with one gallon a minute.

Our buckets were full. Time to plant the bush. Hey, sun was going down. We were almost done.

Toshi pulled up the hill, and Pete lets out a yo-del -del; ay-ye-ae-eee. Toshi comes over and says, "OK Peter, Rik comes to visit and you put him to work?"

Pete smiled, "Look what we did. I could not have done it with out him."

We finished up the job then went into his house to relax. We were both exhausted and dripping with sweat. It was almost twilight, time to shove off. Pete and Toshi walked me out to my truck, where I showed them my long wooden trumpeta. I asked Pete to give it a try. Pete gave it all he had, and then Toshi tries a turn. The old Polish trumpet blasts across the mountaintop. I tell them a Polish folk tale, then sent out a signal blasting out into the Hudson River. We all said goodbye as I pulled down Pete's bumpy drive way.

SINGING WITH THE RAGGLE TAGGLE GYPSIES

The first gypsies, or as they are properly known, Roma, claim to be descended from Punjab musicians in northern India. They came from an ancient warrior caste that possessed their own language, customs, traditions and religion.

Around the 11th century they left India wanting to find liberation from India's rigid caste system and began searching for a place that they could live without harassment. Centuries later they are still looking. Escaping from India, they were free to live their life as they pleased. Well, almost. It seems that many other countries decided that these free roaming spirits were not going to be tolerated, so laws were soon created and enforced. They were told to leave. Some were even threatened with the torching of their caravans. During the Second World War, the Roma, like the Jews, were singled out to be destroyed by the Nazis. Even today just mention the word "gypsy" in Europe and you get a bad reaction: "Just a bunch of thieves," "dirty," "lazy," "we don't allow them to come to our town."

In sharp contrast, they are also admired and loved by many for their incredible musicianship and vibrant folk culture. Today there are over fifteen million Roma scattered throughout the world. While some are still living the nomadic lifestyle, many others have chosen to settle down, and have been absorbed into the mainstream.

As very little of their story is written down, and there are so many misconceptions regarding their way of living, I figured that the best way for me to truly learn about their rich culture was to go straight to the source. I had my chance when I was invited to participate in a huge gathering of Roma and Travelling people in Glasgow, Scotland.

As this was a special festival, my wife Marianna decided to come along. This was her first trip to Scotland and we both knew we were in for a great experience. Open Roads 2000 Romany and Travelers Festival, in Glasgow, Scotland, brought over a hundred performers from all over the world. There were Roma from Russia, Poland, Rumania, the Czech Republic, Slovakia, the Ukraine and a group of travelers and tinkers from England, Ireland and Scotland. The event was planned through a grant from the Millennium Foundation and it incorporated workshops, school programs, and concerts throughout the old working man's town of Glasgow. I was there representing the American hobos and had brought along a poster from the National Hobo Convention, photos and a hobo stick signed by all my friends.

Even before I reached the festival I had some doubts as to the organizers capabilities. She was a young woman without a lot of festival experience and right at the beginning of our arrival I could tell that my fears were well grounded. The festival was a shambles. The performers were there but there was little information available about venues or even performer's hospitality. Marianna and I were being lodged by my old friend Lusia, whom I had met years ago on a trip to Poland. Lusia was married to a fellow named Ben who ran a nearby hotel and, most of the performers were being lodged at Ben's hotel, but the festival had not arranged for any food. Ben, whose family was from India, was outraged and took it upon himself to prepare the food for his guests.

Back at the festival, things did not appear much better. The evening show was over-booked leaving some of the English Travellers with as little as two minutes to perform. It was obvious that something needed to be done. The next morning was scheduled to be another showcase of European Gypsies leaving the travelers out in the cold. One of the travelers, Sheila Stewart, rose to the occasion. She marched down to the festival organizer's office and took over the festival. She then rescheduled the entire day to give every one equal time, then marched the organizer down to a local fish shop and demanded that everyone be fed. I could not believe this woman's perseverance, but she did get everything done. As we sat in the chip shop I broke out my banjo and asked if everyone would join me in a thank you song for the cooks who made the food. As I strummed my banjo I was joined by the entire crew of gypsy Travellers singing "Going Down the

Road Feeling Bad." At once the shop turned into a carnival atmosphere with hands and feet beating to the rhythm of the banjo. The owner of the shop was so delighted that he began calling up his friends and lifting the phone high in the air so they could hear the music.

As we left, we kept singing right out the door and into the bustling city street. From that moment on we were treated like family. We spent the rest of the day inside Glasgow's beautiful old fruit market listening to the hauntingly beautiful songs of our new gypsy friends. Inside the fruit market were two painted caravans, a display of gypsy photographs and a huge decorated stage. The music was just incredible with acts like Raya and her Gypsy Legacy from Russia, Romano Drom and Fanfare Ciocarlia from Rumania, Musafir from India, Kale Bala from Poland, Tackolatoc from the Czech Republic and a host of English, Irish and Scottish travelers, featuring Sheila and Essie Stewart, Ian Mcgregor, Stanley Robertson and the Darlings.

The stage turned into a fireball of energy, filled with hot guitar licks, accordions, trumpets, water jug drums and fancy dancing feet. In all of my life, I had never heard such a wide variety of dazzling musicianship presented on one stage. While it was easy for me to converse with the Travellers, it was a challenge to speak to some of the other European Roma until I tried to talk to them in Polish. To my surprise they all understood some Polish and were happy to talk to me. One fellow said, "We were all wondering who you were." Once our tongues started waggling there was no stopping us. Through my limited Polish, I was able to explain that I was here to sing songs of the American traveler or hobo. They were all intrigued as I pulled out my big scrapbook. They smiled at the faces of the Hobo Kings and Queens and said, "We have Gypsy Kings, too." They looked over my hobo stick signed with the monikers of my hobo friends and asked if the hobos still rode trains like in the movies.

After my show I had to head back to the hotel and a whole group of gypsies poured into the minivan joining me. When I asked the overworked bus driver if she had been enjoying the show, she replied, "What show? I'm the only driver for the festival and have not been able to hear any of the music." With that I reached for my banjo. Within minutes, every gypsy had his instrument out. The group leader smiled and gestured for me to accompany them on a gypsy song and soon the bus was like a rolling festival with guitars strumming, drums pounding and everyone singing and clapping along. Our little jam lasted all the way back to the hotel and the driver was thrilled. On the last day of the festival the fruit market was almost packed. As there were a lot of acts to fit in, the MC had to run the stage like a Swiss watch.

When my turn came I read a wonderful poem by my hobo pal, Buzz Potter, then sang Leadbelly's "The Midnight Special," quickly followed by the old "Hobos Lullaby." When I finished, the crowd roared for more as I broke into a rousing rendition of "Going

Down the Road Feeling Bad." After my performance I was able to just sit and enjoy the rest of the show.

The gypsies were incredible, their musicianship flawless and their stage presence spellbinding. I came a long way to experience this moment but all my efforts were well rewarded by this performance and the new friends that I made.

Now, when I think of the word gypsy it is no longer just a word with a nameless face, but a whole batch of new friends with a wonderful living and breathing folk culture all of their own.

THE SONGWRITER'S NOTEBOOK

Hey, Now I'm A TV Producer!

Here is a true story. A few years ago I was touring over in England. The tour was set up by my friend Tony Nightingale and my old blues-playing pal, Gareth. While I was there, Gareth worked out an interview with West Country TV in Devon. A few months later, he was touring over here and I was helping him with his tour. I wanted to repay the favor he did for me, and get him on TV. At first I was stuck. After all, I could not just call my local CBS affiliate and say, "Hey, I have this great guitar-picking player from England, who is touring in the area. Could you interview him?" (I know this because I did call and did not even get a reply.) Then I remembered a friend who had a grass-roots political TV show on public access TV. I would see him at every rally or speech with his video camera so I called Ed up and got some information and contacts for the station. Next, I called Channel 15 in Burlington and told them my idea. They were interested and said, "That sounds wonderful but what are you going to do for your next show?" My next show? I was dumbfounded. Then they explained that it would be great if I could do more than just one show. Why not make it a series.

They welcomed me into the world of TV by saying," Rik, you are now a TV producer." I spent the next few days working out an idea for the birth of what would come to be known as Song Writer's Notebook. My vision was that, with so many songwriters on the scene, it would benefit our community, and the artists themselves, to have a show featuring their music and a behind-the-scenes look at the world of the songwriter. I called it The Song Writer's Notebook because to any writer, their notebook is the very essence of their being. It is where all the ideas come from and where their songs come to life.

Then I made up a wishlist of guests, including my English blues?playing friend Gareth Hedges. Some were local heroes, but there were also the names of some famous people too. With list in hand, I started making the phone calls to explain the project. To my surprise, and delight, everyone on my list said, "Yes." Next, I sat around my house and watched a few copies of Pete Seeger's show Rainbow Quest, the very show that had inspired me back when I was just starting out. I watched how Pete interviewed his guests and how he combined the interviews with a good mix of music, instruction and education.

The big day came and I contacted the studio and made an opening show. With the help of two cameramen and the studio engineer, I learned how to produce my show in a studio. My first show was an introduction to the series and featured me doing the show myself. During the taping, I asked lots of questions and practiced learning how to work in front of a camera. I knew that I needed to feel comfortable in front of the camera before bringing in a guest. The first show went very well and then the series really started with my first guest, Steve Gillette. Steve did a fantastic job, but he also set a very high standard. After Steve's show, I realized that my guests not only had to be good songwriters but they also needed to have a story to tell. Even to this day, when a songwriter wants to do my show I tell them: "Everyone who has been on The Song Writer's Notebook has a story to tell. What's yours?" Even if the songwriter is unknown and lacks experience, if they have a good story to hang the show on, they're on! This guideline has helped me bring on lots of young musicians.

My early shows were all done in the studio, with the same blue background, potted plants and wooden screen as most Public Access shows are. Soon I found that in order to capture the vision that I was seeking, I had to get out of the studio and take my camera out on the road, right to where the action is. I soon learned from the in?house engineers how to put together a show from scratch by video-taping my own shows and then doing my own off?line editing. Since that time, I have done about eighty shows featuring the many facets of the world of music -writers like Tom Paxton, Mary Macaslin, Anne Hills, Pete Seeger, Utah Phillips, Margaret MacArthur, Ellis Paul, Small Potatoes, Rachel Bissex, Guy Davis, Roy Bookbinder and the Rose Tattoo, just to name a few.

My show has also covered topics like hobos, video-taped in boxcars and train yards and an interview with the hobo minstrel. We've also featured the Celtic Connection Festival and the Open Roads Festival of Gypsies, both taped in Glasgow, Scotland, the Phoenix Heritage Folk Festival, the Champlain Valley Folk Festival, here in Vermont, the New Jersey Folk Festival, the Sloop Clearwater Pumpkin Festival, a live concert with Pete Seeger and friends at the Bitter End, Around The Camp Fires at Falcon Ridge, a visit with the Aston-Martin Owners Club (OK, I couldn't resist a chance to spend a day riding around in a few vintage Aston-Martins, and feel like James Bond), and an hour long visit with the CF Martin Guitar Company.

It's hard to believe that the simple idea of helping out a friend has turned my life around but, thanks to Channel 15, my little show has a life of its own and has given hundreds of songwriters a chance to have their voices heard.

TRAMPS LIKE US

In August, 2002, I played the Clearwater Festival in Asbury Park. My set was scheduled for 2:00 PM. Someone said a special guest might show up, and if he did, he would perform at 1:30.

As my set time loomed closer, I noticed a fellow, dressed in bright blue pants, who resembled a young version of the rock star, Bruce Springsteen. I figured this guy might be connected with Bruce and realized that Bruce must be the mystery guest who was going to appear at our festival.

While I was waiting backstage I observed a quiet guy with a baseball cap pulled low over his face. I walked over to him and said it was great that he was at the festival. He smiled and said, "Yeah, I'm glad to be here!" I told him his presence was going to really help the festival and Asbury Park, and he said, "Yeah, that's why I came."

Then I said, "There's only one thing wrong." Bruce looked at me and asked, "What's that?"

I laughed and said, "You'll be stealing my crowd. I'm going on at two, and you'll have the whole festival at your stage." Bruce smiled. "I'm only going to do five songs," he said. "You'll have plenty of time to get the crowd back." Then we both laughed.

We talked about my little TV show The Song Writer's Notebook and I told him I was impressed by his album Nebraska. He said he had recorded Nebraska on his Tascam Porta Studio in an old farmhouse not far from there. He said, "When I was doing that album I recorded the songs as a demo as I always do, but when I brought it back to play it with my band it just didn't work. So I thought I'd just record the same songs as a solo in the studio, but again, it just didn't have the same feeling as what I had captured on my little portable studio. I ended up just enhancing the original demo cassette, and if you listen really close you can hear the squeaking of the chair that I was sitting on when I made the tape. But what I was really searching for in Nebraska didn't turn up 'til years later when I made another album, The Ghost Of Tom Joad.

As Bruce talked, he kept moving back and forth, testing and setting up the stage. "You sticking around?" he asked me. "Well, where else am I going to go?" I said. He told me he was going to ask for some help on the third song and said if I was there to come on up and join him. I asked what he was going to sing, and he said not to worry, just come up.

By the time Bruce hit the stage, the festival had filled in 'til it looked like an ant colony. Bruce was fantastic; he made that stage come alive with just his guitar and harmonica. The crowd was rocking. When he called for help on the third song, the stage filled up in seconds. Bruce motioned me over and smiled as he revealed the lyrics, taped to a music stand for one of his classics, "Blinded by the Light," covered in the early 70s by the group

Manfred Mann.

The song started with just Bruce singing the verses and then having his new pick-up choir join in on the chorus. As the song built in intensity, the electricity on stage was enough to light the Empire State Building! Bruce was having the time of his life, smiling and grooving to the music and enjoying the raw energy. When his lyric sheet fell off the music stand we all rushed to help him. He was laughing, encouraging us to repeat the choruses until the words were back in sight.

On Bruce's other side was a festival volunteer named Joellen. She amazed everyone by knowing every word to the long, complicated song. Bruce seemed delighted; near the end of the song he told Joellen to take the next verse. She blew everyone away with a flawless execution. After thunderous applause we left Bruce to finish off his set. He closed the show with a beautiful rendition of a song called "My City of Ruins," about his love for Asbury Park.

Mayhem reigned when Bruce stepped off the stage, with his legion of fans yelling "Bruce! Bruce!" He stayed on and signed autographs, posed for photos and even talked to fans on the cell phone. But after talking with him for a while I could tell that he would have liked to just blend in and listen to the other performers. As I really did not want to taint the good vibes we had with any kind of fan worship, I just walked away to do my set.

The next morning I found a wonderful gift. Hanging on the festival pressboard was a copy of the morning's newspaper. The front cover of the Asbury Park Press showed Bruce, me, and a few others singing. All day people stopped me to say, "Hey, Rik! I saw your picture with Springsteen, pretty cool!" Sometimes dreams do come true.

REMINISCENCES OF THE PHILADELPHIA FOLK FESTIVAL
THEN AND NOW

As I walked into the hospitality room of the 40th Philadelphia Folk Festival, I was struck with wonder by a large display of photos from the year they now lovingly refer to as The Mud Fest. That was back in 1971 and it was the first folk festival that I had experienced. I can still remember the excitement of pulling into the tent-filled campground surrounded with the sound of banjos, guitars and fiddles filling the air.

Back in those days, the Philly Folk Fest was a rat's nest of folk singers singing all kinds of old chestnuts as well as wonderfully obscure old songs. It was at Philly that I learned many of my banjo tricks and learned hundreds of songs that I still play today. After the evening shows, multitudes of folkies would be on the prowl hunting for another hot jam around the flames of the campfires that dotted the hillside. Even some well-known performers were camping out and it was possible to sit around and learn right from folks like The High Woods String Band or even John Prine or Steve Goodman. I would spend hours just standing within a large circle of friends singing and strumming away, playing 'til the light of day.

During the daytime workshops, the audience was able to get a chance to mingle with some of their favorite performers and also meet a few new faces. I can still remember my very first sight of Utah Phillips. He was standing in the muck and mire, dressed in his leather pants and wide brimmed hat spinning out the most outrageously funny stories I ever heard. Years later Utah admitted to me, "Whatever made me think that I should wear leather pants in the middle of the summer? Why, I was sweating my a** off." Of course, to me, at the age of 15, he was just the coolest thing on this planet.

Along with Utah, were folks like Michael Cooney, Paul Geremia, John Hartford, Janis Ian, Steve Goodman, John Jackson, Bill Monroe, Doug Kershaw, Mike Seeger, Pat Sky, Doc Watson, Heddy West, Rosalie Sorrels and Dave Van Ronk, just to name a few. I was getting a crash course on folk music all in one place and loving every minute of it. Needless to say I was very impressed and inspired. For me and for many others, the true spirit of "Folk" came alive for that short weekend. It were as if we were all part of a beautiful dream, the kind of dream that you wished would last forever.

That was many moons ago. Now, many of my childhood dreams have come to pass and instead of being a fan, out in the crowd, I'm one of the folks standing on the stage, trying to hand out a few songs or stories to help our circle grow.

Playing the 40th Philadelphia Folk Festival was a real treat. It was an honor to be working with so many of the performers that first inspired me as well as all the new ones that are turning heads in the contemporary music scene. This year seemed to be a family affair, as many of the veterans of the old guard were now filling the ranks with their offspring. Arlo brought along his kids Sarah Lee and Abe, as did David Bromberg. Pete Seeger's grandson, Tao, was there appearing with Jay Unger's daughter, Ruth, in The Mammals. With Sarah Lee and her husband Jonny in RIG, plus the infectious bluegrass speed of Nickel Creek, these new faces of folk lit up the stage with their youth and enthusiasm, and also gave us comfort that there were plenty of new links to come.

Along with these young upstarts were a host of old farts like Utah Phillips, Arlo Guthrie, Roy Bookbinder, Tom Rush, Janice Ian, Michael Cooney, Judy Collins, Tom Paxton, and Richie Havens. Every time these mentors took the stage they showed us why they have endured, for their performances were as sweet as fine vintage wine. There were also a bunch of us folks who were too old to be young but not old enough to worthy of the realm of "crusty old farthood," that included Small Potatoes, Tempest, Solas, Laurie Lewis, Laura Love Band, Anne Hills, Kim and Reggie Harris, Kat Eggleston, Ruthie Foster, Annie Wenz and of course yours truly, Rik Palieri.

This year's festival was a cornucopia of merriment and variety. There was something for everyone; from the nitty-gritty blues of Roy Bookbinder, Chris Smithers and

Jimmy Johnson, sea shanties from the Liverpool Judies, Klezmer music of Strauss and Warschauer, plus Celtic, bluegrass, and some great singer/songwriters.

Some of my personal highlights included Janis Ian's incredible evening performance where she combined her high tech wizardry with down-home humor to create one of the most stunning and moving performances of the festival, as well as Tom Paxton and Anne Hill's Friday night concert. It is amazing to think of someone like Tom Paxton singing other songwriters' songs when he has written so many gems but both Tom and Anne had decided to honor other writers and did just that with some beautiful renditions of songs by Bob Gibson, Malvina Reynolds and Gill Turner. Utah's performance was testament that this guy can truly hold the audience in the palm of his hand. With just his unplugged guitar and rusty old pipes The Golden Voice Of The Great Southwest worked his magic on the crowd and once again left them begging for more.

I also had the privilege of working together with Utah and Roy Bookbinder in a workshop that was almost like a ping pong match of wits and talent. Another highlight for me was leading the Thursday campfire sing-a-round with Terry McGrath and later, on Sunday, working with Annie Wenz in a workshop called Instruments of Joy.

It was after doing the workshop with Annie, when people crowded around to ask me questions about the instruments that we played and asking for advice on how to play them, that I realized just how far I had come from the mud-filled festival of 1971 and, to borrow a phrase from my pal Al Grierson, that now "The Circle Was Complete."

FRIENDS FOR LIFE

I was down in southern New Jersey doing a few school shows when I heard the news that my first wife, Claudia, was in a hospice center not too far away. It had been about eight years since we had ended our relationship but, even though we both went our separate ways, we had stayed in touch. She often came to my shows and we visited when we could.

Even, before our break up, Claudia was exhibiting the early signs of her illness. She, like my old friend Mike, had a brain tumor. At first it was benign, but as the years passed it turned cancerous. Claudia went thorough all the different types of chemo that she could, but soon the doctors told her that she was running out of time. A few years ago she moved in with an old friend of mine, in New Jersey, to be close to her oldest brother. She lived in New Brunswick continuing to live out her life, doing her artwork and sometimes teaching until just recently a stroke hit her and she had to be hospitalized.

When I pulled into the hospital parking lot, I decided to bring my instruments and play her a bit of music, as I knew that Claudia loved music. I walked down the corridor and asked for her room. The nurse on duty pointed me in the right direction and I soon found Claudia lying in her bed watching TV. She recognized me at once and smiled as I sat down beside her. Her face still looked young and pretty, almost like she did when we first met. Unfortunately the stroke had paralyzed her right side and she could only speak in small two syllable words. Even though she could not talk as well as she used to, she still could communicate her feelings with her deep emerald eyes and with the nodding of her head.

After a while I asked her if she wanted to hear some music. She smiled and said, "Yeah." I pulled out my guitar and started to play one of her favorite songs, "In the Pines." Then, all of a sudden, the most remarkable thing happened. She was singing along. It surprised everyone in the room, including her, but the part of her brain that contained music and songs was not affected. When I finished the song she said, "More." We kept singing for about an hour until we noticed the hallway was blocked with patients trying to get their wheelchairs into Claudia's room. Soon the head nurse told me that I had to stop singing as I was causing a disturbance and it wasn't fair to give just one person a private concert. I could not believe it but I was getting thrown out of the hospital for singing. I asked the nurse if I could at least sing one more song and she said, "Alright, but then you have to go, because visiting hours are now over." Claudia was still smiling when I told her, "Well, it looks like I will have to go, but here is one more song just for you."

Friends for Life

Friends for Life, That's what we'll always be
Friends for life, just you and me
Through all of life's changes
Through all of our lives
We both realize, we're friends for life

Friends for life, in good times and bad
Friends for life, the best friend I ever had
Through all of life's changes
Through all of our life's
We both realize, we're friends for life

Friends for life, in laughter and in pain
Friends for life, until we meet again
Through all of Life's changes
Through all of our lives
We both realize w'ere friends for life

After I finished the song the nurse walked back in and I kissed Claudia on the cheek and walked out the door. I am sad to say that I never saw her again, as she passed away about a month later.

SINGING AT THE HOBO JUNGLE
AND HOPPING TRAIN WITH THE KING OF THE HOBOS!

I made it out to the Windy City and pulled my truck/camper into a small grassy area near the Pullman museum and historic Florence Hotel. I parked next to a few tents that made up the jungle. Hobos like, Luther, The Jet (Hobo King 97-98) Danville Dan, Texas Mad Man, Back Woods Jack, Mr. Bojangles, Red Bird, Express, Quiet Mike, and King of the Hobos 98-99, Liberty Justice were already jungled up so I spent some time getting to know every one as we set up camp.

It wasn't long till another group of Bo's came in fresh off a freight train from Minnesota. Hobo King 98-99 "Frog," and two past queens, Minnesota Jewel and Connecticut Shorty, rode in piggyback (That means riding in a flatcar underneath a truck trailer) with Adman, and had made the trip in about 12 hours. After warm greetings, we all headed out to the Florence Hotel for a lump (some food) then finished off the evening playing in the bar along with a sassy trio of women called Aunt Flo. The show lasted late into the evening with a program chock full of train songs, stories and hobo poetry.

Later that night the cops came. Four cop cars with cops in bullet-proof vests, and big guns walked over to check us out. After a lot of talking, about if we could camp or not, they soon threw up their hands and said, "OK, but next time get a permit." Then the chief asked, "Are you people really hobos?"

As the night went on more and more cops came to check us out and eventually some joined us for a bowl of hobo stew and secretly shared their love for trains. Within a short time we were like old friends.

The next morning, a few of us walked around the historic neighborhood of old brick buildings. We checked out the spot that, up until recently, (it was lost in a huge fire) housed the building that built the famous Pullman sleeper coaches. It's just a pile of bricks now, but there are plans in the works to have it fully restored. This area was built by the Pullman Company for its workers, and is on the Chicago Historic Register. It's a nice, clean, friendly neighborhood with just the right atmosphere to host our hobo gathering.

This was the third year, so already locals were strolling by to get a taste of hobo stew or buy a hand carved walking stick. Years ago, hobos would carry a stick, tie their clothes in a small bag and attach it to the stick. These sticks helped the hobo carry his belongings without taking on too much weight. Today's hobos make these sticks to sell to the public. Hobos are often asked to sign the sticks and usually spend more than a few minutes telling their story before placing their autograph. It's nice to see the young kids listening with wide eyes as the old Bo's relate the hobo lore, then walk off proudly holding their hobo sticks.

As the day turned into night, we entertained the public with songs, stories and crafts, fresh hobo stew and a few bottles of Night Train, around the jungle fire. Then we all exchanged the news of the whereabouts of some of the Bo's who could not make it to Pullman and talked in memory of those who had "caught the west bound"(died during the year.).

On our final day together, we walked down to a local bar and sang for the customers. The bar owners fed the ever-growing army of hobos in exchange for a program of music and stories. The locals got a big charge out of experiencing this very colorful crowd, with our old hats, bandannas, and tattoos. They clapped with joy and danced around the room as we sang for our lunch. We beat on our banjos, thumped our guitars and wailed on our harmonicas as the waiter kept filling our pitchers with beer and placing food on the table.

After the big meal, we marched over to the old church to get ready for the big show. Luther The Jet acted as MC and kicked off the show with Aunt Flo. These talented women did an excellent job with songs of traveling, rocking guitar rhythms, bluesey harmonica and great stage presence. I soon came up and did a few of my songs then joined in a fantastic jam, playing my didgeridoo with Liberty and Aunt Flo to the old classic "Ruben's Train."

After a short break, Banjo Fred Starner started things off with a bit of frailing banjo and some of his original songs about hobos played on the 12-string. He was followed by a glorious rendition of "Hallelujah, I'm a Bum" played by Luther on the 1882 vintage church pipe organ. We all joined Luther and sang so loudly, we made the rafters ring. Next hobo poet, Buzz Potter did some moving poems of his days riding the freights, followed by a grand fanfare with everyone back up on stage singing Woody's "So Long It's Been Good to Know You."

After the show every one packed up their tents, but my hobo adventure was not yet over. My old pal, Danville Dan, asked if I could join him at a small gathering up in North Freedom, WI at the Railroad Museum so I packed up my gear and drove up to Wisconsin.

Every year the Mid Continental Railroad hosts a Hobo Day, by inviting Hobos to ride the old steam trains and sing for the passengers. For the big event, they hook up a whole line of boxcars and invite the whole town to take a ride and sing with the hobos, then sing around the jungle campfire.

As I came early, I had the chance to ride the trains for a few days with "Danville Dan" singing in the coaches, but I soon found myself riding the "hobo way"

My good friend, Liberty Justice had a little skit worked out. While the passengers were boarding he would hide out in the yard then "catch it on the fly" (hop the train while it's moving) then sneak onto the train. The conductor would play along with the gag, and pretend that he caught Liberty. Liberty would sing a song of forgiveness, to the crowds delight, then pick up his guitar and sing for the rest of the journey.

After watching him a couple of times he said, "Rik, you want to give it a try?" So Liberty and I walked down the tracks and disappeared into the woods while the passengers were getting aboard the train. The conductor warned the passengers "Watch out for hobos. They have been seen in the area." One passenger caught a glimpse of us and said, "I think I see one." When the brakeman came to look, Liberty and I clucked like chickens. The brakeman smiled at us and said, "No hobos. Just some lost chickens."

He gave the "High Ball" signal to the engineer, the steam whistle blew and the iron wheels chugged and clanked as the train started to roll. The engine roared by as we jumped out of the woods, running toward the moving cars. Liberty said, "Rik, remember, left hand grabs the iron bar, and then throw your right foot onto the train steps. You only have one chance."

The train was rolling as I threw out my arm and caught the iron bar, my foot jammed into the corner of the metal step while the motion of the train pulled my body inside. Once we were inside the train, the passengers screamed out, "Look, hobos!" and the brakeman chased us down through the train cars and nabbed us. He then said, "What should I do with them?" Some passengers said "Throw them off the train" but he said, "No, I have a better idea. We'll make them work off their ticket by playing music." He handed Liberty his guitar and me my banjo and we broke into "This Train Is Bound For Glory, This Train!"

More hobos kept turning up for the climax of the hobo freight car ride on Saturday evening. I had to go to another gig in Milwaukee, but made it back just in time to experience the ride. The engineer blew the whistle as my truck pulled in the train yard, so I quickly grabbed my banjo and headed straight for the train.

Many of the local townspeople were all lined up to climb the ladder into the dusty old boxcar. There was real electricity in the air, as old Danville Dan was lifted inside the car. Dan smiled and said," It's been a long time since I've been in one of these things," then brought out his guitar and kicked us off with one of the old favorites. "Going Down The Road Feeling Bad." The boxcar was filled with excitement as the last riders boarded the car and the whistle blew. Dan and I played on, as the train began to shake, rattle and roll. The old boxcar squeaked and groaned, kids screamed with delight, Lady and The Tramp's dog, Smokey, howled, as we all were bounced around the box car.

On our return trip, Liberty and I leaned against the dusty boxcar wall and led everyone in a songfest, singing all the way back to the old train depot.

After our ride, all the musicians gathered back at the jungle for a bit of music. Liberty, Captain Dingo, Danville Dan and I kept things moving along until a local woman came and blew us away with her hauntingly beautiful voice and snappy guitar playing. She also brought along her didgeridoo and asked me to join her in a duet. We laid these two hunks of long hollowed out logs on the ground and blew out the exotic winds of the Australian aboriginal people into the starry night. It was the perfect way to end the evening, by giving thanks back to the spirit world and to mother earth for all the good things in life that she brings to us. As the campfire embers burned low I bid farewell to my new friends and then left with the morning sun.

THE SLAUGHTERHOUSE AND KRANKENHAUS TOUR OF GERMANY

I left the states, back in early January 2002, for Merry Old England and another tour sponsored by my long time friend and Folk Radio DJ, Tony Nightingale. Tony and I had a plan to debut my new CD Hard Traveling, an album featuring some of my favorite old folk songs that I had recorded the previous year with my old pal Gareth Hedges. Tony's idea was a month of shows with Gareth and I performing the songs we had recorded together. After our tour in England, our plan was to continue our CD tour over in Germany for another month sponsored by Bernd Haber and Laura Records.

On the very day that I arrived in London, I had to jump on a bus and ride up to Derby in the Midlands for my first performance, a live spot on BBC radio on a program called The Folk Waves. My friend, Gareth, turned up just in time to join me on the program and with little more than a "Hey, let's tune up" and "Are you in tune?," we were off to a running start. With the magic of live radio, the show went so well that we got another booking while we were still in the studio. Thus, the next three weeks were filled with a amazing array of gigs in schools, village halls and folk clubs - some forty-nine shows in only three weeks. The shows went off without a hitch and before we knew it we were heading back to London for a few days rest before the part of the tour over in Germany.

At this point, Gareth came down with a whale of a cold or that is what we thought it was. He went to the doctor and found out that he had a virus. The doctor assured him that if he took it easy he should be able to continue the tour. The next day we drove over to the White Cliffs of Dover and took the ferry to France. That night we were planning to stay with a friend near the German border. Well, something went wrong. Gareth's friend's had a family feud in our honor, and by the time we found out, it was almost midnight. With that bit of last-minute news, it left us no choice but to pull out the sleeping bags and try to sleep in the car. Oh, it was not a really cold night but we were not in the tropics either. Poor Gareth shivered and shook all night long and, in the end, I'm sure that night did Gareth in. The next two days in Berlin went fine but it was obvious that Gareth's health was failing. By the time we reached our host's house Gareth could not get out of bed and was in serious trouble. I realized that Gareth was really sick and that he needed a doctor fast. Wilfried, our host and head of Laura Records, got the message and called the doctor. After a full examination the doctor said that we had to get Gareth to the hospital immediately. Once in the hospital, (called the krankenhaus) we were told he had double pneumonia, was in really bad shape and that if we had waited much longer, Gareth would have died.

At this point, I realized that I had to either figure out how to continue the tour or cancel it all together. The next week was filled with many agonizing visits to the hospital watching my friend's condition worsen. The sad realization was that Gareth was not getting better and now the pressure was mounting as our next performance date was just a few days away. After a great deal of thinking, Wilfried volunteered to help and offered to drive me to the shows and try to play an accompaniment to my banjo. We spent a few days rehearsing and after going over all the songs at least once, we hit the road together. On the road, Wilfried turned out to be not only a fine musician and songwriter in his own right, but also a great traveling partner. We soon found out that not only were our shows working well (performing together) but we were also building a strong friendship

The days trickled by and after another week, Gareth was given a clean bill of health and was well enough to come out of the hospital. Even though the doctors let him go, they were worried that Gareth was going back on tour, a task they were sure he could not live up to. After Gareth was released, we tried to play at a few clubs, as a duo again. But the smoky clubs quickly took their toll on Gareth's frail health. By the end of the week, Gareth was so exhausted that he chose to cancel out of the rest of the tour to recuperate at a friend's house. Lucky for me, Wilfried was willing to help me finish off the tour so once again we loaded up the green Laura Records bus, and traveled off down the Autobahn together, playing shows in old castles, schools, pubs and jazz clubs.

The tour, despite all it's troubles, was going along with a great deal of success. Every venue was filled with good crowds and we were getting return engagements even before we left the buildings. Besides touring, I worked on a new CD, on Wilfried's record label Laura Records, and did many interviews with both radio and German newspapers.

Despite the heavy workload, I did get to spend some time sightseeing and enjoying the German lifestyle, by meeting and spending time with Wilfried's family and friends. One surprise took place early on a Tuesday morning when I was invited to a pig butchering party! That morning, a pig was slaughtered and we were invited to help out at Wilfried's wife, Iris's family farm .

OK, it is not usually my scene to sit around with a bunch of folks in bloody aprons and chop up pig meat, but when in Rome, or should I say Germany, you've got to go with the flow. At our little party, a small group of us stood around a long table, covered with salt and spices, cutting and rolling the meat into sausage while occasionally sipping a few shots of whisky. For our reward, we were able to take all the pigs meat we could carry, so we sort of "pigged out" on pig meat for the rest of my stay while Wilfried's family had meat for months to come.

Another special moment was the day that Wilfried, his wife and youngest son, Simon, and I all went to spend the day in Eisenach, the town where my wife's mother grew up. What a beautiful town it was, with it's own grand old castle called the Wartburg. What intrigued me most was the room, where legend has it, a singers contest took place. It was back in 1206 that troubadours came from all over Europe to compete. It was great to stand in the very place where it all happened so many years ago and imagine the voices of the old minesanger filling the castle walls.

For our final show, we played at the Slaughter House. No, not the one back at the farm, but a small club in Wilfried's own town of Eiseinberg. There, from a dimly lit stage, Wilfried and I sang to a host of friends, and even a few of Gareth's doctors and nurses, while they toasted us with rounds of good tasting German beer.

At last, my tour had come to the end and Wilfried drove me down to the train station. There, standing on the platform, with me loaded down with my banjo, guitar and backpack, I bid a sad farewell to my new friend. Wilfried stood and waved as the high speed train whisked me down the tracks, across Germany, to Paris. In Paris, one very tired old folksinger had to carry his heavy load through the narrow Parisian streets and then board his final train that rode the rails under the sea, through the Chunnel, to London.

580 LEO STREET

Ever since I was a boy, I thought of my Grandma Wojdyla's house as the meeting place. Grandpa bought the house when the family first emigrated from Poland. It was just a typical New Jersey two-story house painted white and nothing on the outside would ever make you wonder about the people who lived inside. But for our family it was something special. It was where we would come to celebrate birthdays, Thanksgiving, Easter and the Christmas holidays. When anyone in the family needed a place to stay you knew that you would always be welcomed at grandma's.

Relatives from Poland lived here, as well as most of my siblings, after they finished school and were searching for their way in the world. I even spent a short time living at grandma's when I had the idea of working for the nearby Oscar Smith Auto?harp Company. (That only lasted for one week!) And then later, stayed to work for one of grandma's neighbors making authentic Native American jewelry but that's another story.

As grandma grew older, I would often stop in to see her on my way to do a show. She was always glad to have the company and would start cooking up mountains of her tasty Polish soul food. Links of Polish sausage, stuffed cabbage, Polish dumplings filled with cheese and mushrooms and bucket loads of black tea. Even though she could barely speak English, she was always there smiling, reading your fortune with a deck of cards and cooking up more food than you could possibly eat.

Reaching ninety years of age, grandma was slowing down. She'd had a bad fall and could not even walk to get her groceries. At this point my family began to worry about her so they tried to take her with them to their house in Florida to enjoy the sunshine, but she just did not want to leave her home.

For the last couple of years, my parents had been coming up to the old house and trying to help her out. Unfortunately, one family member was not happy about this and felt that they should mind their own business and go back home to Florida. It's interesting that this same relative was the very one who was causing a lot of the problems and even taking advantage of grandma.

By March of 2002, my parents had had enough, and this time they were going to really get to the bottom of the situation, so they drove their car up from Florida and planned to stay with grandma until they could get her life back in order. The same weekend they came, I was also in the area doing a show in New York. I was happily surprised to hear that they were in New Jersey and I decided that we could all meet for dinner at my sister's in Bloomfield.

That evening we all had a great time visiting as we sang a few songs together, shared some food and just enjoyed being a family. When I said goodbye the following morning, little did I realize the horror to come.

After I finished my show I headed back to Vermont but kept in touch with the family by phone. The next week, my mother and father started working at getting Grandma's life back in order. My mother scrubbed the house from top to bottom and was just beginning to straighten out grandma's financial affairs. Everyone was feeling good about the situation. Well, almost everyone.

On Saturday morning, around seven, a mysterious fire broke out. My father said later, "I heard something coming from a back room where Joe, another friend of grandma's, was staying." When my dad looked into the room he saw that the floor was covered in small flames. Joe had one bad eye and was in a panic. My dad saw that my mother had taken grandma out of the house, leaving by the front of the house, so he thought that they were safe and went to help Joe out of the room. At first, the fire looked controllable so my dad went outside to get the garden hose to try and put out the blaze. The fire heated up and was becoming more than they could manage, so my father called for help. Just at that moment a police cruiser went by, saw the flames and called to get more help.

As my dad left the house, my mother for some unknown reason went back inside the burning house to get something. Perhaps it was because she did not see my father yet or she had left something behind that seemed so important that she took a chance to retrieve it. At this point Joe yelled, "Stephie went back in the house." When my father realized that his wife was still in the house he too ran inside the burning building. My dad said, "I ran in the house calling for mom, but I couldn't find her. The smoke was so black and thick, that I could not see anything. I made it to the kitchen and I started to get dizzy so I knew that I had to leave before I passed out." As my father reached the door the fireman arrived on the scene. One fireman shouted, "Is everyone out?" and dad replied, "No, my wife is still in there." Dad was covered with black smoke and cinders and was crying out to the fireman, "I think she's in the bathroom. Try the bathroom." A few minutes later one fireman yelled, "She's here." My mom was lying face down in the hallway. Forty percent of her body was burned with second and third degree wounds, her hair was turned to black cinders and she was unconscious.

By this time, seven fire engines, with an army of twenty-seven firemen, were all on the scene fighting the blaze. The police had blocked off the area while the fire was intensifying. My dad was being held back by the policeman and could barely see two firemen struggling to get my mother's burnt body out of the flames. The street was now a maze of fire trucks and police cars with horns and sirens squealing as the fire scorched the morning sky. From a distance, my dad watched helplessly as a rescue helicopter flew overhead and rushed his wife off to the hospital. It took hours before the fire was under control but in the end the house that was such a big part of my life was left in ruins and my mother was in critical condition in the ICU burn unit.

PLANT A TREE

Even though my grandmother survived the fire without a scratch, she did not stay on this earth very long after the fire. She had nowhere to go, her home was destroyed and she was being shuffled back and forth between her children. Almost a month after the fire, she had a stroke and died. We had a small service for her, not far from her house, in the same cemetery in which my grandpa is laid to rest. As she was ninety when she passed, she had outlived most of her old friends so only the family was invited to her burial. It was a beautiful May day, the sun was shinning and there was a feeling of peace and tranquility in the air. When I arrived with my father and sister, they helped unload my guitar and Polish bagpipes from the trunk. When the funeral director saw me holding my pipes he asked me if I was going to play some music. I told him that I had prepared a little musical tribute to grandma and if he did not mind I would like to follow the priest's service. The service began with my playing the Polish bagpipes and walking towards her casket. A priest said a few words and some prayers then sprinkled her coffin with holy water. After the priest had concluded grandma's last rites, I stepped up to her casket and said, "Everyone here has at one time or another, enjoyed sitting around grandma's kitchen table. She welcomed all of us into her humble home, to eat and sleep and she never turned anyone from her door. She cooked up mountains of Polish kapusta, sausage and glomupki while telling our fortunes with her worn deck of cards. She was not wealthy but she shared everything that she had with those she loved. Today we are joined together for the last time by our grandmother."

"Grandma loved music and today I would like to honor her in a small musical tribute." At that point I faced her coffin pumped up my bagpipe bellows and played a slow "Air" over her casket, then sang out an unaccompanied mountaineer's ballad, with my loud falsetto voice ringing over the tombstones. We had hoped to plant a tree for grandma but it was against the rules of the cemetery so, instead, I took out my guitar and sang my song "Plant a Tree" and noticed that right behind her grave site was a mighty oak glimmering in the sunlight. It turned out that she had chosen this site years ago, because of that tree, so we did not have to plant a tree as she already had one. As the last notes of my guitar rang over her, we paid our final respects and each went our separate ways realizing that we will never be able to sit around grandma's kitchen table again.

PLANT A TREE
Words & Music 1993 by Rik Palieri

When it's time to leave this earth,
Give my ashes to the dirt.
Dig a hole, on a mountainside
And plant a tree with me inside.

Chorus
Plant a tree, Plant a tree
Plant a tree and think of me.
I'll be standing by your side.
Plant a tree. I'll never die

Shower me with sun and rain,
'til my roots start to grow again.
You won't miss me when I'm gone
I'll be with you all year long.
Chorus

I'll be there in winter, I'll be there in spring
From the first snow fall, 'til the robin sings.
Through the hazy days of summer, till the leaves begin to fall
I'll keep on growing, true and tall
Chorus

When your children sing and play,
Let them through my branches sway.
Jump and roll in autumn's leaves
Carve their names for all to see.
Chorus

The years will come and the years will go
'til I'm so old I cannot grow.
Then chop me up for wood to burn,
But save a seed so I may return.

As we walk through natures chain,
There's many things we can't explain
So if I die before my time,
Remember me for all human?kind.

Last Chorus:
Plant a tree, Plant a tree
Plant a tree and think of me.
I'll be standing by your side,
And we'll keep reaching
for the sky.

COMING HOME

It had been almost six months since the tragic fire at my grandmother's house and finally it seemed like this story might have a happy ending. The good news was that my mother was able to walk out of the hospital and had gone back to her home in Florida. Mom was slowly recovering with the help of my sister, Tina, my dad and the therapist at the rehab center. Now that she was able to walk again, and even drive, it was time that she got her old car back from New Jersey. Before she left the hospital, she had asked me if I could drive it down to Florida and I had promised to do just that, as soon as my summer bookings were over. As the last shows were crossed off my calendar it was time to keep my promise. At first I was just going to drive down and fly back, but as Marianna had a few vacation days left, we decided to bring Koza along and make the trip into a fun family vacation. The plan was that Marianna would drive my mom's car, while I drove my truck/camper, then drive back together and do a bit of camping and sight seeing on the way home.

Before the end of the summer, Marianna had convinced me that I had to retire my old pickup truck, Apache. I really did not want to do it, as I loved my old truck, but I also realized that the old girl had over 200,000 hard traveling miles on her and, even though she was still running strong, most of her parts were still original. It was only a matter of time before she would start breaking down. I knew that I could not take the chance on taking her on another cross-country tour and, since traveling is what I do, I just had to let her go off to find a new owner and live a new and hopefully less demanding life.

Marianna had worked out all the details for a suitable replacement but my heart was heavy with the thought of losing one of my best and most reliable friends. On the day I was to pick up the new truck I could feel our paths beginning to part as I cleaned the seats and removed my "Moonlight in Vermont or Starve!" bumper sticker from her tail end. Standing in my driveway, I looked her over and remembered the day we first brought her home. Oh she was a beauty, shiny fire engine red with a white racing stripe running down her metal panels, gray interior, pile carpets, radio and tape player. Now, some ten years later, I could see that her red war paint was fading, the seats were worn, the carpets caked with dirt, and her racing stripe was now peppered with specks of rust and rot. But when I thought of all the miles she has on her, she was still in fine shape. Just like any old-timer, if she could talk, it would take her many hours and at least a few tanks of gas, to tell you about all the traveling she had done:

Blizzards in the Dakotas, twisters in Texas, black ice in Iowa, dust storms in New Mexico, she'd crossed the Mississippi, climbed the Rockies, drove through the swamps of Louisiana, sat with herds of buffalo in Kansas, run with wild mountain goats in North Dakota, chased lizards through the hot desert sands of Death Valley, camped out at hobo jungles and driven smack dab up a high canyon to rescue another vehicle on the Standing Rock Reservation in South Dakota. This old truck had visited every state in the lower 48 at least once, crossed both the Mexican and Canadian borders, camped out in Yellowstone, saw the Badlands, slept in ghost towns and even spent a few times climbing up and down Pete Seeger's bumpy drive way.

As I drove her down to the car dealer, memories of all our travels flashed through my head. By the time I reached the parking lot, I had to wipe a few tears away from my face before I could clean out the glove box and sign all the papers for my new truck.

After the paperwork was finished, I gave her a final pat on the hood and thanked her for being so reliable and trouble free through all our travels. Then I just had to walk away. Apache was a good ole truck!

Marianna had picked out a new Toyota pick-up that would try to fill old Apache's wheels. This new truck was sure a fine looking beauty, but it would take a bit more work to get this truck ready for its new job. In order to carry my camper, I had to make a few trips down to my local garage, Bob's Auto. There, they welded long metal bars onto the undercarriage to carry the load, and screwed eye bolts into the fenders, to hook on the long chains to get my camper to fit on tight and secure. Now, with my camper on and the truck ready to travel we were ready for its first long road trip all the way down to Florida and back.

On a breezy Thursday night, at the beginning of September, we loaded up the camper, made a little bed for Koza behind the seat and hit the road. It took two days to drive through the south lands, sleeping in truck stops, 'til we reached the little town of Palm Bay where my parents live. As we rounded the corner of their street, my sister Tina's kids came out to greet us. Soon the whole family was outside exchanging hugs.

My family was so glad that we had made the long trip safely. They were also happy to have their car back as now it was handy to have another car for mom to drive back and forth for her treatments. Since her return to Florida, my mother was working at reclaiming her life. Her wounds were still large and uncomfortable, but she was doing her best to keep up her spirits and also working out at the rehab center every other day. That night my family had cooked up a big batch of Polish-style potato pancakes, sausage and dumplings and, even though my mom's hands were not that strong she insisted on helping with the meal. It was good to be together with my family and know that we had somehow survived this tragedy.

As usual, after dinner, our family gathered round the kitchen to sip endless cups of tea and tell stories. After retelling some of our favorite family stories and catching up with the news, our conversation turned to the more serious stories about the fire. After re-telling the events that took place when the fire first broke out, my mom told me something rather strange. She said, "Now that I am beginning to heal, some of the memories of the fire are coming back to me. When I was standing in the middle of the blaze, I felt like I was dying. Perhaps for a few seconds I did die, but then I saw an image, it was you, Rik. You were riding a white flying horse. You had come to save me. I don't remember much more, but they say that sometimes when you die, your first child comes to you, maybe this is some sort of a sign."

I looked at my mom covered from head to toe in red and purple scars and said, "Well, whatever it means, we are all here for you now." She laughed, "Yes, you are." I said, "The doctors told us that you had a very good chance of not making it, but I guess you weren't ready to leave us yet, or maybe you are just a stubborn old Pollack." She laughed again and said, "Yes, I am."

The next day we were told that my father had planned a little party. Ironically the house that was next door had burned down a few years ago and instead of building a new house the town decided to make the lot into a little neighborhood park. The park was used often for birthday parties for the children, but my family wanted to host a block party to not only celebrate our visit but also celebrate my mother's survival.

My father had invited all his friends and just about every family who lived on the street. My mother bought enough food to feed the whole block, and my sister Tina spent most of the day cooking. The neighbors arrived, young and old, black, white and Hispanic and all sat together eating a feast of BBQ, chicken and ribs, hotdogs, hamburgers, beans, potato salad and chips. After everyone chowed down, I strummed my banjo as a gang of kids danced around the picnic tables, singing and beating out a rough rhythm on a metal trash can. After the kids wore out, some of the older folks brought along their guitars and sang some old pop songs and some wonderful songs in Spanish.

The party lasted into the early evening hours. Then, when the sun went down and mosquitoes came out, Tina and her kids put away the food, cleared the tables, and we all went inside for some more tea and stories. That night we stayed up late and tried to squeeze in every story we could before bedding down for the night, for we knew we would be leaving in the morning and it would be a long time 'til we could be together again.

Parting is never easy, especially when you live almost on the opposite sides of the country so it was with a great deal of sadness, and a quite a few tears, that my family stood outside their house, took a few photos and waved goodbye. We backed up the truck waved, and yelled, "So long" and drove down the street, headed for the highway.

We were now on our way home. It was still early in the day but we knew that we had a long days ride ahead, so we took turns as we dashed up the Interstate past miles of Georgia swamps, through South Carolina and into the rugged hills of North Carolina. We spent the night with my old pal Mike and his wife Shelly, then headed North up the Blue Mountain Highway through Virginia, then made it back onto the Interstate. We made a short stop in Pennsylvania to see a steam train museum and then headed through up state New York and straight up to the Vermont state line.

As we were driving through the Green Mountains we saw a large flock of Canada geese headed south. As I listened to their loud honking and watched them beat their wings into the chilly autumn winds, I wondered if they were flying back on the same route we had just come. As I thought about the bird's migration instincts, I could feel that these fine feathered friends and I had a lot in common.

Yes, just like these birds I too had something inside me that made me want to migrate, spread my wings and fly off to far distant places. Travel was in my blood and bones and even though I was happy to be home, I knew that it wouldn't be long before I had to spread my wings and once again fly off down the highway.

The Road Is My Mistress

(Chorus: After each verse)
The road is my mistress, siren of darkness,
cloaked in black midnight she bids me from home
In arms ever winding, I'm lost in her magic,
destined to follow where ever she roams

Goodbye New England, I'm off on your highway past green fertile farmlands
and fat Holstein cows, threading my way along the old Hudson,
I see New York City, I'm on the road now.

When I'm on the road and leave my life behind, I seem to spend my time
trying to get back home,
But when I return, my thoughts shift and yearn for an open highway and the
song of the road.

Another lost week in the hills of the badlands,
I'm slipping in quick sand my pockets threadbare.
The diesels are humming while my guitars strumming,
a song of the road wishing you were here.

Through rusty red mountains from Casper to Cody
on snake-twisted rivers to Idaho Falls
Just one more old night in this lonely old truck stop,
I'm backing this rig up and I'm heading home

The End

Breinigsville, PA USA
04 October 2009
225258BV00002B/3/A